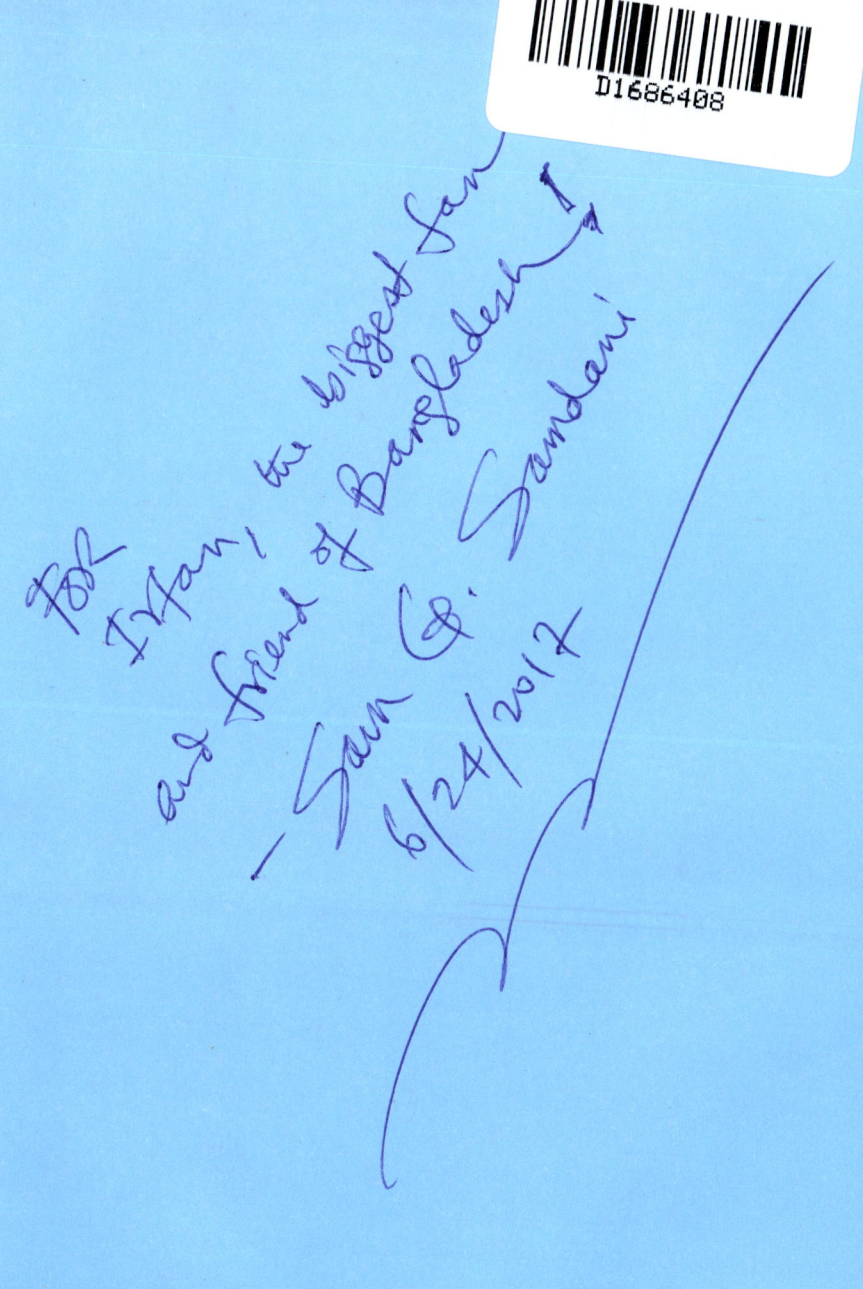

For Iffat, the biggest fan and friend of Bangladesh!
— Sam G. Samdani
6/24/2017

Going Digital

GOING DIGITAL: Realizing the Dreams of a Digital Bangladesh for All is perhaps the first book which traces the background and development of Information Technology in Bangladesh since installation of the first computer in 1964. The style of presentation is very innovative. The introduction of avatars (e.g. Karim 2021, Samdani 2031, Quamrul 2021) enables the authors to leapfrog into the future and look back at some of the developments which have taken place.

The experiences of Bangladesh as well as some weaknesses in policy implementation have been analyzed and suggestions have been made to fully exploit the opportunities for use of ICT in accelerating socio-economic development to realize the vision of Digital Bangladesh by 2021. The book should be very useful for policy makers, ICT professionals, academics and all persons interested in ICT.

Professor Jamilur Reza Choudhury
Former Professor, Bangladesh University of Engineering and Technology (BUET)
Founding Vice Chancellor of BRAC University
Convener of National ICT Policy Formulation Committee, 2008

GOING DIGITAL

Realizing the Dreams of a Digital Bangladesh for All

Habibullah N. Karim
Quamrul Mina
Gulam Samdani

 The University Press Limited

The University Press Limited
Red Crescent House
61 Motijheel C/A, P. O. Box 2611
Dhaka 1000, Bangladesh
Fax : (88 02) 9565443
E-mail: upl@bangla.net, upl@btcl.net.bd
Website: www.uplbooks.com.bd

First published, 2011

Copyright © Authors, 2011

All rights are reserved. No part of this publication may be reproduced or transmitted in any form or by any means without prior permission in writing from the publisher. Any person who does any unauthorized act in relation to this publication may be liable to criminal prosecution and civil claims for damages.

Cover design by Najib Tareque

ISBN 978 984 506 034 9

Published by Mohiuddin Ahmed, The University Press Limited, Dhaka. Book design by Ashim K. Biswas and produced by Abarton, 354 Dilu Road, Moghbazar. Printed at the Akota Offset Press, 119 Fakirapool, Dhaka, Bangladesh.

This book is dedicated to:

My late father Abu Nayeem M Jahed who always encouraged me to write from very early on, to my mother Sultana Zabinda A Jahed who painstakingly saw to all the creature comforts and motherly care for me and my two sisters Rokeya and Rofiqua, to my wife Fatima Yasmin who despite holding down a highly demanding full-time job puts up with my nagging demands effortlessly, and to all the children of the digital era who one day will realize the potential of our nation by harnessing information technologies.

–Habibullah N Karim

My loving parents, siblings, my wife Farah and our three daughters—Anika, Priyanka and Liana—who make life interesting and keep me inspired to write a book like this. And to my dear childhood alma mater Dhaka Residential Model School & College and its teachers who taught me how to dream and get things done methodically and humanely.

– Quamrul Mina

Sarah (aka "Sneha") H. Samdani, the ultimate virtuoso with all things digital: May all your dreams, digital or otherwise, always come true! Your loving dad will always be hovering just beneath your wings as your imagination takes flight to worlds where even the sky isn't the limit!

– Gulam (aka "Sam") Samdani

Contents

Foreword xi
Why This Book —The Questions and Answers xiii

Chapter 1 **Learning to Leapfrog as Digital Bangladesh** 1
    1.1 The promulgation of the current concept of Digital Bangladesh 4
    1.2 Early adoptions of IT—1964 onwards 4
    1.3 Bangladesh's failures and missed opportunities in IT so far 8
    1.4 Bangladesh's current position and rankings in IT 11
    1.5 Bangladesh's current development agenda in ICTs 14
    1.6 A leapfrogger joins the economic development marathon 23
    1.7 The tale of two countries with two very different trajectories 28
    1.8 How the internet has changed everything 30
    1.9 How to fish in the networked ocean of opportunities 34
    1.10 Broadband connectivity is the virtual bridge to Digital Bangladesh 35
    1.11 Showcasing the mobile enablers of digital transformation 39

Chapter 2 **Reporting Live from Where the Digital Future has Already Happened** 43
    2.1 What happens when digitization gets a Darwinian leg 52
    2.2 The underpinnings of our 'digital big bang theory' for Bangladesh 53
    2.3 Learning from where the future has already happened 56
    2.4 The evolving transformative roles of the mobile phone 62
    2.5 Building on what works in Bangladesh and beyond 74

Chapter 3	**Creating the Roadmaps and Policy Instruments to Enable Inclusive Economic Prosperity**	81
	3.1 The regulatory and policy landscape for ICTs	82
	3.2 Rounding out the missing links	88
	3.3 How to bridge the gaps in regulatory and policy landscape	90
	3.4 Upholding the BRIDGE to a Digital Bangladesh for all	92
Chapter 4	**Tapping into the Various Sources of Capital for Productive Investment**	95
	4.1 Start with a bankable idea	98
	4.2 Funding organizations active in Bangladesh today	103
	4.3 Surveying the broader investment landscape	107
	4.4 Reading the mindsets of various investor types	110
	4.5 Capitalizing on the disciplining effect of debt	111
Chapter 5	**Bridging the Knowing-Doing Gap Through Disciplined Implementation**	117
	5.1 Acknowledging the political context of Bangladesh	118
	5.2 Key steps in the implementation process	121
	5.3 What would it cost to build a Digital Bangladesh?	141
Chapter 6	**The New Face of Bangladesh Looking Back from 2021**	145
	6.1 The occupational hazard of a forecaster	147
	6.2 What Google's strategy taught Bangladesh	148
	6.3 An underdog's chance to leapfrog	150
	6.4 The rites of passage for a Bangladeshi blogger	151
	6.5 A (re)view of the shape of things that came to Bangladesh	155
	6.6 Education as co-created experience of knowledge and inspiration	157
	6.7 The mobile phone as the all-purpose connectivity tool	160
	6.8 When mobile apps rule the world	163
	6.9 Dropping in and out of many avatars in one lifetime	167

6.10	When broadband met Bangladeshi entrepreneurship	170
6.11	Cognitive surplus put to productive use over the internet	176
6.12	Internet access as a legal right for everyone in Bangladesh	177

Chapter 7 Let's Get Reset and Go Digital! — 179

7.1	How to keep going and not stop short of the finish line	180
7.2	Always play fair and square	182
7.3	Dare to care for what constitutes your digital legacy	185

Bibliography — 189
Acknowledgements — 197
Glossary of Terms — 199
Index — 211

Foreword

In my 2007 book, *Creating a World without Poverty: Social Business and the Future of Capitalism*, I discuss in one chapter about the transformative role of digital technologies in poverty reduction in particular and economic growth in general. The enormous potential of digital technologies in transforming the poverty situation of the country has to be brought to the attention of policymakers and entrepreneurs alike in Bangladesh and beyond.

I am glad to see that the authors of this well-researched book have crafted a realistic roadmap for our nation's socioeconomic renewal and cultural well-being. They deserve our kudos for making this often too-technical a subject not only easy to understand but also a joy to read.

As thoughtful and well-informed experts on digital technology-based innovations that can drive inclusive economic growth, they have cast the net far and wide to help us identify and capture meaningful growth opportunities for Bangladesh. They highlight the issues and challenges people face in adopting or adapting to the constantly evolving "new and improved" digital technologies.

This book deals well with the interaction of digital technologies with the policy instruments devised by the public sector and the emerging business imperatives for the private sector to help bridge the much-maligned digital divide.

The illustrative case examples and "back from the future" vignettes will appeal greatly to those who are looking for a counterweight to the flood of purely numbers-driven reports and self-serving white papers that are now so fashionable and yet so often missing the mark.

I encourage you to read this book not just for the fun but also for the compelling case it makes for all of us to work together towards a digital poverty-free future.

In short, let's get reset and go digital!

Professor Muhammad Yunus
Founder, Grameen Bank

Why This Book—The Questions and Answers

> "The man who does not read good books has no advantage over the man who can't read them."
>
> – *Mark Twain (1835-1910)*

Reader: *If books could talk, they would be the first to tell you that most people do not read them even if they have received one for free as a gift from someone. So why have you decided to write a book not on something as topical as how to get rich overnight, but on something as dry and technical as Bangladesh and digital technologies?*

Samdani: *It's indeed a pity that even those who can read, often don't. In that sense, as Mark Twain pointed out, there is often not much of a difference between those who can read (i.e., who consider themselves literate) and those who can't. Our hope is that by reading this book you'll be able to take full advantage of the increasingly transformative roles of digital technologies in your personal and professional life.*

Although this book is mostly about how digital technologies will transform Bangladesh over the next decade or so, it should be better viewed as being not about Bangladesh or even digital technologies per se, but about life. That is another way of saying that what matters most is the practical point of it all, which is neither primarily to educate nor entertain (although there is some of both ingredients judiciously sprinkled throughout the book), but to change.

And the change we hope for is not only people's enjoyment of, or facility with, digital technologies for their own sake. It is change in the way we understand experience, how we are informed, change in the way we are governed with or without our consent, and the way we think about our roles in an increasingly globalized society. After all, the book happens to be just one form of the content, which might as well be converted into an audio format for those who prefer that particular mode of learning (aural vs. visual). Who knows, it may someday inspire a multimedia production in the form of a forward-looking documentary or a docudrama of sorts!

> "Reading is a means of thinking with another person's mind; it forces you to stretch your own."
> – Charles Scribner, Jr. (1921-1995)

Quamrul: We expect to continue our conversation with you, dear reader, online at www.GoingDigitalBook.com where you can read our blogs, and post comments and questions. In fact, we hope to build a vibrant online community that will be the virtual eyes and ears to keep track of the ongoing and proposed projects and policies toward realizing our dreams of a Digital Bangladesh by 2021.

Reader: Hmm. That's fascinating. Tell me more about when will these technologies and the cool apps we hear about be available, and more importantly, affordable to me.

Karim: A lot depends on how quickly we as a nation can get our act together to invest in building the necessary digital infrastructure. Assuming a concerted effort is made by all the stakeholders in the public and private sectors, we believe Bangladesh can become a bona fide digital nation in 10 to 20 years.

Reader: Wow, 10 to 20 years sounds great.

Quamrul: Ah, but wait. As we'll discuss later, in those 10 to 20 years we'll have at our disposal dramatic new digital technologies that we currently do not have nor can we even imagine what they will be. Keep in mind that we will not jump into the digital future of Bangladesh we describe in one big leap. Rather, it will come in countless small steps. Given that digital technologies are subject to exponential progress (see Chapter 2 for more on this phenomenon), these steps will come faster and faster.

Samdani: For the Tarzan fans among us, another way of looking at the situation may resonate a little better. It's often called the Tarzan strategy, which refers to the pragmatic policy of clinging to the vine that holds us off the jungle floor and not letting go of the one we've got until we've got the next vine firmly in hand. However, the problem is that we can get mired in the thorny underbrush of existing operational frameworks and outdated and costly infrastructures. What's worse is that our economic foundation may be based on the assumptions suited for the old analog era, not the new digital world powered by open systems, collaborative innovation, and networked intelligence.

> "Every man who knows how to read has it in his power to magnify himself, to multiply the ways in which he exists, and to make his life full, significant and interesting."
> – Aldous Huxley (1894 -1963)

Reader: In that case, how should we proceed? What are the steps we need to take now so that we are ready to take advantage of the new digital technologies when they become available and affordable?

Samdani: As we have been putting the book together, we've been fortunate enough to have avatars of our future selves visit us from time to time and share just how exciting the digital world of the future will be. Samdani 2021, Karim 2021, and Quamrul 2021 will tell us about "cloud computing" and "apps-driven digital lifestyles", which will all be realities in Bangladesh 2021. For example, the cloud computing paradigm (inspired by the cloud symbol that is often used to represent the internet in flowcharts and diagrams) will obviate the need to own a lot of the physical infrastructure, thus enabling us to avoid much of the traditional capital expenditure by renting usage from a third-party provider. We'll consume resources as a service and pay only for resources that we use.

> "When you reread a classic, you do not see more in the book than you did before; you see more in you than there was before."
> – Clifton Fadiman (1904-1999)

Many cloud-computing offerings will employ the utility computing model, which is analogous to how traditional utility services (such as electricity and water) are consumed. Sharing rapidly depreciating computing power (from financial accounting standpoint) among multiple tenants will improve utilization rates, as servers will not unnecessarily be left idle, which can reduce costs significantly while increasing the speed of application development.

Karim: By 2031, more advances in digital technologies will have begun to bring fundamental changes to our lives, altering almost every aspect of how we live. We'll turn to Karim 2031, Quamrul 2031, and Samdani 2031 for help in explaining how these technologies transform our lives in 2031. We often use the metaphor of bridges to talk about the transformational changes ushered in by digital technologies.

Samdani: This book will be your guide to Bridge One, which is what we need to do right now to catapult Bangladesh onto the status of a digital nation by 2021. Bridge One will take us over a moving frontier because the scope and scale of digital technologies are expanding at an accelerating pace.

> "The way a book is read—which is to say, the qualities a reader brings to a book—can have as much to do with its worth as anything the author puts into it. Anyone who can read can learn how to read deeply and thus live more fully."
> – Norman Cousins (1915 -1990)

Quamrul: Bridge Two will take us to the full flowering of digital technologies in Bangladesh 2031. Naturally, our visibility into the shape of Bridge Two will be limited due to the uncertainty of the choices we and others will be making in crossing Bridge One. The important point to keep in mind is that we must first build and cross Bridge One before we can earn the right to build Bridge Two.

> "A book is the only place in which you can examine a fragile thought without breaking it, or explore an explosive idea without fear it will go off in your face."
> – Edward P. Morgan (1910-1993)

Karim 2021, Quamrul 2021 and Samdani 2021: We thought now would be a good time to introduce ourselves.

Reader: Wow, where did you guys come from?

Samdani 2021: We're avatars of our future selves.

Reader: Hmmm, so what advanced digital technology allows the three of you to talk to me from the future?

Samdani 2021: Actually, we're using a very old technology. It's called poetic license, which allows us to share with you some perspectives on general trends, but we cannot comment on specific developments or events without forfeiting the precious privilege of our poetic license.

Reader: I see. You still look like yourselves in 2011. You really haven't aged much in the past 10 years.

Karim 2021: That's right. We're in our late fifties now, but thanks to the dramatic advances in anti-aging medicine that have taken place over the first two decades of the 21st century, we're still doing quite well.

Samdani 2031: And you'll be happy to see that we're still doing fine in 2031, when we're in our late sixties. If you take care of yourself the old-fashioned way for a while longer, you too can be "young at heart" like ourselves well into the 2030s and beyond.

Reader: Wow, there are nine of you now! But your older arrivals look even younger than you did in your late forties.

Quamrul 2031: That's because slowing down the aging process was the best we could accomplish in the early 2020s. Now age reversal is a reality.

Reader: I am not going to ask you about the winning numbers for lottery jackpots or anything like that, but I am really psyched to learn more about who will be "running the show" in our digital future. Is it going to be a supercomputer like Hal featured in the movie, 2001: A Space Odyssey?

> "There are books in which the footnotes or comments scrawled by some reader's hand in the margin are more interesting than the text. The world is one of these books."
> – George Santayana (1863 -1952)

Samdani 2021: *If you were to stop and ask people from all walks of life, "Who is running your life?" the answers may range from "I am the captain of my own ship," to "I have surrendered my destiny to Allah, and He is the one who is in charge of my life." Moreover, if you were to ask the same people, "Who is running the country?" the answers may be no more predictable.*

> "Read, everyday, something no one else is reading. Think, everyday, something no one else is thinking. Do, everyday, something no one else is silly enough to do. It is bad for the mind to be always part of unanimity."
>
> – Christopher Morley (1890- 1957)

Karim 2021: *Newton described the relationship of mass and distance to gravitational attraction between objects with such precision that we can use the law of gravity to plan spaceflights. During the Apollo 8 mission, astronaut Bill Anders responded to the question of who was flying the spacecraft by saying, "I think that Isaac Newton is doing most of the driving right now." His response was understood by all to mean that the capsule was simply following the basic laws of physics described by Isaac Newton three centuries earlier.*

Quamrul 2021: *Our view is that we humans cherish our "free will" too much to surrender it to physics. Protecting and defending our personal freedoms and national sovereignty will be our responsibility—and ours alone—unless, of course, we're foolish enough to abdicate this responsibility to willingly subjugate ourselves to the tyranny of an Orwellian dictator—be that in the form of a digital entity or not.*

Samdani: Before we get carried away with the dark sides of digital technologies, of which there are many, let's first understand what our technology options are, what they can do to dramatically improve our lives, and what we can proactively do to maximize the upsides while minimizing the downsides of digital technologies today and in the future.

The late Marshall McLuhan, a Canadian scholar who has been famous for creating thought-provoking concepts like "the global village" and "the medium is the message" viewed language assembled into a book as a probe. He said, "When information is brushed against information, the results are startling and effective." One of the aims of this book is to produce such creative abrasion that will spark truly fresh and bold ideas in your mind

> "In a very real sense, people who have read good literature have lived more than people who cannot or will not read. It is not true that we have only one life to live; if we can read, we can live as many more lives and as many kinds of lives as we wish."
>
> – S. I. Hayakawa (1906 -1992)

and galvanize you all into taking collective action to overcome whatever obstacles may come in the way.

Reader: Sounds good.

Karim: Our hope is that you'll be able to treat this as a casebook of actionable ideas to help catapult Bangladesh into the new Facebook era and beyond. To this end, let's now turn to the chapter on "Learning to Leapfrog as Digital Bangladesh."

Samdani: Dear readers, you'll have to wait until Chapter 2 to learn how to claim your $80-trillion prize by closely reading and fully understanding the contents of that chapter. How's that for a tip on getting rich overnight through a thorough reading of a book chapter, i.e., by buying into the logic of "going digital" before you go to sleep tonight?

Chapter 1

Learning to Leapfrog as Digital Bangladesh

"Never before in history has innovation offered promise of so much to so many in so short a time."

– *Bill Gates (b. 1955)*

There are two takeaways from this chapter:

What's all the fuss about the digital age? Well, it happens to be a big deal, even after we strip the digital qualifier to our current era of some of the usual hype associated with it. Recent research indicates that if equipped with a robust digital backbone soon enough, a more open and economically vibrant Bangladesh could leapfrog to the world stage with the status of a middle-income country (MIC) in about a decade.

At a more personal level, are you already beginning to feel like an awkward "immigrant" among the "digital deshis" shopping for the best deals online, reading blogs or watching videos on something called YouTube for the latest news and views, and staying in touch with like-minded friends and business partners across the globe via e-mails and Facebook postings? Then we must forewarn you that this is just the beginning. You need to develop a basic understanding of the distinctive features of today's digital technologies driving the globalization of culture and commerce, and keep up with the goings-on in our ever-shrinking digital "global village."

What is Digital Bangladesh about? It's about equipping ourselves to make the most of the accelerating pace of technologies by incorporating digital hardware, software and 'humanware' into 'everyware' with the utmost care to make them accessible to all.

Before getting to learn how to leapfrog, let's take a brief (de)tour around defining what it is by enclosing the wilderness of an idea that has little or nothing to do with physical leaping or a frog as such within a wall of words (so to speak). It turns out that the concept of leapfrogging originated in the context of economic growth theories that promulgated sustainable development for developing countries by way of accelerating their economic development by skipping inferior, less efficient, more expensive, more polluting technologies and industries and moving directly to more advanced ones.

A case in point is digital communication in developing countries like Bangladesh by moving directly from having few telephones to having widespread mobile or cellular phones, thus skipping the stage of copper-wire landline telephones altogether. The city of Rizhao in China is another case of energy leapfrogging at a city level where almost 100% of the households at the central district reportedly use solar water heaters, and most of the lighting and traffic signals are powered with photovoltaic solar power. What's more, Rizhao city was recognized by the United Nations as one of the most habitable cities in the world in 2009.

The idea is that leapfrogging enables today's developing countries to avoid the more expensive or environmentally harmful stages of economic development and thus bypass the need to follow the more polluting development trajectories of the industrialized countries. Thus the adoption of solar energy technologies by developing countries illustrates leapfrogging by them as they avoid repeating the mistakes of today's highly industrialized countries in creating an energy infrastructure based on non-renewable fossil fuels and "jump" directly into the Solar Age instead. In other words, the leapfrogging concept proposes developing countries could learn from the experiences of industrialized countries, and restructure their growth and development to address potentially expensive and environmentally irreversible damages from an early stage.

The social dimension of the leapfrogging concept entails diffusion and adoption of modern technologies that would not only reduce costs and adverse environmental impacts, but also contribute to the realization of the United Nations-initiated Millennium Development Goals (MDGs)—e.g., eradicate extreme poverty and hunger, achieve universal primary education, promote gender equality and empower women, reduce child mortality rate, improve maternal health, and develop a global partnership for development with measurable targets to be achieved by the year 2015—by promoting greater access to resources and technologies to people who currently lack such access.

The good news is that Bangladesh has already achieved several targets of the eight-point MDGs and claims to be on track to achieve many of the other goals within the deadline of 2015. The country's achievements particularly in minimizing the child mortality rate under the MDG targets earned high marks when the UN decided to formally acknowledge the performance in the form of an award during a three-day special summit on the MDGs in New York on September 20, 2010 as convened by the UN General Assembly.

> "Learn from the mistakes of others. You can't live long enough to make them all yourself."
> – Eleanor Roosevelt (1884-1962)

Now the question is, could leapfrogging as Digital Bangladesh dramatically improve the odds of our achieving additional targets in MDGs by 2015 and beyond? Of course, this is not a rhetorical question—one asked merely for effect with no answer expected—since we believe the answer is an emphatic yes! What's more, we envision the actionable ideas of Digital Bangladesh catapulting her status from currently being a low-income country (LIC) to that of a middle-income country (MIC)—the coveted "middle class" member of the global economy—by 2021, perhaps not a moment too soon to celebrate the occasion of the 50th anniversary of our independence.

With that much resting on our success as Digital Bangladeshis, it's perfectly natural to pose the question, what is Digital Bangladesh after all? At the risk digressing a bit, this question reminds us of a story featuring Albert Einstein when he was monitoring an exam for graduate physics students and was told that there was a problem with the test since the questions on the exam were the same as the ones on the previous year's test. "That's okay," the famous physicist replied, "the answers are different this year."

Although today's digital technologies may not be as profound and cosmic in their implications as the theories of relativity and quantum mechanics, we believe they are as fast-changing (if not even more so) as physics was during the early decades of the 20th century to warrant different answers every year! Naturally, the best we'll be able to offer you in this book are our good-faith efforts with vintage 2011 answers and have you, dear reader, come up with yours for the intervening years as we approach 2021. But before we get to develop our individual visions of realizing the dreams of a Digital Bangladesh, let's take stock of its origin in a nutshell.

1.1 The promulgation of the current concept of Digital Bangladesh

While campaigning for national parliamentary elections in 2008, the Bangladesh Awami League (AL) came out with a party manifesto. First published on June 12th, 2008, it has henceforth been billed as the most forward-looking campaign manifesto ever. The manifesto formally endorsed "Digital Bangladesh by 2021" as the primary development goal of the Awami League led coalition for the nation and laid bare several milestones along the way. The voters, a third of whom have never seen a ballot before, were elated by this technology-centric future of the country and voted the AL to an over-whelming majority in the parliament. After AL formed the government on January 6th, 2009, the high expectation of the citizens, especially the young generation, on the fulfillment of the visions of "Digital Bangladesh" has outweighed everything else (additional details on the manifesto are available in Appendix).

> "Ever since I could remember, I'd wished I'd been lucky enough to be alive at a great time—when something big was going on, like a crucifixion. And suddenly I realized I was."
>
> – Ben Shahn(1898-1969)

Of course, historical evolution of the concept of Digital Bangladesh can be traced back to some five decades of the country's achievements in information technology (IT). What follows is a high-level chronology of the landmark events and significant developments (or lack thereof as missed opportunities). Indeed, Bangladesh can take pride in a number of achievements in IT so far.

1.2 Early adoptions of IT—1964 onwards

Use of computers in Bangladesh as research and data manipulation tools goes back more than 45 years. The first known computer installation in the country was an IBM 1620 at the Atomic Energy Commission in 1964, followed by an ICL 1902 at the then United Bank Limited (UBL) in 1966. Today computers are widely used in offices, businesses, educational institutions, at home and in the field. Bangladesh Computer Samity (www.bcs.org.bd), the industry association of information technology vendors, estimates that more than 300,000 computers are sold per year, a count that has seen a positive 20% annual growth in recent years.

This estimate is based on the fact that Intel (BD) Ltd. reportedly imported more than 250,000 CPUs in 2008, a number that does not include central processing units (CPUs) used in completely built units (CBUs) of branded computers imported into the country or non-Intel CPUs used in computers here or the grey market for Intel CPUs. The Intel figure for 2007 was more than 190,000 (Source: Mr. Mustafa Jabbar, President, BCS, 2010-11). Most IT majors, such as Dell, HP, Intel, Microsoft, Nokia, Oracle, Samsung and others have a direct presence here. There is also a large growing market for original equipment manufacturer (OEM) IT products sold under various local and foreign trade names.

The ICT industry in Bangladesh has seen mixed growth over the years. Some landmarks are highlighted below.

Machine dialogue—Volvo example

In 1986, Mr. Nurul Ghani Chowdhury, a UK-trained software professional, set up a business application development firm in Dhaka. He trained a team of young and promising software engineers and started developing an enterprise resource planning (ERP) application suite for vehicle manufacturing process. The business plan seemed a bit odd as there was no vehicle manufacturer in Bangladesh then (even today there isn't any such manufacturer although some claim some form of assembly operation with very little value addition). Mr. Chowdhury's firm was named Machine Dialogue Ltd. and in 1989 he successfully sold his ERP application to Volvo Motor Company of Sweden. In 1990 several Volvo personnel were flown into Dhaka to get training on the Machine Dialogue software application.

Things could not look more promising for the software industry in Bangladesh which was clearly under the radar at that time. But then Machine Dialogue crumbled. Habibullah Karim, one of the co-authors, ran into Mr. Chowdhury in Las Vegas (at the 'COMDEX Fall' IT exhibition) many years later in 1998 when he narrated this story about how his company folded—"things were going very well in 1989 but then all of a sudden I lost three-fourth of my development team as they migrated to the USA. The universities here were not yet turning out computer science graduates and I did not have the time to retrain another team and provide the contractual services to Volvo. In the end I lost my contract and I decided to relocate to the USA myself." What a sad ending to such a great start. Then again such has been the saga of the software industry of Bangladesh ever since.

IBCS Primax —ICI example

In 1989, another British trained software professional Mr. Abu Ahmed left his high-paying job with the pharmaceuticals division of the British chemical company ICI (Imperial Chemical Industries) and set up a software company in Dhaka named IBCS-Primax (BD) Ltd. He convinced his erstwhile superiors at ICI to outsource some of their software development needs to his startup operation in Bangladesh. Things were looking good until the IT services wing of ICI was spun off in 1991 and the new owners of the operation discontinued the outsourcing contract with IBCS-Primax. After some struggle, especially after the sudden demise of its founder in 1997, the company has emerged as the leading supplier of products and services on the Oracle database platform.

Technohaven—Railway example

Technohaven was a relatively small but significant player in the new-fangled IT industry of the mid-eighties Bangladesh. The country was groaning under the yoke of the dictatorial rule of a military general turned politician. The economy was struggling to keep ahead of stagflation and use of computers was stifled under the direction of martial-law-styled National Computer Committee (NCC) without whose approval no government office could even purchase a personal computer. In this IT-hostile environment, Technohaven started promoting the idea of PC-based systems for offices and factories in place of traditional and proprietary mini and mainframe computer systems that were much more expensive to buy and even more so to maintain.

One of the large clients Technohaven bagged in the course of this market promotion was Bangladesh Railway. Towards the end of 1989, Technohaven proposed several groundbreaking IT projects to Bangladesh Railway. These included a computer-based reservation and ticketing system for the inter-city trains. Bangladesh Railway started planning for such a system in 1990 and finally in 1992 called for tenders inviting bids for a nationwide reservation system on a build-operate-and-transfer (BOT) scheme. Technohaven was the lone domestic bidder among eleven. In the end Technohaven's design prevailed based on cost and local condition considerations and was awarded the work through an open tender. Technohaven ran the gauntlet to build the system from scratch in nine months flat.

This was the first time a major IT project was undertaken by a local company and broke the myth that local IT firms are merely traders of technology products. The Railway reservation system remains one of the country's most notable IT projects to date that undertakes more than a million reservations a month on the indigenously designed and built system. Technohaven is also the designer and builder of the customer billing and collection system of the largest gas utility in the country that processes nearly 1.5 million bills and payments a month.

Voter ID —Caretaker government project

Bangladesh today has the distinction of having the single largest biometric voter database in the world. More than 90 million voters were enumerated with their identification particulars, pictures, fingerprints and signatures compiled into a single voter registration database during 2007-2008. The work was carried out by the Bangladesh Election Commission and executed on its behalf by the IT directorate of the Bangladesh Army. This voter database with biometric identification features was instrumental in ensuring fair play during the December 2008 parliamentary election that saw the AL win by a landslide on the promise of "Digital Bangladesh by 2021."

PC second only to TV in households

In 1997 Bangladesh Computer Samity embarked on a major public relations campaign to make computers more affordable by withdrawing all import duties and taxes on computers. In its final putsch to win over the financial policy czars of the country, BCS arranged a seminar in December 1997 where the finance minister was invited as the chief guest. The keynote speaker at the seminar was the late Dewang Mehta, the legendary president and CEO of the Indian software industry association called NASSCOM. In his great story-telling riposte to the finance minister's entrenched trifling opinion of IT as anything but a significant tool for economic growth and progress, Mr. Mehta passionately challenged the Bangladesh finance minister to act faster than his the-then-Indian-counterpart Dr. Manmohan Singh (now the prime minister of India) who apparently sat on the proposal to lower import duty and taxes on computers for two years before positively acting on it.

The Bangladesh finance minister, the late Mr. Shah A M S Kibria was so moved by the appeal that he declared that he would act on it in two days and not two years. True to his word, all duties and taxes on computer software were withdrawn immediately afterward and it has remained that way ever since. In early 1998 Mr. Kibria was ecstatic when he was sent the pictures of his grandson via internet within hours after birth although he was born half the world away in the US. According to his son Dr. Reza Kibria, this incident combined with prodding from his son-in-low Dr. Allen Littlefield, a computer scientist, prompted Mr. Kibria to readily approve the withdrawal of all duties and taxes on computer hardware as well which was formally announced in the FY 1998-99 budget. With the lifting of import duty and tax, computers became cheaper by at least 20-40% and more importantly the psychological barrier to computers as a sophisticated geek tool was overcome. Students started to buy computers first in trickles and then in droves. Today PCs are only second to TVs as one of the most popular household electronic products.

1.3 Bangladesh's failures and missed opportunities in IT so far

From the above list of achievements it was easy to surmise Bangladesh would scale the heights of IT fortunes the way India, the Philippines and lately what Vietnam have done. Unfortunately that is not the case. Despite fits and starts and great promise at all times, the Bangladesh IT industry has been a victim of policy apathy and investment drought that has brought the industry crawling to a market size of US $300 million (Japan International Cooperation Agency or JICA study 2008) of which only a third accounts for software and services. Some of the biggest failures and missed opportunities are as follows:

Focusing only on import of computer technology for far too long

The local IT entrepreneurs have largely focused on import and distribution of computer products—a trend that was further given an incentive with the complete withdrawal of import duties and taxes on computers. This policy intervention—while made at the behest of the IT industry players—acted, strangely enough, as a strong disincentive for setting up manufacturing plants for any computer products, even accessories. This also highlighted only the tangible aspects of computer technology, that is, hardware while diluting the importance of software and services. What's more, piracy of software products is rampant and use of computers beyond their use as office equipment is trailing computer usage curves in countries of similar economic standing.

Not getting the Fortune 500 firms to open development centers yet

One of the major failures of the Bangladesh IT industry is the lack of any significant global players in the software and IT services market. The offshoring attraction to India, the Philippines, Vietnam and other developing countries was greatly enhanced by the setting up of captive software development and IT services centers in those countries by global majors such as British Airways, GE, HSBC and Microsoft. After the nuclear tests by India and Pakistan in 1998 when there were widespread talks of economic and trade sanctions on these two nations, the Philippines, Vietnam and even a civil-war-torn Sri Lanka cashed in the nuclear chip to bring home some IT off-shoring business. However, Bangladesh drew a blank. (As a note of optimism, of late, Samsung Mobile Phones Division has opened an offshore development center in Dhaka for mobile content and applications in 2010; GE executives paid a visit to Dhaka in 2009 while Telenor spun off the IT division of their Bangladesh operations as an IT services firm named GPIT in January 2010.)

Not recognizing the IT wave early on

There was a sizable number of highly educated and motivated entrepreneurs that started IT ventures in the country in the early eighties. By the early nineties this group of entrepreneurs swelled to more than a hundred. However, most of these IT ventures focused on providing IT products and systems as opposed to services and locally developed software. The market for computer products was growing and there was easy money to be made from selling computer hardware and packaged software. The lure of easy money drove more and more entrepreneurs to enter the market and intoxicate the corporate world with personal computers based on the latest processor from Intel or the latest operating system from Microsoft. Very soon there was a glut of pirated software applications all the way from AutoCAD, dBase III and Lotus 1-2-3 to WordStar and WordPerfect flooding the market. The computer hardware vendors kept on pushing the latest this or latest that, garnishing them with all kinds of free-of-cost (FOC) pirated software applications.

The profit margins on computers were fat and vendors did not mind providing all kinds of free services, warranties and more FOC software applications for the asking. In this scenario when the computer vendors tried to introduce payment-based services for anywhere from routine maintenance to custom software development, they were met with strong rebuffs from a clientele used to getting away without paying for software and services for too long. If the older vendors insisted on charging for software and services, there were always a slew of new vendors waiting in the wings to take their place and continue the mad rush of FOC software and services and get by with profits from hardware sales alone.

This hardware-centric expansion of the computer market here completely blindsided the entrepreneurs to the grand possibilities of software and IT services at both the domestic as well as the overseas markets. In the mid nineties, the IT entrepreneurs in Bangladesh were caught completely off-guard by the new wave of software off-shoring happening on an increasingly rapid pace in the so-called three Is—India, Ireland and Israel.

Failure to take up on McKinsey's offer to draw up the IT roadmap

McKinsey & Company drew up the IT roadmap for India in the mid nineties and then helped implement the roadmap. The advocacy done by McKinsey through road shows and widely disseminated country reports greatly helped build the Indian brand for IT services. Habibullah N Karim, the founding secretary general of Bangladesh Association of Software & Information Services (BASIS), with the help of his school buddy Gulam (aka "Sam") Samdani at McKinsey & Company (co-authors of this book), arranged to have a similar study done by McKinsey at a fraction of the cost incurred by India for the study. McKinsey offered to do the roadmap as somewhat of an "investment" for Bangladesh in 1998. Unfortunately, BASIS could not convince the government to fund the study and the industry association itself was not financially strong enough to do it on its own. Such a roadmap is yet to be done by Bangladesh.

Failure to build IT firms large enough befitting our economy

Bangladesh today boasts an economy that has reached 12 figures (around 100 billion in current US dollars). In India, the software and

ITES industry accounts for 1.5% of GDP (India's Information Technology Sector: What Contribution To Broader Economic Development? By Nirvikar Singh, UC Santa Cruz, 2003). In the USA it is estimated to be higher than that. Even at 1.5% the software and ITES industry's size in Bangladesh should be US $1.50 Billion. However, in reality the number is one-tenth of that. Due to this dwarfish size of the software and ITES industry, IT is not considered a major player in the economy despite all the feel-good and romantic policy support this industry enjoys. To make IT matter, this industry must break out of midgethood and gain bulk soon or it will become irrelevant. Today there are several hundred software and IT services firms in Bangladesh (more than 400 of them are members of BASIS) but due to the small market size most firms fall into the SME category and very few have broken the 100-employee mark.

For an industry estimated to generate around US $100 million to 150 million in revenues a year, the general assessment is that it's a highly fragmented market with too many small to midsize firms in all sub-sectors of the IT services industry causing severe price wars, acute revenue attrition and an increasing number of failed IT services projects—all of which are causing a vicious cycle of anemic growth, loss of goodwill and loss of market share to foreign IT services firms.

> "The empires of the future are the empires of the mind."
> – Winston Churchill (1874-1965)

1.4 Bangladesh's current position and rankings in IT

PC units sold per annum and computer market stats: An estimated 300,000 computers were sold in 2009 in Bangladesh according to the Bangladesh Computer Samity—the national industry association of computer vendors. The sales numbers are increasing at an estimated rate of 20% a year.

PC penetration rate: After televisions, computers are the most popular household electronic gadgets in the country. An estimated 2 million PCs are in use today which puts PC penetration at an unflattering 1.3%. However, the rising popularity of smart mobile phones skews the penetration rate curve north. There are approximately 76 million mobile phones in use today (source: BTRC; June 2011), of which around one-tenth are smart phones. If smart phones are included then the penetration rate goes up to 5%.

Telecom penetration rate: Before the days of cell phones, there was only the state-owned land-line operator called BTTB which over the last century (since 1898) built up a nationwide telephony network serving only around 800,000 customers. The penetration rate was the lowest in South Asia. Today, total landline customers have doubled in a matter of 5 years due to opening up of the sector to the private sector. (All private landline licenses have been on suspension since 2010 due to 'illegal' carrying of international voice traffic over IP.)

But the real diva of telecom growth was not the landline operators but the cell phone operators for whom the market was opened up in 1996. By the turn of the century cellphones have outstripped landlines as the primary means of telecommunications and today outnumber their fixed variety by a factor of 76. Today because of cellphones, the telecom penetration rate is a respectable 49%. The telecom sector is still slated for high growth over the next few years and the penetration rate is expected to reach 75% by 2013, at the present rate of growth.

Bangladesh ranks 118 out of 133 countries in the latest study (2009-2010) of the World Economic Forum's assessment of the overall network readiness of nations. This truly is sad especially since we are at the bottom of the SAARC region (just above Nepal at 124 to be sure as Bangladesh moved up 6 notches from a year ago). India ranks 43 while Pakistan trails at 87.

Our hope is that with the launching of two Wi-Max broadband services, a number of fiber-to-the-home broadband services and increasing coverage of 2.5G (and in due course 3G and 4G) mobile broadband services, we will soon have much higher internet penetration rate which is an important consideration for network readiness. There is also a rising number of data service providers with ever wider coverage coming into play.

Since the WEF network readiness index influences IT services growth to some extent, there ought to be a targeted roadmap of WEF ranking escalation for Bangladesh over the next few years. We are of the view that Bangladesh can advance her ranking by at least 50 places within the next 4 years with appropriate policy support and nothing more.

According to BASIS, the software and IT services industry is growing at nearly 25% a year based on the growth of membership and procurement trends both inside and outside the country. The hardware market is growing at 20%, according to BCS as mentioned earlier. In internet service, the traditional stranglehold of ISPs, a host of telecom operators and broadband service providers entering the market have extended the reach and affordability of such service. The biggest growth is expected here in the next several years as both private and public sector enterprises roll out more and more expansive and cost-effective data/internet services throughout the country. If we have to put a number here for the expected growth rate, we imagine it would be in triple digits.

The overall software and ITES market is estimated to be worth more than BDT 10 billion or US $150 million of which around 22% is export revenue, according to BASIS. The export growth last fiscal year was 32% while domestic growth was around 23% giving the overall industry a 25% growth in 2009 (July to June). But according to a World Bank study done between late 2008 and early 2009, this industry has

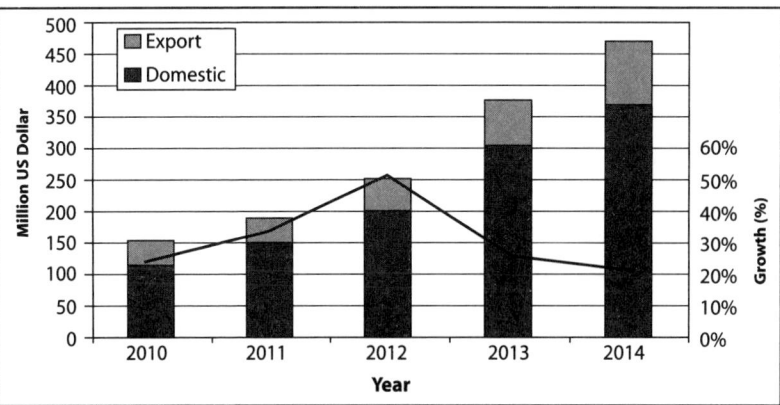

Bangladesh IT Services Market Projection 2010-2014

Year	Revenue (in million Dollar)	Export (in million Dollar)	Growth (%)
2010	$150	$35	25%
2011	$188	$40	33.33%
2012	$250	$50	50%
2013	$375	$70	25%
2014	$469	$100	20%

the hallmarks to grow rapidly with export revenues reaching US $500 million a year by 2014. In another study conducted by the International Trade Centre (ITC) in 2007-2008, the ITES industry exports are poised to reach US $150 million by 2011 and generate new employment of 20,000 ITES professionals. Japan International Cooperation Agency (JICA) instituted a study in 2008 that ranked Bangladesh second only to India in South Asia in terms of IT services export readiness and growth potential.

On the domestic front, the government has allocated BDT 1 billion for e-government projects under a separate budget head for the first time in fiscal year 2009-2010 (repeated in FY2010-2011 and FY2011-2012). The public sector procurements of IT services should see a sharp rise in the next 3 years, increasing the overall local market by a factor of 5 in the next 5 years. By 2014, the overall software and ITES market in Bangladesh should reach nearly half a billion US dollars, a fifth of which will be from exports.

An important positive impact from Bangladesh's participation in the ITS and ITES markets would be on the status of women. For example, women account for about 65% of the total professional and technical workers in ITS and ITES in the Philippines. In India, women made up 30% of the ITS and ITES workforce in 2007—a much higher rate of female participation than in the services sector overall—and this share grew to 45% by 2010. More than half of call center employees are women. In both countries, women fill a greater number of high-paying jobs in ITS and ITES than in most other sectors of the economy.

1.5 Bangladesh's current development agenda in ICTs

ICT Policies 2002 and 2009: Back in the late Eighties computer use in the public sector i.e. in government offices was highly regulated by an ad-hoc committee called the National Computer Committee (NCC) which had its mandate directly from the office of the president of the republic. However, in 1988 a forward-looking military officer named Col. Azizur Rahman from the Army Corps of Engineers, who had formerly been with military intelligence, drew up a plan to set up a national body promulgated by law to promote (and not regulate) the use of computers in government offices. He drew his inspiration in this from similar institutions in other countries in Asia, notably Singapore and India. This new setup was formed as Bangladesh Computer

Council (BCC) in 1989 with Col. Aziz, then just retired from the Army, as its first Executive Director (CEO).

An eleven-member Council acts as the supervisory board and is chaired by the cabinet minister in charge of the ministry of Science and Technology. The Science & Technology Ministry has been renamed as Science & ICT Ministry since 2002. The BCC in the late Nineties worked on formulating a national policy to promote and harness ICTs. It put together a draft by 2001 which was approved in principle (subject to scrutiny by the secretaries committee) by the-then Awami League-led government the same year. In late 2001 the Bangladesh Nationalist Party led coalition came to form the government. The new government did some consultation with the various stakeholders of the ICT industry and the cabinet finally approved the first ICT Policy of the nation in 2002.

However, BCC and the Ministry of Science & ICT failed to take into account most of the inputs given by the ICT industry. The ICT Policy 2002 also had some structural flaws in that it did not segregate policy matters from strategic objectives and action plans. This resulted in incongruous goals and policy paradigms. For example, back in 2002 when the PC penetration rate was less than 0.5% and the internet penetration rate was south of 0.3% the Policy proclaimed the outlandish goal of achieving a "Knowledge Society"—where advanced know-how is the newly tapped factor of production alongside land, labor and capital—by 2006. Equally unrealistic was the goal of reaching US $3 billion in annual exports of ICT services within four years when in 2002 the revenue from such exports was less than US $3 million.

In 2007 there was a military-backed caretaker government in place to prepare the nation for the parliamentary elections. Among some of the good initiatives of this interim government while the election commission was busy preparing the national voter database from scratch, was the Better Business Forum—a public private partnership initiative to address business environment issues including regulatory and policy issues through joint committees populated by public and private sector representatives. Among the many recommendations the BBF put forward to the government for immediate implementation was the one to review the ICT policy adopted by the government in 2002 and update it.

The 2008 ICT Policy Review Committee was headed by Professor Jamilur Reza Choudhury, then Vice Chancellor (President & CEO) of BRAC University, Dhaka and consisted of 27 members representing all ICT stakeholder groups in the industry, academia, government and non-profits. As the representative from the software industry Habibullah N Karim argued for a fresh ICT Policy instead of reviewing and updating the previous one citing several structural weaknesses in the policy document. The committee accepted his arguments and formed a working group with him as the convener to examine the 2002 policy and draft a new one.

The new draft ICT policy put together by this working group was formally endorsed by the main ICT Policy Review Committee and was forwarded to the government in October 2008; this was eventually adopted by the newly elected Awami League led government as the ICT Policy 2009 in March. The new policy is structured like a pyramid with a singular vision of turning the country into a middle income country within a decade and into a developed country within 30 years by accelerating the economic growth through use of ICTs. The singular vision is supplemented by 10 core objectives cutting across all socio-economic fields which are expanded into 56 strategic themes that steer 306 action programs to achieve the objectives and the vision laid out in the policy.

The government in the mean time has reconstituted the national ICT Task Force headed by the prime minister as the Digital Bangladesh Task Force while the prime minister's office (PMO) is closely supervising and coordinating the implementation status of the 306 action programs provided in the ICT Policy 2009. There is a lot of hope and excitement in the ICT industry as well as the government and the people in general on the ensuing digital future of the country.

Human resource (HR) development

For ICT to flourish and for the ICT industry to become the driver of economic growth in Bangladesh, it would require a rapid influx of highly trained and motivated ICT professionals in the industry that employs around 30,000 professionals, according to BASIS. An increase of at least another 50,000 professionals is envisaged by 2014 in the World Bank study of 2008. That's more than 10,000 new professionals being inducted a year. The impending skills shortage becomes clear in light of the fact that all the universities combined turn out around 5,000 computer science and engineering graduates while a couple of thousand more come out with degrees in closely related fields such as telecommunications and electronics engineering. However, most of them do not have job-specific ICT skills for which they need to undergo skills-gap training.

In most countries such training programs are conducted both by the government or state-run vocational training institutes and by private companies. In Bangladesh, though, the number of companies large enough to afford in-house training centres are not too many (only a few dozen companies employ more than 100 professionals). In view of this situation, BASIS proposed the formation of a government sponsored ICT Professional Skills Assessment and Enhancement Program (IPSAEP) in 2007 which eventually evolved into the ICT Capacity Development Company (ICDC) in 2010, a proposed company wholly owned by the state through the Bangladesh Computer Council (BCC). This project, if and when it gets going, will only cater to skills development for the software sector.

> "Time is nature's way of preventing everything from happening at once. Space is nature's way of preventing everything from happening to you."
> – Unknown

We need to have similar skills training for IT Enabled Services (ITES) sector as well, a sector that is growing very fast indeed driven both by local demand as well as exports. A two-year study undertaken jointly by the International Trade Centre (ITC), Bangladesh Export Promotion Bureau (EPB) and BASIS on the ITES market carried out in 2008-2009 found strong growth in Graphic Design Services (GDS), an ITES subsector where some firms registered triple digit growth consistently during the study period.

Market access development

Despite the strong demand for software and IT services from many developing nations such as India, Pakistan, the Philippines, Sri Lanka, Vietnam and others, Bangladesh has to date remained outside the mainstream destinations for such services outsourcing. Even though Bangladesh featured prominently in the JP Morgan's "Frontier Five" or Goldman Sachs' "Next 11 Emerging Markets", country rankings on IT services outsourcing by industry monitors such as IDC and AT Kearny fail to mention Bangladesh.

BASIS in partnership with EPB has been participating in IT outsourcing expositions such as OutsourceWorld in London and New York, EasyFair in Denmark and JOFIS/SODEC in Japan since 2003. Gartner finally took notice and included Bangladesh in its 2011 list of 30 potential IT services destinations. Bangladesh registered a 32% growth in export receipts on account of software & IT services exports to North America, European Union, Middle East and other destinations in fiscal 2009 (July 2008 to June 2009). There are presumably several factors contributing to this apparent apathy of the IT services cognoscenti towards Bangladesh, the most important of which is lack of market access development in any systematic manner.

Since formation of BASIS in late 1997 (when one of the authors was its founder secretary general), EPB and BASIS have jointly organized participation of Bangladeshi firms in IT exhibitions in USA, Germany, Denmark, UAE, and Japan. In BASIS's very first overseas IT exhibition at COMDEX Fall in Las Vegas in November 1998, eight member firms participated. Some of these firms came back with sales leads that generated the first wave of systematic export of software and IT services from Bangladesh.

But the sailing has been far from smooth either back then or even now. At this first ever overseas exhibition BASIS and EPB were poorly prepared and the Bangladesh country stall did not have any decoration beyond the bare-bones structure and signage provided by the fair authorities. There were few visitors the first day. As the coordinator of BASIS member firms, Habibullah N Karim brainstormed with his colleagues on how they might improve the situation and agreed that if they provided some free candies, as done by many other exhibitors, visitors would come. Accordingly, they bought a glass bowl but forgot to buy the candies the next day. Seeing the empty bowl some visitors asked if they were there to collect relief for Bangladesh flood victims! Incidentally, the timing was right for some flood relief action as Bangladesh had a devastating flood that year in September.

The BASIS team was back to the drawing boards on what to do. The-then BASIS treasurer Atique-e-Rabbani came up with a brilliant idea that since people at the show think they were there for flood relief, they should put up a sign that says that 'We write software too!'. Immediately the signage was done and put up. That incidentally became one of the lead stories in the next day's COMDEX daily news. After 12 years and reaching a little beyond US $30 million in annual exports, the IT services entrepreneurs here still get the feeling that most of the world do not know that "we write software too."

BASIS has been participating in anywhere from 3 to 5 international marketing events (exhibitions, seminars and road-shows such as Global Sourcing in New York, CeBIT in Germany, EasyFairs in Denmark, Sodec in Tokyo, Gitex in Dubai, etc.) each year since the late nineties but accelerated IT services export growth seems to have run out of steam in recent times. Having made inroads into 30 countries around the globe, exports in FY2009-10 (July to June) were US $35.36 million which is marginally more than the figures for the previous year. The export figures are really insignificant when one compares them with other industry exports. Even cut-flower exports, that does not even merit a position in the top ten export industries of the country, ranked above IT services. This is despite dogged optimism expressed by international development agencies on the bright future of IT services both for export and domestic markets.

The World Bank in a study conducted in 2008 concluded that Bangladesh IT service exports will reach more than half a billion US dollars by 2014 and create more than 50,000 IT services jobs. Japan International Cooperation Agency (JICA) in a regional survey carried out in 2007 concluded that Bangladesh is the most competitive for IT services in Asia and overall ranks only behind China and India at competence in this industry. JICA was equally optimistic about the jute processing industry that has reached US $500 million mark in exports for the first time this year, whereas IT services exports have been languishing at late twenties early thirties range (in million US Dollars) for 5 years now. International Trade Center (ITC) also conducted a study in 2007-2008 with the conclusion that IT enabled services (one derivative of IT services) will reach US $150 million in exports by 2011! Even Gartner listed Bangladesh as one of the 30 most potential global sourcing destinations for IT services in early 2011. How could so many international observers go wrong in their assessment of our IT services industry? We will dig into this issue in more detail later in this book.

Entrepreneurship development

The IT industry saw a trailblazing growth in the number of first generation IT entrepreneurs between the mid eighties and now—IT industry associations such as Bangladesh Computer Samity (BCS) and Bangladesh Association of Software and Information Services (BASIS) saw their memberships rise more than twenty fold during this period. This huge growth in ICT entrepreneurship is due principally to the romanticism of rags-to-riches stories of many a software firm across the border rather than the intrinsic growth prospect of the industry here. As mentioned before, this has given rise to a multitude of under-capitalized also-rans that is not helping the cause of an ICT-led economic boost. Nevertheless, the strength of entrepreneurial numbers in ICTs needs to be nurtured within an institutional framework because failure of these entrepreneurs will set the industry back even further.

We need to look upon the fragmentation as an advantage rather than an impediment and we have to find the right kind of industry ecosystem to strengthen them. We are reminded of a story a business associate once told one of the authors while visiting Taipei many years ago. He said the running joke in the island state is that if anyone throws a rock from the sea onto Taiwan, it's bound to land on the head of either a Ph.D. holder or a company CEO. In other words, the Taiwanese people value high academic accomplishment and are highly entrepreneurial. That value system has propelled Taiwan from the shackles of extreme poverty in the early fifties (General Chiang Kai Shek fled from the advancing Chinese Red Army and formed the Taiwanese Republic in 1947) to a thriving economic powerhouse of the twenty-first century. Maybe this is the model we need to emulate in the IT services industry in Bangladesh, since here you are bound to find a plethora of CEOs and plenty of highly educated workers.

e-Government initiatives

According to the UK-Intellect (British IT services industry association), the British Government accounts for almost half the IT industry revenues and is automatically the single largest buyer of IT services there. Although we lack proper statistics for Bangladesh, we estimate that the government procurement of IT services is a hefty chunk of the industry revenues. Government's share is anywhere from a third to around half of the market despite the lack of a coordinated and strategic push from the top.

Government departments and affiliated organizations in Bangladesh have been buying ICT products since the sixties in an increasingly bigger volume but buying ICT services such as business process consulting, software development, staff training and adaptation, facilities management outsourcing etc. has been lacking to a large extent.

Based on the recommendation of Professor Jamilur Reza Choudhury in his report on prospects of establishing a software export industry in mid 1997 and taking a cue from the Indian 'ICT Task Force', the Bangladesh Government also formed a high-level task force in the year 2000.

In 2002, co-author Habibullah N Karim as the then president of BASIS submitted a proposal to the ICT Task Force to initiate an e-government program by allocating specific funds for it. The ICT Task Force accepted the proposal in principle and allocated BDT 800 million to start off the program, named 'Support to ICT Task Force' under the Ministry of Planning. This was the first time the government initiated a central e-government implementation program. However, the placement of the program under the planning ministry caused technical and administrative difficulties resulting in huge delays in the utilization of the fund. After six years and 30-odd projects, the program was discontinued in 2008.

The ministry responsible for ICT development is the Ministry of Science & ICT, which oversees a fully functioning technical setup called the Bangladesh Computer Council. In the new ICT Policy 2009, this ministry was made the focal point of all ICT activities within the government. Accordingly in the 2009-2010 fiscal year, as per demands from the ICT industry, the finance ministry allocated BDT 1 billion for ICT development to the Ministry of Science & ICT. This was mostly utilized for setting up ICT infrastructure within the government, such as the first tier-3 data center of the country and computer laboratories in selected government schools. This ministry has received similar funds for the 2010-11 and 2011-12 fiscal years and is likely to continue receiving such funding at least within the tenure of the present government running up to 2013-2014.

On the other hand, the Prime Minister's Office (PMO) runs an ICT program with technical assistance from the UN Development Program. This program, though initiated in 2007 to augment the government's "access to information (A2I)" capacities, has transformed itself into a full-blown ICT advisory and piloting organ within the PMO. In terms of creating heightened awareness on ICTs among the government functionaries, the A2I program has had some success but its role vis-à-vis the mandated roles of the Ministry of Science & ICT and the BCC remain unclear. The principal secretary of the PMO is the executive head of the ICT Task Force (the Prime Minister is the statutory/administrative head of the task force) while the chief private secretary (called PS 1) to the Prime Minister is the head (called project director) of the A2I program.

The A2I program is coordinating and assisting the government efforts at putting together the strategic document for implementing the Digital Bangladesh vision (more on this in Chapter 3) and has the flexibility to draw upon industry expertise through consulting assignments funded by the UNDP. However, as it is outside the purview of the regular government machinery for ICT affairs and as it wields enormous clout being part of the PMO, there is a certain mystique about the program in the public mind. Despite the missionary zeal of the A2I staffers in promoting e-services to citizens, the project is still a temporary setup with funding from UNDP ensured up to June 2011. For the Digital Bangladesh initiative to remain a core agenda, the government needs to tie up these loose ends under the newly mandated ICT Ministry (as per decision number 3.2.5 of the Digital Bangladesh Task Force meeting held on 03 August 2010) which is expected to start operations soon. On way to carving a full-fledged ICT Ministry out of the three present Ministries of Information, Post and Telecommunications, and Science and ICT, the government has separated the ICT functions into a separate Division headed by a secretary in May 2011.

Online business/e-commerce initiatives

Bangladesh entered the realm of e-commerce early on with excited entrepreneurs trying to carve out a market for online trading at the turn of the new century. Following in the footsteps of Amazon.com, several vendors started hawking books online, such as 'munshigi.com'. However, due to lack of online payment systems these businesses foundered. The only online business that has thrived is a copy of the jobs.com in USA and naukri.com in India named bdjobs.com. However, very recently the county's central bank (named Bangladesh Bank) has lifted the artificial sanctions on online credit and debit card transactions (the statutory order was issued in early 2010). The BRAC Bank, an SME-focused commercial bank owned by the largest NGO in Bangladesh and Dutch-Bangla Bank, a regular commercial bank, has launched e-commerce payment settlement platforms for Visa/MC debit/credit cards at the end of 2010 which are starting to get some traction now.

In this sphere however, Bangladesh has barely scratched the surface. It's estimated that 84% of internet users in the US conducted at least one online purchase during the final quarter of 2010, and in a 2010 survey conducted by KPMG in India, 38% of the respondents said they used mobiles to shop while 43% for financial transactions. Clearly, in Bangladesh we have a very long way to go no doubt but we suspect this market will grow at breakneck speed for several reasons. First, more than ten million Bangladeshi diaspora around the world are eager to buy Bangladeshi gift items both for near and dear ones living in the country as well as in faraway lands. Second, large urban centers such as Dhaka and Chittagong have been ripe for online purchases for many years now with their congested roads and chronic traffic jams. An explosive growth of online offerings is right under our noses.

> "Do not attempt to walk through life without a dream, without a hope, without a goal to achieve success."
>
> – *Luis Noboa Naranjo (1916-1994)*

Digital lifestyle initiatives

Executives carrying smart phones with internet connectivity, students and salespeople toting laptops and netbooks with wireless gateways to the internet, yuppie crowds milling about coffeeshops, restaurants and hotel lobbies with wi-fi hotspots, it's all happening all over the country. Digital lifestyle is here to stay. The naysayers and cynics are missing the elephant in the room! In many ways this new lifestyle is changing the way we do things and look at things. Nobody blinks an eye to purchase an e-ticket from airlines at thousands of taka or carry out online stock market trades worth millions of taka without any physical papers changing hands. Such unmistakable signs of the coming of the digital era are only heightened by the desire of the current government to make Bangladesh the place of everything digital by the year 2021—a vision appropriately dubbed "Digital Bangladesh." However, if we were to make it a demographically and economically inclusive initiative, we have a long way to go.

1.6 A leapfrogger joins the economic development marathon

If Bangladesh were a marathon runner, where would you place her relative to the world's leaders in overall standards of living and quality of life? Well, no less an authority on such matters than the World Bank has recently applauded the speed and stamina with which the country has pulled herself from the back of the pack to a place within sight of the leading countries. Yet it wonders when Bangladesh will manage to get a second wind on her back and propel to the head of the field.

Even if you discount the "cheerleading" aspect of the World Bank's role here, this optimistic assessment resonates with us in light of the fact that Bangladesh has made impressive gains in poverty reduction and social and human development since 1991 although these achievements are often overshadowed by rising concerns about the quality and equity in public and social services.

What's more, the country pulled off these achievements in spite of worsening governance—that is, the decision-making processes in the administration of the government—over the same period since Bangladesh often ranks near the bottom in cross-country comparisons relating to governance. This odd coexistence of development success with governance failure has given rise to the so-called "Bangladesh paradox": How could the pro-poor development achievements of Bangladesh even be possible, given the poor state of governance?

Well, the English word "paradox," derives from a Greek word, *para*, meaning beyond and *dox*, meaning common opinion. Put yourself in the shoes of a logical purist facing a paradox as simple as this: How could one cross a stream or river and still not get wet? Then, of course, a pragmatic Bangladeshi comes along and suggests using a floating object (e.g., a raft or a boat) or building a bridge, in order to be able to cross the stream and still stay dry.

We believe that this simple resolution of the paradox of "crossing a stream without getting wet" explains many, if not most, of the factors underlying the Bangladesh paradox. Could it be that Bangladeshi people in general, and entrepreneurs in particular, have simply improvised the equivalents of the proverbial boats, bridges and ladders to cross the apparent chasms and overcame the barriers often created by the poor state of governance? However, there's no getting around the fact that no one can jump a 20-ft chasm in two 10-ft jumps, and therefore, boldness in vision and action will be required to bridge the gap between where Bangladesh stands today and where it wants to be in 2021.

The good news is that a number of internet-enabled digital technologies could provide the much-needed "second wind" or "kicker" for the leapfrogging Bangladesh by expanding the virtual bridges for its growing number of mobile-phone-savvy "netizens." What's more, these netizens could learn to leapfrog with both feet - not just run at a limping pace—across the virtual bridges toward the head of the global economic development race.

The mixed news is that a 2007 World Bank report—*Bangladesh: Strategy for Sustained Growth*—projected that given a second wind, Bangladesh could join the ranks of middle-income countries (MICs) in little over a decade. This aspiration required Bangladesh to nudge its annual gross domestic product (GDP) growth rate from the recent average of 6% "to a challenging but not impossible 7.5%". That's because, the World Bank says, the country has the necessary assets: much-improved economic fundamentals; success in implementing many first-generation reforms; a young, rapidly growing labor force; and an established entrepreneurial culture. In other words, despite the widely acknowledged and critical weakness in governance, Bangladesh could build on its impressive record of achievements to date, especially in harnessing sound economic and social policies to pioneering social entrepreneurship.

To pick up the pace in the development marathon, says the World Bank, Bangladesh will need to deepen its industrial base, further its economic integration with global markets, and unleash the growth potentials of its major urban centers while creating new opportunities for the rural poor. Indeed, broad-based economic growth will be key to transforming the country by reducing and eventually eliminating extreme poverty. It is the surest way to generate the resources it needs to address illiteracy, poor health, and other development challenges, and thus to emerge from dependence on foreign aid.

Indeed, there is direct correlation between the openness of a country and its standard of living. Research conducted by economist Jeffrey Sachs and the Harvard Institute for International Development found that openness was decisive for rapid growth. It turns out that open economies "grew 1.2 percentage points per year faster than closed economies, controlling for everything else, because the more open you are, the more integrated you are into today's global network of ideas, markets, technologies, and management innovations."

The potential for additional 'leapfrogging' boosts to the GDP of Bangladesh comes from a recent (2009) World Bank econometrics analysis of 120 countries, suggesting that for every 10-percentage-point increase in the penetration of broadband services, there is an increase in economic growth of 1.3 percentage points. The impact can be even more robust once the penetration reaches a critical mass. Combining these two effects—openness of the economy and a 10% increase in broadband access—could produce an aggregate GDP growth rate of over 8.5% in place of the current secular trend of 6% growth in Bangladesh. Even without the 'kicker' from broadband penetration, there is international precedence for such performance, e.g., GDP growth in China has averaged over 9% since 1975, while Thailand and South Korea each attained 8% growth for two decades before the 1997 East Asian financial crisis. In some sense, the new kickers from increasing broadband penetration could provide Bangladesh some "margin for safety" with its open-door policies with the rest of the world.

Bangladesh has achieved 6% average growth over the last decade. This is despite a major political upheaval and chronic governance problems during the said period. Economic and political observers reckon Bangladesh can accelerate the growth rate by 2-3% with a reasonable improvement in the quality of governance. In a study carried out by Dr. Hossain Zillur Rahman in December 2010 on behalf of the largest chamber in Bangladesh—the Dhaka Chamber of Commerce & Industry (DCCI), the growth projection is slated at 8% over the next two decades in order for the Bangladesh economy to become the 30th largest in the world by 2030. The ICT Policy 2009 on the other hand envisions lifting the average growth rate to 7.5% through leveraging ICTs so that Bangladesh can reach the status of a middle income country (MIC) by 2021. The DCCI study vindicates the economic goals set in the ICT Policy 2009 which now essentially is the policy blueprint for the "Digital Bangladesh" initiative of the government. Whereas the ICT Policy 2009 aims for MIC status by 2021 and high-income-country status in 30 years, the DCCI study calls for quadrupling the size of the economy in 20 years to attain the coveted economic rank.

We however, need to look at historical evidence of any large nation achieving such growth over a long period of time. Japan did it in the seventies, the Four Tigers (South Korea, Taiwan, Singapore, Malaysia) did it in the eighties, China of course has done it in the nineties and it appears that India might do it in the 2010s. Whether Bangladesh can do it in its present political ecosystem begs an answer.

The World Bank classifies countries according to their per capita income—countries with average per capita income of at least US $10,725 (nominal dollars) as High Income Countries (HIC) and countries with per capita income of less than US $785 (nominal dollars, without adjustment for purchasing power parity) as Low Income Countries (LIC). With the GDP for Bangladesh pegged at a little over US $100 billion, the average per capita income for her citizens in 2010 stood at about US $685/yr (nominal dollar basis). The country is also rated the 48th largest economy in the world as per GDP purchasing power parity (PPP) basis and 77th largest trading nation. Industrial contribution to GDP is 28%; external trade is 40% of GDP. We are no longer in the position that we were in 1975-1990 but, unfortunately, we are still considered as one of the least developed countries in the world due to a low economic base and a high level of poverty.

The present government has set "Vision 2021" to move Bangladesh to a middle income country (MIC) by 2021; however, many feel that the MIC status for Bangladesh may arrive by 2014 indicating that Bangladesh's economic performance may have been underestimated and as such the economy will out-perform expectations due to a sound economic foundation that has been achieved over the last 20 years. The other interesting fact about Bangladesh's economy is the large informal economy that exists but is not accounted for in the formal analysis of its economy. Some economists estimate that the informal economy is as large as a third of the economy (Source: *The Shadow Economy of Bangladesh: Size Estimation and Policy Implications* by Prof Kabir Hassan of Univ. of New Orleans, USA) but due to lack of effective regulations and difficulties in enforcing them make it hard to account for the informal part of the economy.

The Bangladesh economy until 1990 failed to gather much needed growth; average GDP growth rate was stagnant at less than 4%. But after restoration of democracy in 1991, the economy started to gain momentum and economic growth showed commendable performance over the last 20 years. Impressive growth above 5% for the last two decades has indeed taken the economy to a new growth trajectory—contributed to by steady agricultural production, increased export earnings, healthy expatriate worker remittances and vibrant domestic demand.

GDP growth picked up to 6.2% in 2004 from a rate of 5.2% in 2003. After slowing down to 5.5% the next year, GDP picked up steam to post a 6.6% growth rate in 2006 and remained above the 6% level before declining to 5.8% in 2009 and climbing back up to 6% in 2010. The steady growth of GDP in the context of the global meltdown exhibited the resilience of our economy yet at the same time revealed our relatively small exposure to the external shocks.

Strong resilience during global financial meltdown added an important seal to the strong fundamentals of the economy. The Asian Development Bank (ADB) in one of its reports has indicated that Bangladesh's economy can grow by an additional 1% if the Dhaka-Chittagong Economic Corridor (DCEC) can be upgraded and developed into a modern communication link between the two major cities of Bangladesh where it is estimated to have 65% of country's economic activities—the DCEC is considered as the "economic life line" of Bangladesh. It is also estimated that the current power and energy crisis is also eating up close to 1% of Bangladesh's growth.

Taking the two above assessments, we can estimate that Bangladesh can aim to achieve 8% growth rate quite easily. However, in order to achieve such growth rates, investment to GDP ratio also needs to increase from 25% to 40% percent. This will not be an easy task as a large amount of investable resources will need to be mobilized to raise the rate of investment to 40% of GDP.

1.7 The tale of two countries with two very different trajectories

To appreciate what broad-based economic growth—or lack thereof—can do, look no further than the contrasting trajectories of Ghana and South Korea. In 1950, South Korea's per capita income was roughly US $770 in dollars of 1990 purchasing power; Ghana's was considerably higher, at US $1,120. During a time span of six decades, per capita income in South Korea rose dramatically to US $30,200 (purchasing power parity basis), while Ghana's crept upward to just US $1610 (comparable to Bangladesh at US $1,600 in 2010).

In 1950 life expectancy in South Korea exceeded that in Ghana by only four years. The gap has since grown to 20 years. Most citizens of both countries lived on less than US $2 per day in 1950. By 1998, 78 percent of Ghanaians, but less than 2 percent of South Koreans still lived in such poverty. Similar gaps emerged in education, health, and other measures of well-being. Due largely to their contrasting records in economic growth, South Korea has achieved transformational development, whereas Ghana remains at a much earlier stage of this process. South Korea has become a significant and constructive actor on the world stage as well as one of the top cross-border trading partners with the leading economies of the world. South Korea supports development in other countries through its own foreign aid program now while Ghana remains dependent on foreign assistance.

We have heard this anecdote many times now that after the Korean war of the early fifties, a delegation of South Korean businesspeople and government functionaries were brought to Dhaka, then the capital of East Pakistan (E.P.), to see the development works here and learn from them since USAID (the sponsors of the visit) felt that Bangladesh (E.P. then) was a model of development that other poor Asian nations should emulate. When co-author Habibullah N Karim visited South Korea in March 2008, one senior KOTRA (Korea Trade and Investment Promotion Office) executive confirmed the story. In 1955 the per capita GDP of East Pakistan (now Bangladesh) and South Korea were not too dissimilar. Since then a sustained high growth rate has propelled South Korea to the status of a high income country with a per capita GDP of US $30,200 whereas Bangladesh is languishing at US $1,600 per capita GDP (purchasing power parity basis). This together with the Ghana comparison before shows the importance of smart governance and open market economy to the sustained development of nations. This example also shows how economic growth increases incomes and improves livelihoods and that while poverty alleviation measures can assist in short term income redistribution, unless they are coupled with economic growth, longer term prospects for poverty reduction are dim.

While economists often differ with respect to how best to go about achieving economic prosperity, most agree that economic growth occurs as societies accumulate savings and equip workers with greater and better physical capital (e.g., factories and infrastructure) and human capital (i.e., skills and knowledge), and use these assets ever more productively to produce goods and services of increasing value. It turns out that among these sources of growth, increases in productivity account for most of the differences in economic growth among countries.

Productivity grows as owners of the means of production—who are, almost by definition, entrepreneurs operating at all scales—find ways to squeeze more output from a given set of inputs. They do so by adopting more efficient production methods, applying technical knowledge to create better products, changing their product mix, and so on. Needless to say, capital accumulation and productivity growth both result from the independent efforts of millions of individual producers, constantly working to create new, better, and less costly goods and services through ingenuity and investment. Those efforts, in turn, are guided by the incentives that producers face, which are strongly affected by public policy enforcement of contracts and property rights, the prevalence or absence of corruption, and other aspects of economic governance.

If a Rip Van Winkle economist, a distant cousin of the legendary Rip Van Winkle, were to wake up today from his 20-year slumber, he would probably nod his head broadly in agreement with everything we have said above. However, what would astonish him the most is the increasing role of information and communication technologies (ICTs) in advancing the growth of national economies worldwide through enhanced efficiency and productivity, and expanded market reach for even the poorest of the poor. It is within this context that we would like to draw your attention to the new ICT-driven opportunities that are not purely limited to, and accessible only by, the larger multinational corporations (MNCs), but they are also open to small, medium and micro-enterprises (SMMEs), which directly serve as both the backbone and relentless growth drivers of developing economies like Bangladesh. Indeed, our Rip Van Winkle economist friend is probably going to be amazed by how creative the SMMEs have been in leveraging ICT's to directly alleviate poverty by increasing income levels and creating jobs for millions in Bangladesh. However, as a practitioner of the "dismal science," Mr. Van Winkle economist may also start worrying about the growing "digital divide" and the "information poverty" it engenders throughout Bangladesh and elsewhere. The good news is that "digital deflation" may win over the prospect of the digital divide very soon.

1.8 How the internet has changed everything

Today, voice can be translated into digital data packets using Voice over Internet Protocol (VoIP), for example, then sent over digital networks to remote locations—often thousands of kilometers away—and, upon receipt, translated back to voice. Even television is not immune to digitization. In the US, for example, all television signals and television sets were converted to digital in 2009. As a result, TV viewers are now increasingly opting to surf the internet and chat with people from different locations while watching a TV program.

Courtesy of www.BDeshTV.com, a pioneering initiative launched in July 2010 by a group of non-resident Bangladeshis (NRBs), including one of your authors (Quamrul Mina), from Austin, Texas, you can now view scheduled as well as on-demand TV programs and high-quality videos for education and entertainment from anywhere in the world using a broadband internet connection. This is one more example of digital deflation winning over the prospect of digital divide since the online offerings tailored for the Bangladeshi audience from all walks of life worldwide are available essentially for free as long as the viewers have a broadband connection. The goal is to build a technology platform and an innovation ecosystem where program producers, artists, designers and engineers in Bangladesh and abroad (e.g., London, New York, Sydney, Rome, Dubai, Riyadh, and Tokyo) will be able to collaborate seamlessly, creating exciting job opportunities, particularly for the younger, tech-savvy workforce. What's more, with the integration of Facebook, MySpace and Twitter, BDeshTV is designed to work well with various social network platforms.

That's now possible because with everything becoming digital, television, voice telephony and the internet can use similar networks. The transmission of hitherto different services (e.g., telephony, television, and internet) via the same digital network is known as convergence. Experts indicate that once the digital infrastructure and the hardware, be it a computer or a telephone or another device, have been set in place, the cost of communications and information exchange will be virtually zero. Distance will no longer decide the cost of communicating electronically. This explains why, for example, the cost of a three-minute transatlantic call ranges from zero (via Skype or Vonage, for example) to less than US $0.25 in 2009 vs. US $0.84 in 2003 and nearly US $800 in today's money 50 years ago!

Of course, with the advent of the internet, which is a network of networks (aka the "mother of all networks"), a global set of connections of computers that enables the exchange of data, news and opinion has become a platform for new ways of doing business, a better way for governments to deliver public services and an enabler of lifelong learning. Unlike the telephone, radio or television, the internet is a many-to-many communication medium. The digital cognoscenti will remind you that the internet is not a thing, a place, a single technology, or a mode of governance: it is an agreement. In the language of those who build it, it is a protocol, a way of behaving. What is startling is the dramatic spread of this agreement, sweeping across all arenas of modern life that rely on the exchange of symbols.

The internet has become the fastest growing mass medium. In only four years the number of internet users reached 50 million. In contrast, it took radio 38 years, television 13 years and the Personal Computer 16 years to reach the same milestone. Despite its explosive growth, however, only about 25% of the global population has had internet access as of second quarter of 2009. What's more, this confirms the famous observation of William Gibson, a futurist: The future is already here—it's just unevenly distributed. The regional distribution of internet access is as follows: Africa (6.7%), Asia (18.5%), Europe (50.1%), Middle East (23.7%), North America (73.9%), Latin America/Caribbean (30%), and Oceania/Australia (60.1%). Even within a single region, wide disparities exist. For example, in Asia, Bangladesh stands at the bottom decile with 0.3% of the population having internet access, while South Korea tops the list at 77.3% (Japan at 74%, Pakistan at 10.6%, Indonesia at 10.4%, and India at 7%).

> "People overestimate what can be accomplished in the short term, and underestimate the changes that will occur in the long term. With the pace of change continuing to accelerate, we can consider even the first decade in the twenty-first century to constitute a long-term view."
>
> – Ray Kurzweil (b. 1948)

However, if all the mobile phone users in Bangladesh could connect to the internet, then penetration immediately jumps above 30%! Why is internet penetration important? Well, the little-known fact is that the internet is increasingly becoming an "innovation commons", a shared resource that enables the creation of new and innovative goods and services. Thus, the internet can be likened to designer clay whereby its use is limited only by the imagination and skill of the designer. This unique characteristic is due to the fact that the internet is designed using the end-to-end (e2e) principle. That is, the intelligence in the network is at the ends, and the main task of the network is to transmit data efficiently and flexibly between these ends.

Experts point to at least three important consequences of an e2e network on innovation. First, because applications run on computers at the edge of the network, innovators with new applications need only to connect their computers to the network to let their applications run. Secondly, because the design is not optimized for any particular existing application, the network is open to innovation not originally imagined. Thirdly, because the design has a neutral platform—in the sense that the network owner can't discriminate against some packets and favor others—the network can't discriminate against a new innovator's design.

Consequently, the internet as an "innovation commons" has made the transformation to the information age possible. As long as the e2e principle is not violated, the internet is democratizing in the sense that it redistributes power from central authorities (governments and companies) to individuals. Thanks to the internet, everyone can be a producer of content, create a new software application, or engage in global activities without the permission of a higher authority.

Think of the internet as a layered platform (actually the phrase "platform stack" is a part of the common parlance of modern programming) that allowed Tim Berners-Lee to single-handedly design the World Wide Web in 1989 by freely building on top of the open protocols of the internet. In his own words: "I just had to take the hypertext idea and connect it to the Transmission Control Protocol and domain name system ideas and—ta-da!—the World Wide Web." The first web site was built at the CERN (i.e., Geneva-based European Organization for Nuclear Research) and put on line on August 6th, 1991. In other words, he did not have to engineer an entire system for communicating between computers spread across the planet since that problem had been solved years before him.

Similarly, when Chad Hurley, Steve Chen, and Jawed Karim (three former employees of the online payment site PayPal) sat down to create YouTube in 2005, they built the service by stitching together elements from three different platforms: the Web itself, of course, but also Adobe's Flash platform, which handled all the video playback, and the programming language Javascript, which allowed end users to embed video clips on their own sites. Indeed, their ability to build on top of these existing platforms explains why three guys could build YouTube in six months, while an array of expert committees and electronics companies took twenty years to make HDTV (i.e., high-definition television) a reality!

1.9 How to fish in the networked ocean of opportunities

Another most celebrated recent case study in the innovative power of the stacked platform of the internet has been the rapid evolution of Twitter, a social networking service. Its creators, namely Jack Dorsey, Evan Williams and Biz Stone, benefited from the existing platforms just as the YouTube founders did. For example, Twitter's legendary 140-character limit is based on the limitations of the SMS mobile communications platform that they rely on to connect Web messages to mobile phones. But perhaps the most fascinating thing about Twitter is how much has been built on top of its platform since the founders dreamed up the service in 2006. Of course, when it first emerged, Twitter was widely derided as a frivolous distraction that was mostly good for telling your friends what you had for breakfast.

Now it is used to organize and share news about world events (e.g., the political protests in Iran, Tunisia, Egypt and throughout much of the Middle East), to route around government censorship, to provide customer support by large corporations and a thousand other applications that did not occur to the founders themselves, thanks to people finding a new use for a tool designed to do something else!

This "repurposing" of Twitter has resulted in redesigning the tool itself. For example, the convention of replying to another user with the @ symbol was spontaneously invented by the Twitter user base. Attaching geographic data to a tweet by your GPS (i.e., global positioning system) powered mobile device allows a real-world social network "Foursquare" to automatically distribute to all its users who have recently visited the nearby restaurants or public spaces. What's more, your tweet pops up immediately as a pushpin on the countless Twitter maps that developers have created over the past few years. Thanks to such user-generated innovations, following a live feed of tweets about an ongoing event, be that political debates or TV episodes, have become a central part of the Twitter experience. You may wonder, what are the users going to do with these trails of user-generated data? That's anybody's guess! However, keep in mind that without the follow-on innovations that built on that platform, this mode of interaction would have been technically impossible during the first year of Twitter's existence.

Another little-appreciated "side effect" of the internet has been that our planet is increasingly donning an electronic skin with the internet as a scaffold to support and transmit its sensations. Indeed, this skin is already being stitched together with millions of embedded electronic measuring devices ranging from thermostats to pressure gauges, pollution detectors, cameras, microphones, glucose sensors, EKGs, and electroencephalographs. These will probe and monitor cities and endangered species, the atmosphere, our ships, highways and fleets of trucks, our conversations, our bodies and even our dreams.

According to some futurists, ten years from now, there will be trillions of such telemetric systems, each with a microprocessor brain and a radio. They'll be in constant contact with one another. But the communication won't be at our plodding verbal pace. In fact, fifty kilobits per second is slow since these machines will prefer to talk at gigabit speeds and higher—so fast that we humans will catch only scattered snippets of the discussion. The next logical questions are: What will the earth's new skin permit us to feel? How will we use its surges of sensation? For several years—maybe for a decade—there will be no central nervous system to manage this vast signaling network. Certainly there will be no central intelligence. But many scientists believe that some qualities of self-awareness will emerge once the Net is sensually enhanced and emulates the complexity of the human brain.

1.10 Broadband connectivity is the virtual bridge to Digital Bangladesh

Lest we should get ahead of ourselves too soon, however, we need to build first the bridge to the global innovation commons, else be prepared to accept being on the wrong side of the widening digital divide separating the information-rich from the information-poor of the world. The Organization for Economic Cooperation and Development—an international organization of 30 countries that accept the principles of representative democracy and free-market economy—defines the digital divide as the difference between individuals, households, businesses and geographic areas with regard to their opportunities to access ICTs and their use of the internet for a wide variety of activities. It is the gap between those who have real access to ICTs and who are able to use it effectively, and those who don't have such access.

More and more, developing countries are recognizing that they cannot compete in the new global market unless they take advantage of the ICT revolution. Countries that do not undertake measures to enhance their ICT infrastructure run the risk of not just being marginalized but also being completely left behind in the new global order. The experiences of a number of countries, like Singapore, Malaysia and South Korea, demonstrate that bold actions in bringing their countries into the digital age pay off.

It is already received wisdom among those who are working to bridge the digital divide that providing access to technology is only one of many obstacles that must be overcome. Internet access is not enough. Critics argue that content is one important aspect of the digital divide that has been neglected. The four content-related barriers to greater internet uptake across society are: local information barriers; literacy barriers; language barriers; and cultural diversity barriers.

Since local content is often determined by the commercialized interest of the content providers, they tend to focus on content that delivers attractive returns on their investments. Thus, internet users from developing countries, such as farmers, rarely find information that is relevant to them. What often compounds the challenge further is that non-profit, community-based initiatives to create content all-to-often face sustainability problems.

The literacy barriers include not only basic and functional literacy but also technological literacy. Older people who may be literate may find using a computer and accessing the internet an intimidating experience. A related concern is creating inexpensive content that is accessible to all, including illiterate people. Perhaps this aim will be achieved through voice recognition technologies.

Given that most of internet content worldwide (over 68% according to some estimates) is in English, the language barrier compounds the literacy issue. In the business domain, English is even more dominant, with over 94% of links to pages on secure servers.

Of late, a new focus on social inclusion is shifting the discussion of the digital divide from gaps to be overcome by providing ICT tools to social development challenges to be addressed through the effective integration of the tools into communities, institutions, and societies. Clearly, what is most important is not so much the physical availability of computers and the internet but rather people's ability to make use of those technologies to engage in meaningful economic and social practices to compete in a "flattening" world.

In his 2005 best-selling book, *The World Is Flat*, Thomas Friedman recounts a journey to Bangalore, India, when he realized globalization has changed the core economic concepts of commerce. In his opinion, this flattening is a product of the convergence of personal computers with broadband connection and the rise of workflow software that enables people to collaborate and participate in the global economy like never before. He termed this period as Globalization 3.0, differentiating this period from the previous version Globalization 1.0 (when countries and governments were the main protagonists) and the Globalization 2.0 (when multinational companies led the way in driving global integration). Friedman recounts many examples of companies based in India and China that, by providing cheap skilled labor from typists and call center operators to accountants and computer programmers, have become integral parts of complex global supply chains for companies such as Dell and Microsoft.

One beneficial "side effect" of all three versions of globalization is that developing countries are no longer losing out from ever-faster technological change. This is because science and technology are rapidly improving the lives of the poor as well as the rich people.

Indeed, the strongest force propelling globalization has been the swift adoption and wide diffusion of technology. For example, modern medicine with its toolbox of antibiotics, vaccines and Oral Rehydration Therapy (ORT) has improved the most basic indicator of well-being: staying alive. Although sometimes controversial because of their unintended long-term consequences, several proven technologies, e.g., high-yield rice, hybrid wheat, fertilizers, pesticides, and chlorination of water have allowed people from developing countries to expect to live two-and-a-half times longer than in 1900.

Not all of the technologies came from the developed world, however. Some of them have been home-grown, too. For example, ORT—a simple mixture of molasses and salt dissolved in water that prevents dehydration—was developed in Bangladesh, and saved millions of babies from dying of diarrhea in Bangladesh and elsewhere. Before ORT, the standard treatment used to be an intravenous drip, costing up to US $50 per baby. Thanks to mass production of packets of oral rehydration salts since the 1980s, the cost has come down to less than 10 cents each.

This diffusion is similar to the growth driven primarily by wireless technologies and liberalization of telecommunications markets worldwide over the past 15 years that have brought about an unprecedented increase in access to mobile phones. At this point in time, more than 4 billion handsets are in use, and astonishingly enough, three-quarters of them are in the developing world. Why this explosive growth in developing countries? Perhaps less surprisingly for those of us from Bangladesh, these phones can compensate for inadequate infrastructure, such as bad roads and slow postal services, and allow information to move more freely, making markets more efficient and unleashing a new tech-savvy form of entrepreneurship.

The mobile phone market is especially important for developing countries like Bangladesh where it is growing most rapidly, especially among the rural poor. The World Bank estimates that mobile communications have a particularly important impact in rural areas, which are home to nearly one-half of the world's population and 75% of the world's poor. As a result, mobile operators are taking innovative approaches to reach rural customers, such as offering village phone programs throughout Bangladesh, low-denomination recharges for pre-paid phones in East Africa, and combined voice and agricultural information service in China. It turns out that the mobility, ease of use, flexible deployment, and relatively low and declining rollout costs of wireless technologies enable them to reach rural populations with low levels of income and literacy.

Recent economic research indicates that the direct contribution of the mobile phone industry ranges from 1.4 percent to 5.3 percent of an emerging market's GDP. This impact, for example, is higher in the Philippines, a country with high service penetration and a high degree of service innovation, than in other countries such as India, where penetration and quality of service are known to be low. However, the indirect contribution of the mobile industry to the economy can range several times higher than this observable GDP effect, because it includes GDP contributions from other companies in the wireless sector, such as handset manufacturers and retailers, content providers, and equipment manufacturers, as well as what we call the "end-user surplus." This surplus includes not only direct productivity gains related to the use of mobile communications, but also indirect consumer benefits such as peace of mind, security, and access to family.

1.11 Showcasing the mobile enablers of digital transformation

Take the case of a taxi driver in Dhaka, for example, who shares his cab with another driver in alternating 12-hour shifts. Buying a mobile phone improves his productivity because he now receives six or seven calls per month from regular passengers, which saves him from spending about four hours a week seeking passengers. He uses his mobile phone to contact other taxi drivers if, for example, he needs to ask directions to unfamiliar destinations. This person also uses his phone to stay in touch with his family and friends, and his employer benefits as well: the company now provides an instant lost-and-found service to passengers.

For this taxi driver, the benefits of going wireless take two forms, which together we call the end-user surplus. The first involves greater productivity. McKinsey research suggests that the economic value to high-mobility enterprise end-users in China was around US $34 billion in 2005, with a productivity increase of around 6% being one of the key factors. The corresponding value creation scaled to the GDP and mobile penetration levels of Bangladesh amounts to about US $1 billion (in nominal terms; or more than US $2 billion on purchasing power parity basis) in 2009.

To estimate the second, less tangible benefit—exemplified when workers contact their family and friends with mobile units, the above analysis used historical Average Revenue Per User (ARPU) as an indicator of an user's individual willingness to pay. This consumer portion of end-user surplus equals ARPU at the time a customer subscribes to wireless services minus today's ARPU, and assumes the user's willingness to pay does not change over time. Thus, a Chittagong mobile subscriber who purchased the service in 2000 for, say, Tk. 500 a month, now pays only Tk. 400 a month (because of competition and other factors) has saved a total of Tk. 100 a month.

Admittedly, any estimate of intangible benefits will be a rough calculation, but this one relies on actual data—the amount customers have demonstrated they will pay. In fact, McKinsey researchers consider their estimate to be conservative, since many users would pay higher rates if necessary. Moreover, as technology, network coverage, competition amongst operators, and network quality improve over time, this form of surplus should increase.

These factors massively amplify the economic impact of the mobile industry—in China alone, in 2005, it generated approximately US $200 billion, or nearly 6% of the GDP of that country. Of this, only a quarter reflected the direct contribution the mobile industry made to GDP; half came from related industries; and the final 25 percent came in the form of the consumer's surplus. Research indicates that other countries have displayed similar levels of total economic impact—from 4.7 percent in India to 7.4 percent in the Philippines.

But there's a catch. Researchers have discovered nonlinear relationships between technological change and economic development. More specifically, the introduction of new digital technologies can have the following effects on society:

- Initial productivity slowdown and delayed productivity payoff from the new technologies
- Destruction of human capital (as many old skills are no longer wanted)
- Technological unemployment (temporary but serious)
- Widening disparities in the distribution of income, which tends to be temporary until the supply of labor catches up to the new mix of skill requirements
- Big changes in regional patterns of industrial location (i.e., globalization)
- Big changes in required education
- Big changes in infrastructure (e.g., the information highway)
- Big changes in rules and regulations (e.g., to protect intellectual property, and enforce antimonopoly conduct)
- Big changes in the way we live and interact with each other

The progressive digitization of mass media and telecommunications content is expected to blur earlier distinctions between the communication of information and its processing, and interaction between people and machines. Digitization makes communication from individuals to machines, between machines, and even from machines to individuals as easy as it is between persons. Also blurred are the distinctions among information types: numbers, words, pictures, and sounds, and eventually tastes, odors, and possibly even sensations, all can be stored, processed, and communicated in the same digital format.

On a societal level, the digital technologies make possible better and cheaper access to knowledge and information. This speeds up transactions and processes and reduces their cost, which in turn benefit citizens and consumers. With the advent of the communications revolution, distance has a different relationship to self-immediacy and experience than it used to have. Put another way, so what if two people are located in different time zones? They can still talk, negotiate, and make deals as though they were face to face. Increasingly, digital technologies are all characterized by their pervasiveness, that is, by their penetration of all domains of human activity, not as an exogenous source of impact, but as the fabric in which such activity is woven.

For ICT to weave its magic, however, it must find a hospitable social and political environment. New technologies threaten existing power and economic relationships, and those that benefit from these old relationships put up barriers to the spread of the new technologies.

Moreover, laws can deter (or encourage) the spread of new technologies. For example, the lack of legal recognition for digital contracts and digital signatures is holding back electronic commerce. It is important to remember that technology is shaped by society as much as it shapes society. Thus, those interested in harnessing the power of new technologies should help create the right environment for it to flourish.

Today, however, the markers of widespread "information poverty" are evident across Bangladesh where the vast majority of the people in the rural areas have little or no access to the information that impacts their daily life. For example, data on water quality, education and health budgets, and agricultural prices are nearly impossible to access. Despite hundreds of crores (or billions) of taka spent each year on providing basic public services like primary education, health, water, and sanitation to poor communities, one cannot help wondering, where does this money go, who gets it, and what are the results of the resources invested? That's where we find a big black hole of information and a lack of basic accountability. How do inputs (i.e., taka spent) turn into outputs (e.g., schools, clinics, and tube wells), and, more importantly, how do outputs translate into results (e.g., literate and healthy children, clean water, and so on)?

We simply don't know the answers to most of these basic questions. But what if we could? What if a mother could find out how much money was budgeted for her daughter's school each year and how much of it was received? What if she and other parents could report how often teachers are absent from school or whether health clinics have the medicines they are supposed to carry? What if citizens could access and report on basic information to determine if the various governmental and non-governmental agencies provide value for the money?

Critics often argue that the "digital divide" is unbridgeable as the rich countries grow richer from their high-tech industries, which allow them to invest in the next generation of high-tech products. However, we beg to differ. We know that as rich countries push out new technologies at a prodigious rate, their high-tech products—mobile phones represent one of the most recent "exceptions" that proves our case—eventually get affordable enough for Bangladeshi villagers to buy them. As we'll show in Chapter 2, the mobile phone technologies are spawning and spreading other technologies and practices in healthcare, banking, education, and entertainment. Increasingly, it's going to be up to the developing countries like Bangladesh to try to catch up and start innovating for ourselves by tapping into the emerging digital world.

The pattern of digitization within and across countries and regions worldwide suggests that while the landscape looks uneven, the concern of a deep digital divide is likely overblown and that greater digitization can substantially boost economic growth. Indeed, sizable "kickers" in the form of increments to GDP growth rates resulting from higher levels of digitization can make a huge difference to Bangladesh's economic fortunes over a period of 10 to 20 years.

Bangladesh already enjoys high levels of mobile phone connectivity throughout the country. Can we use this mobile platform as a stepping stone to leapfrog to the next level? Given that the country's economic prosperity is at stake here, it behooves us to learn as much as possible about what works, what doesn't, what's fundamentally new and different about the digital world today and what it all means for Bangladesh as an aspiring middle-income country (MIC).

Chapter 2

Reporting Live from Where the Digital Future has Already Happened

"Any sufficiently advanced technology is indistinguishable from magic."
– *Arthur C. Clarke (1917-2008)*

There are "four Cs" in terms of key takeaways from this chapter:

What's different about the digital world? CONNECTIVITY. Somewhat technically speaking, what makes the crucial difference is the new network economics where digital connectivity—be that in wired or wireless form—enables innovation-based productivity and quality-of-life-driven prosperity for people from the top to the bottom of the socioeconomic ladder. In other words, thanks to the dramatic way mobile and broadband connectivity is changing how people interact, companies do business and the public sector delivers services, new windows of opportunities are opening up for those who can build their careers or business platforms by leveraging distinctive and innovative ideas, expertise, services, and digital technologies locally, regionally or even worldwide.

What's new now? CONVERGENCE. Indeed, the increasing convergence or confluence, of digital telecommunications, media and computing means ready access and the ability to upload and download a wide range of services, such as voice, video, music, film, radio, games, customer support, customized research and self-publishing through (micro)blogging, for example. This seamless integration across digital technology platforms, content providers and media/multimedia outlets improves dramatically the efficiency and reach of the internet for existing information technology services (ITS) and IT-enabled services (ITES) while providing spare capacity for yet-unknown future IT applications and ITES opportunities.

What does it all mean for Bangladesh? COMPETITIVENESS. By building an integrated system of broadband networks—both fixed and mobile—

and thus getting connected to the already "flattening" world's largest collaboration and distribution platform over the internet, Bangladesh stands to capitalize on a major leapfrogging opportunity for transitioning from today's mostly agrarian to a largely service-intensive knowledge economy over the next decade. We believe this is indeed a once-in-a-lifetime opportunity for Bangladesh that could generate the "biggest bang for the bucks" invested in creating a robust digital infrastructure with more of a level playing field for its economic, social and cultural development. Some of you may recall the lead character in the 1989 rural American film, *The Field of Dreams*, where Kevin Costner as Ray Kinsella dreams about and then succeeds—albeit not without some minor setbacks and detours along the way—in building a baseball [a la cricket] field in the middle of nowhere (i.e., a cornfield). Paraphrasing the whispering voice into the ears of Ray Kinsella, we the authors would like to stick our collective necks out not just in this chapter but throughout the book to convince you, dear reader, of our claim: "If we build it, change will come to Bangladesh."

What's in it for you? CAPITAL. We promise that you'll be entitled to claim US $80 trillion just by reading this chapter and understanding what it means. How's that for a supersize return from an investment of only a few hours of your reading time! (Yes, we know some authors will promise just about anything to keep your attention, but we're serious about this charter with you. However, until we provide a further explanation later in this chapter, please do read the first sentence of this paragraph carefully. As you can tell, we're not quite sold on the efficacy of speed-reading courses. After all, what's the point of investing your time in speed-reading courses if they don't teach you how to speed-think as well?)

What if you could shrink the world to the size of a small village—dubbed Globalpur—of 100 people? With its current human population ratios remaining the same as our wider world, Globalpur would represent a true microcosm of the real world with some startling demographics as follows: The village is populated by 60 Asians (there would be only 2 Bangladeshis), 14 Africans, 12 Europeans, 8 Latin Americans, 5 from the USA and Canada, and 1 from the South Pacific; 51 would be male and 49 female; 82 would be non-white and 18 white; 67 would be non-Christian and 33 Christian; 80 would live in substandard housing; 67 would be unable to read; 50 would be malnourished and 1 dying of starvation every year; 33 would be without access to a safe water supply; 39 would lack access to improved sanitation; 24 would not have any electricity (and of the

76 that do have electricity, most would only use it for lighting at night); 7 people would have access to the internet; 1 would have a college education; 1 would have HIV (the virus that causes AIDS); 2 would be near birth and 1 near death at any point in time; 5 would control 32% of the entire stock of Globalpur's wealth 4 of which would be US citizens; 33 would be receiving, and attempting to live on, only 3% of the village's income.

Even if Globalpur is purely a figment of your imagination, it brings our too-big-to-comprehend world to a scale we can all relate to. Moreover, thanks to the growing penetration of the internet and wireless technology, the "death of distance" has made Globalpur a virtual global village of sorts. What's more, the digital future is already here, albeit unevenly distributed in various parts of Globalpur. In the spirit of illustrating this little-known fact, we've plucked a few snippets of "headline news" covering digital developments throughout our global village with potentially significant implications for how we should think about realizing our dreams of a digitally inclusive Bangladesh:

- *The world created 988 exabytes of digital information in 2010 alone, which is equivalent to 18 million times the amount of information in all the books ever written, or 72 stacks of books reaching from the Earth to the Sun, or 36 tons of books for every living person.* Given that a single exabyte is equivalent to about 50,000 years of DVD quality video, the world's digital output amounted to some 50 million years of video in only one year (2010).

- *Internet Protocol (IP) version 4, the most common version used today, is running out of addresses to assign to devices that can access the internet.* According to a February 2008 BBC News report, 14 percent of the 4,294,967,296 possible IP addresses remain to be distributed. At the current pace, there will be no IP addresses left to distribute by 2011. However, IPv6, can support 3.4×10^{38} unique addresses, or up to 5,000 IP addresses for every square micrometer of the earth's surface.

- *Annual global internet traffic will exceed three-quarters of a zettabyte (767 exabytes) by 2014.* Global IP traffic grew 45 percent during 2009 to reach an annual run rate of 176 exabytes per year or 15 exabytes per month. In 2014, global IP traffic will reach 767 exabytes per year or 64 exabytes per month. The average monthly traffic in 2014 will be equivalent to 32 million people streaming Avatar in 3D, continuously for the entire month.

- *A new milestone will soon be reached when the number of devices connected to the internet is greater than the number of people who use it.* A similar milestone was reached in 1998 when the volume of global internet traffic through the US surpassed the amount of voice traffic. The range of devices using computing and other advanced technologies is staggering, as are the rapid adoption rates for many such devices.

- *DVD players, Digital TVs, and MP3 Players all reached 50 percent of American homes in fewer than 10 years, despite the existence of competing technologies (VCRs, analog TVs, and CD Players) with widespread market acceptance.* In contrast, one of the oldest consumer communications devices, telephones, were not adopted by a majority of US households until 71 years after its introduction. Another technology, electricity, took 52 years to reach a majority of US households. These innovations, however, have laid the groundwork for PCs, VCRs, CD players, and DVD players, each of which took less than 20 years to pass into a majority of US homes.

- *The need to transmit large music, image, and video files is pushing developed markets to adopt third-generation (3G) mobile technology, and a few markets (e.g., Japan and S. Korea) are well down this path.* It is less clear at this point which technical standards for 3G and 4G services will emerge dominant in each region and worldwide.

- *The allure of broadband over powerline (BPL) is strong, especially in less-developed regions, because one (usually extant) network can be used to deliver multiple services.* An estimated 2 billion people worldwide, currently "unreachable" with modern communications equipment, could plug into a BPL network at minimal extra cost.

- *More than 61 percent of the active VoIP (i.e., Voice over Internet Protocol) users who responded to a survey, reported they had discontinued or replaced their traditional telephone lines with VoIP service.* VoIP is a system of standards that allow telephone calls, traditionally made over circuit-switched networks, instead to be sent using internet-based packet-switching. VoIP allows any broadband provider, whatever its platform, to offer telephone services.

- *Despite the rapid growth of video and audio on the internet, e-mail remains the most common activity of internet users throughout the world, while IM (i.e., instant messaging) services are widely used by teenagers and young adults.* From the earliest days of the internet, two of the most revolutionary forms of internet-based communication have been e-mail and IM.
- *The ubiquity of free online news sources has devastated the print news industry as readers and advertising dollars alike migrate to the new platforms.* In response, many newspapers have added online components. The proliferation of free online classified sites such as Craigslist, however, has intensified the level of competition for classified advertising.
- *Online advertising is increasingly stealing market share from other types of advertising.* Although internet advertising has not replaced many of the traditional forms of advertising, such as direct telephone sales, promotions, newspapers, or even direct mail, it is one of the few forms of advertising experiencing rapid growth.
- *Cell phone manufacturers and carriers are using the mobile technology platform to innovate and compete for customers based on ringtones, games, images, and streaming video.* The introduction of the iPhone and its competitors has sparked a rapid growth in mobile gaming and video. The ability to fully, accurately, and infinitely copy, share, and transmit music, made easier by the MP3 format, has changed the music industry and raised many issues regarding the scope of intellectual property.
- *Gaming has matured from its origins in mall arcades and early home computers to encompass consoles, internet-based casual gaming, cell phones, and other mobile devices.* Within the internet sector, massively multiplayer online games (MMOGs), such as Everquest and World of Warcraft, and virtual social worlds (VSWs), such as Second life, have made gaming more interactive and provided new revenue streams for innovators.
- *Some people find the possibilities offered by digital entertainment media disturbing.* Online gambling and gaming have become a popular internet activity for millions. Social networking websites attract millions of children and teenagers, often for hours each day. Virtual worlds such as Second Life allow users

to lead alternate, and not always exemplary, lives in the digital realm. User-produced and uploaded YouTube videos are often deemed to be disgusting or obscene. Although service providers and legislators alike are taking steps to address these issues, the sheer variety and diversity of modern digital media ensures that a debate on the propriety of the modern digital media marketplace will continue.

- *As the internet has matured and users have become increasingly comfortable browsing cyberspace, the activities in which they participate have become more varied.* A blog is an online diary or journal, often accompanied by pictures, links, and other content. A podcast is a recording, usually audio, available on the internet for downloading. However, video podcasts, also known as vidcasts or vlogs, are beginning to proliferate. Tagging is the labeling of blog posts, news stories, or other items on the internet, allowing the content to be recognized and amalgamated with other related content.

- *The popularity of social networking websites has surprised some internet experts.* Facebook is the most popular social networking site worldwide with more than 600 million registered users in 2010. By the time you read this, dear reader, the Facebook visitors population may be far greater than that of the US and Bangladesh combined, as if the site has become a vast and fast-growing "virtual country" with its citizens holding passports with hundreds of different nationalities.

- *Although some sectors have been affected by the internet more than others, virtually all consumer-oriented businesses have been forced to respond to a purchasing public that is better informed about product attributes, availability, and pricing.* A recent survey found that 92.5 percent of US adults regularly or occasionally go online before making a purchase. Moreover, as internet users have come to rely on online product information and reviews, more are becoming regular internet shoppers for an expanding variety of goods and services. Symptomatic of the maturation of online commerce, apparel has replaced computer hardware and software as the largest single category of online retail purchases.

- *The informational advantage of online shopping is especially pronounced for travel, financial services, and health care.* Online travel agencies, such as Expedia and Travelocity, are part of the first wave of successful e-commerce firms, and they continue to be successful even in the face of competition from airline, hotel, and rental car websites. Slower to move online, but now as well-established, are the e-commerce arms of banks and brokerage firms.

- *Providers of health products and services have only recently begun to take full advantage of the internet as a marketing vehicle.* The rise in direct-to-consumer pharmaceutical advertising in the US and the growth of information hubs and support groups for even the rarest of diseases are two more examples of this marketing maturation. In all cases, though, the internet provides consumers with a wealth of information that can make them more sophisticated shoppers.

- *The ease of trading in financial markets using the internet led online brokers to pioneer successful online financial services companies.* Since their inception, the online financial world has become one of the leading industries in developing e-commerce, overcoming customer concerns about online security, business viability, and the quality of financial services offered. In the past several years, the number of consumers banking, buying and selling stocks, and paying bills online has grown rapidly.

- *Increased use of the internet, particularly for downloading digital media and conducting financial transactions, has been accompanied by an expanding array of threats to users' computer performance and personal information.* In many cases, well-established threats such as spam and spyware have been adapted to pose new threats such as phishing e-mails and keystroke-logging programs. There is, perhaps, some irony in the fact that threats to the digital economy rely on technological advances that arise out of the digital economy. Viruses and worms spread through the internet, spam is possible only because of e-mail server technology, and piracy of copyrighted material becomes increasingly problematic as file downloading and data replication technologies improve.

- *Awareness of and concern about internet security does not always translate into effective remedial action to minimize corporate or personal exposure.* A recent report estimated that 82 percent of small business data that was lost or stolen could have been avoided if the business had followed a security plan. The US-based National Cyber Security Alliance predicts that the most severe threats to small business data protection will come from malicious code, stolen or lost laptops or mobile devices, phishing attacks, unsecured wireless internet networks, and disgruntled employees. Similarly, although most U.S. internet users are familiar with cookies and their privacy-related implications, one study found only 28 percent of those who tried to delete cookies from their computers were able to do so.

- *One should expect a constant evolution in the techniques and technologies used both by cyber-criminals and the law enforcement agencies.* Potential new targets include internet feed services such as RSS (Real Simple Syndication), a hallmark of "Web 2.0," which provide new means for hackers to deliver keystroke loggers, Trojan horses, and other malware. The emergence of widespread peer-to-peer (P2P) networks has created an environment ripe for exploitation by malware. A recent study concluded that 47 percent of the malicious code propagated used P2P networks. Interestingly, the known tendency for malware to propagate on P2P networks may help to discourage the distribution of pirated content because users fear infection from downloaded materials.

- *The US Department of Justice defines phishing as a criminal activity in which perpetrators design e-mail or websites resembling those of well-known online businesses in an attempt to fraudulently acquire sensitive personal information.* The attacks deceive internet users into disclosing their bank and financial information, other personal data such as usernames and passwords, or into unwittingly downloading malicious computer code. The volume of phishing attacks has grown rapidly and the methods by which sensitive information is obtained are widely varied. "Vishing" e-mails ask recipients to call a "customer service" phone number and reveal their account number and password, presumably in order to receive some purported benefit. "Spear phishing" attacks are targeted at users in a particular business or organization with the intention of acquiring employee information that would allow a third party to log into the organization's computer system. "Pharming" involves the creation of deceptive sites that resemble well-known sites and host malicious code capable of redirecting traffic intended for the real site to the fraudulent one.

- *Offshoring has become a viable option for companies providing information services.* Outsourcing occurs when a company hires an external company to complete internal business processes. When the external company is located in a different country, the outsourcing is often referred to as offshoring. Offshoring is utilized by a wide variety of businesses and for a wide variety of products.

- *While China is considered to be the leading manufacturer of inexpensive goods, India is seen as the number one provider of inexpensive business and IT services.* India's IT services industry employed 2.5 million individuals directly and ~10 million indirectly, and reached US $50 billion in 2010, accounting for 3.5% of India's GDP.

With the above wide-ranging sample of the goings-on across our digital world today, it's natural to wonder, how is our digital future likely to evolve? It turns out that the answer hinges on a somewhat provocative question: Can technologies have sex? Well, at the risk of sounding slightly facetious, we say yes! Want proof? How about the birth of information and communication technology (ICT) when information technology (IT) met, or mated with, [tele]communication technology? And that changed everything, ushering in "the death of distance" and making it possible to declare that "the world is flat." That's because these technologies enable us to recreate ourselves through the very personal way we use our new ICT-based tools and how we relate to one another as human beings. What's more, as if extensions of ourselves, these new tools and technologies now equal new perceptions of the world around us.

Need a concrete example of how a tool can become an extension of ourselves? Take the case of the increasingly ubiquitous mobile phone. What other object do you habitually carry around with you and use all the time, and when it's misplaced you become restless and begin to feel as if you're disconnected from the rest of the world? Then what has this tool become if not an extension of yourself? Yet, when did you acquire your first mobile phone? Five or ten years ago? Can you think of a reason why anyone else in Bangladesh and beyond will not behave the same way when this technology reaches them?

2.1 What happens when digitization gets a Darwinian leg

When technologies start having sex, the rules of biological evolution get a new twist. The result is technology evolution with the acceleration of the pace of development and exponential growth in the diversity of digital products and services as part of an evolutionary process in the Darwinian sense, albeit a loosely coordinated or collectively human-directed one. Thus, assuming that the current trends in ICT evolution continue, we fully expect that within our lifetime almost every living human adult, and most children, in the world will own, or at least have access to, one mobile phone, or smartphone, or Personal Digital Assistant (PDA), or whatever we end up calling this versatile tool. By way of comparison, keep in mind that neither the pen nor the typewriter came even close to that level of adoption, nor did the automobile. That will put global connectivity, immense computational power, and access to all the world's knowledge amassed over many centuries, in everyone's hands.

> "Computer science is no more about computers than astronomy is about telescopes."
> – Edsger W. Dijkstra (1930-2002)

The world has never—ever—been in that situation before. This simple tool has the potential to change forever how we live our lives, the way wealth is created and power is shared across the globe. Indeed, we believe it is the ultimate democratizing technology.

Now imagine the impact of this new tool on someone in a part of the world that has not had telephones, computers, the internet, or even easy access to libraries. We'll let your own imagination support our case that this is a game-changing technology on a hitherto unknown global scale. This is a form of globalization that includes worldwide wireless internet access with all knowledge digitized and available to everyone. This implies a global economy with free markets in which anyone can trade with anyone else without interference from states or governments. Ultimately, this transforms our planet into an entity where all states are digital democracies in which everyone has the franchise. Although that "end state" is currently nothing more than a vision, let's imagine Bangladesh among the pioneers in this brave new digital world. After all, we invented microfinance for the world. Why not make the next revolution be with microprocessors!

True, access is limited and expensive today. But with increased bandwidth and the prospect of inexpensive, wireless personal reading devices, we believe the "netroots" change will soon come to Bangladesh on a much broader scale. To understand why, first you need to appreciate the power of what we call the digital "big bang."

2.2 The underpinnings of our 'digital big bang theory' for Bangladesh

You're right, dear reader, if you guessed that we're not talking about the big bang theory of modern cosmology here, which builds on the idea that our universe first flared into existence some 13.7 billion years ago from a submicroscopic pinpoint of false vacuum in the nothingness and expanded at a rate beyond human comprehension, doubling every 10^{-34} seconds. Our version of the "big bang" theory in the digital domain is better known as Moore's law, based on an observation by Gordon Moore, the co-founder of Intel back in 1965 that since the invention of the integrated circuit in 1958, the number of transistors that can be placed economically on a microchip has increased exponentially, doubling approximately every two years. Ever since Moore's enunciation of the geometric progression, as opposed to the linear or arithmetic progression, in semiconductor technologies, almost every measure of the capabilities of digital electronic devices, e.g., processing speed, memory capacity, and even the number and size of pixels in digital cameras, is linked to Moore's law since all of these are improving at (roughly) exponential rates as well. This has dramatically increased the usefulness of digital electronics in nearly every segment of the world economy.

To appreciate the significance of the exponential progression in digital technologies, it is important to ponder the nature of exponential growth. A simple way to illustrate this concept is through the tale of the inventor of chess and his patron, the emperor of China. In response to the emperor's offer of a reward for his beloved game of chess, the inventor asked for a single grain of rice on the first square, two on the second square, four on the third, and so on. The emperor quickly granted this seemingly benign and humble request. One version of the story has the emperor going bankrupt as the 63 doublings ultimately totaled 18 million trillion grains of rice. At ten grains of rice per square inch, this requires rice fields covering twice the surface area of the Earth, oceans included. Another version of the story has the inventor having been decapitated by an angry emperor.

It is important to realize that as the emperor and the inventor went through the first half of the chess board, things were fairly uneventful. The inventor was given spoonfuls of rice, then bowls of rice, then barrels. By the end of the first half of the chess board, the inventor had accumulated one large field's worth (4 billion grains), and by then the emperor did start to take notice. It was when they progressed through the second half of the chessboard that the situation quickly changed. Incidentally, with regard to the doublings of computation, that's about where we stood in 2001—there have been slightly more than 32 doublings of performance since the first programmable electronic digital computers were invented during World War II.

In case a chess board arithmetic is too exotic for you, consider this parable that may be closer to home, especially for those of us born and brought up in rural Bangladesh (which was the case for one of your authors): A fish farmer wants to stay at home to tend to his pond's fish and make certain that the pond itself will not become covered with the wild water hyacinths, which are said to double their number every few days. Month after month, he patiently waits, yet only tiny patches of water hyacinths can be seen at the pond, and they don't seem to be expanding in any noticeable way. With the water hyacinths covering less than 1% of the pond, the fish farmer figures that it's safe to take a vacation and leaves with his family. When he returns a few weeks later, he's shocked to discover that the entire pond is taken over by the water hyacinths, and his shoals of fish have perished. By doubling their number every few days, the last seven doublings were sufficient to extend the hyacinths' coverage to the entire pond. This is because seven doublings extended their reach 128-fold. This is the nature of exponential growth that even our friendly fish farmer can appreciate!

Although technology tends to compound its growth in an exponential fashion, we humans live mostly in a linear world. As a result, technological trends are not noticed during the time period when small levels of technological power are doubled. Then seemingly out of nowhere, a technology explodes into view. For example, when the internet went from 20,000 to 80,000 nodes over a two year period during the 1980s, this progress remained hidden from the general public. A decade later, when it went from 20 million to 80 million nodes in the same amount of time, the impact was rather conspicuous. With more than 1.7 billion nodes (i.e., internet users) worldwide as of 2009, we are beginning to see that our world has suddenly transformed.

Now, moving beyond digital hardware, let's apply our "big bang" theory to software developers. The thesis here is based on the notion that knowledge products in general, and software in particular have different economics than hardware or physical products. Let's take the case of developing a piece of software like Microsoft's Excel. Of course, there is a large one-time cost involved in writing this useful piece of software. Once it's completed, however, the cost of distributing it to customers is low. Let's say it cost Microsoft US $1 billion to write and test, and then sell to retail shops for US $110 per copy. Assume that the box, the manual and the CD-ROM cost US $10, leaving a gross profit of US $100. Breakeven economics is reached when ten million copies are sold. Each additional copy is virtually pure profit. After selling the second ten million copies, Microsoft will have doubled its money on its initial investment, and after 110 million copies are sold, it will have 1,000 percent profit (again, on a gross basis). Later, Microsoft decides to distribute this piece of software online and charge for downloads from its website, in which case each additional copy may have a cost of goods sold (COGS) of just a few cents! While this popular application software is in its growth phase, Microsoft's financial statements will show increasing returns—its costs are behind it and the profits roll in. Most likely, Microsoft may attempt to repeat this success with another "killer app" and keep its revenues from the original software rolling in by issuing version 2.0, 3.0, 4.0 and so on.

Another aspect of the digital big bang theory is that market leaders get more than their fair share of the high-quality opportunities that a new technology unleashes. In other words, they are in a position to enjoy economies of scale, to earn higher margins as a result, thus have more financial capacity to make new investments. In a high-growth environment, the results can be dramatic. Indeed, market leaders such as Microsoft and Google have benefited from this effect.

Extensive analysis of the history of technology suggests that contrary to the intuitive and linear view, technological change overall is exponential. As a result, we won't experience 100 years of progress in the 21st century; instead, it will be more like 20,000 years (at the rate prevailing in the year 2000) of progress since the digital "big bang" impacts from chip speed and cost-effectiveness also increase exponentially. The implications of this digital big bang theory for those considering technology investments are indeed profound.

To appreciate the impact of our digital big bang theory, it's best to put the rapid changes in digital technologies into perspective. The oft-quoted observation goes like this: If, over the past 30 years, transportation technology had improved at the same rate as information technology with respect to size, cost, performance, and energy efficiency, then an automobile would be the size of a toaster, cost US $200, go 100,000 miles per hour, and travel 150,000 miles on a single gallon of fuel.

Another little-known factoid about the Moore's Law is that although it was initially made in the form of an observation and forecast, the more widely it became accepted, the more it served as a goal for an entire industry. This vehemently drove both marketing and engineering departments of semiconductor manufacturers to focus enormous energy aiming for the expected increase in processing power that presumably one or more of their competitors would soon actually attain. In this regard, Moore's Law has become a self-fulfilling prophecy for digital device makers. Similarly, if we believe in the power of the digital "big bang" and work together to realize the full potential of Digital Bangladesh, the country's economic, social and cultural transformation could also become our self-fulfilling legacy for the current and future generations of residents as well as non-resident Bangladeshis (i.e., RBs and NRBs).

2.3 Learning from where the future has already happened

The good news is that the impacts of the digital big bang are already being felt in Bangladesh and elsewhere. And we can learn a lot about what works and what doesn't from the growing array of proven initiatives and pilot programs launched around the world. One such example: the Social Development Network in Kenya is developing a simple budget-tracking tool that allows citizens to track the allocation, use, and ultimate result of government funds earmarked for infrastructure projects in their districts. The tool is intended to create transparency in the use of tax revenues and answer one simple question: are resources reaching their intended beneficiaries? Using tools like Google Maps, they are able to overlay information that begin to tell a compelling story.

Google.org, which receives significant resources, including 1% of Google's equity and profits in some form, as well as employee time, to address some of the world's most urgent problems, has been working through its partners in East Africa and India, to support, catalyze, and widely disseminate this kind of information to public, private, and civil society stakeholders that can use it to see more clearly what's working, what's broken and what are the potential solutions. Leveraging platforms like Google Earth and Google Maps can help organizations disseminate their content widely and let people see and understand what was once invisible or cloaked in secrecy.

Once information is visible, widely known, and easy to understand, it's not difficult to see why citizens will pay more attention to leakages in the service delivery pipeline and feel empowered to propose solutions. That's because you can't change what you can't see. The power to know plus the power to act on what you know is the surest way to achieve positive social change from the bottom up. And considering the magnitude of resources invested in delivering public services each year, experts estimate that a 10% improvement globally would exceed the value of all foreign aid.

Additionally, social media literacy will make this not only possible but more likely. Since the infrastructure for global, ubiquitous, broadband communication media has been laid down along with the internet ensuring the democracy of access, the number of internet users has been growing from a thousand to over a billion in less than three decades. Just as the most important after-effects of the printing press were not in improved printing technologies but in widespread literacy, we believe that the next important breakthroughs won't be in hardware or software but in social media know-how.

Of course, the Gutenberg press itself was not enough. Mechanical printing had been invented in China centuries before the European invention. But for a number of reasons, a market for print and the knowledge of how to use the alphabetic code for transmitting knowledge across time and space broke out of the scribal elite that had controlled it for a millennia. Historians tell us that from around 20,000 books written by hand in Gutenberg's lifetime, the number of books grew to tens of millions within decades of the invention of moveable type. The rapidly expanding literate population in Europe began to create science, democracy, and the foundations of the industrial revolution.

Today, we're seeing the beginnings of scientific, medical, political, and social revolutions, from the instant epidemiology that broke out online when SARS (Severe Acute Respiratory Syndrome) became known to the world in 2003, to the use of social media for political campaigns in the 2008 US presidential election and for organizing "netroots" revolutions in Tunisia, Egypt and throughout much of the Middle East in 2011, for example. But we're only in the earliest years of social media literacy. Whether universal access to many-to-many media will lead to explosive scientific and social changes depends on further developing the know-how.

Would the early religious petitioners during the English Civil War, and the printers who eagerly fed their need to spread their ideas have been able to predict that monarchs would be replaced by constitutions within a few generations? Would Francis Bacon and Isaac Newton have dreamed that entire populations, and not just a few privileged geniuses, would aggregate scientific knowledge and turn it into technology? Would those of us who used slow modems to transmit black and white text on the internet 20 years ago have been able to foresee YouTube?

We hope that the new tools and social media literacy will soon change our perceptions of the world in profound ways. Today, when we think of the world's teeming billions of humans, the specters of overpopulation, poverty, disease, political instability, and environmental destruction tend to overwhelm our minds. We tend to be immobilized by the thought that they are the cause of most of the planet's problems. What if that perception were to change? What if the average human were able to contribute more than consume? To add more than subtract? Think of the world as if each person carries a balance sheet. On the negative side are the resources they consume without replacing, and on the positive side are the contributions they make to the planet in the form of the resources they produce, the lasting artifacts-of-value they build, and the ideas and technologies that might create a better future for their family, their community and for the planet as a whole. What if they could turn the sum of their balance sheets positive?

What might make that possible? One key reason for hope is that so far we have barely scratched the surface of human potential. Throughout history, the vast majority of humans have not been the people they could have been. Take this simple thought experiment. Pick your favorite scientist, mathematician or cultural hero. Now imagine that instead of being born when and where they were, they had instead been born with the same in-built-but-untapped abilities in a typical poverty-stricken village in, say, the France of 1200 or the Bangladesh of 1980. Would they have made the contribution they made? Of course not. They would never have received the education and encouragement it took to achieve what they did. Instead they would have simply lived out a life of poverty, with perhaps an occasional yearning that there must be a better way.

Needless to say, an unknown but vast number of those grinding out a living today have the potential to be world-changers if only we could find a way of unlocking that specific potential. Knowledge and inspiration might be the two ingredients to do just that. That's because if you come across ideas that could transform your life, and you feel the inspiration necessary to act on that knowledge, there's a real chance your life will indeed be transformed. What's more, knowledge has an important property: Unlike money or any other material things, when you give it away to enrich or inspire someone else, you don't lose it. In terms of our personal balance sheets, donating our knowledge and excitement about something can enrich someone else's balance sheet without depleting mine by one iota.

Of course, it needs hardly any reminding that there are many scary things going on in today's world. But one that is truly thrilling is that the means of spreading both knowledge and inspiration have never been greater. Five years ago, an amazing teacher or professor with the ability to truly shape the lives of his or her students could realistically hope to impact maybe 100 people each year. Today that same teacher can have his or her words spread on video to millions of eager students. There are already numerous examples of powerful talks that have spread virally to massive internet audiences. You can experience the excitement of knowledge even from those who are no longer with us. Itching for a dose of inspiring lectures on physics today? You can tune in to late Richard Feynman, the world's most famous teacher of physics via YouTube, for example, any time from anywhere—for free!

Most major universities now provide extensive courses online, many of which are free. Offering virtually all of its courses for free on the Web, Massachusetts Institute & Technology's (MIT) OpenCourseWare (OCW) initiative has been a leader in this effort, which has already had a major impact on education around the world. Sajid Latif, an educator in Pakistan, has integrated the MIT OCW materials into his own curriculum. His Pakistani students are reported to have been able to regularly attend—virtually identical—MIT classes as a substantial part of their education. Brigitte Bouissou, a math teacher in France, once wrote, "I want to thank MIT...for [these] very lucid lectures, which are a great help for preparing my own classes."

Academic Earth (http://academicearth.org/) provides answers our educational establishments by not simply expanding distance learning offerings, it enables students to access lectures for free by some of the leading professors and thinkers from the world's top academic institutions, such as the University of California at Berkeley, Columbia, Harvard, Maryland, Michigan, MIT, Norwich, NYU, Princeton, Stanford, UCLA, UNSW, USC, and Yale.

Another highly successful venue for self-directed learning for students of all ages is the Khan Academy, a US-based non-profit educational organization created in 2006 by Bangladeshi American educator Salman Khan (his father is from Barisal, Bangladesh and mother was born in Kolkata, India). With the stated mission of "providing a high quality education to anyone, anywhere," the www.khanacademy.org website supplies a free online collection of more than 2,300 micro lectures (as of June 2011) via video tutorials stored on YouTube teaching mathematics, history, finance, physics, chemistry, biology, astronomy, and economics. Even Bill Gates, Chairman of Microsoft, admits to logging into this website for an occasional refresher course on math or science!

> "Civilization advances by extending the number of important operations we can perform without thinking about them."
> – Alfred North Whitehead (1861-1947)

Driving this unexpected phenomenon is the fact that the physical cost of distributing a recorded talk or lecture anywhere in the world via the internet has fallen effectively to zero. This has happened with breathtaking speed and its implications are not yet widely understood. But it is surely capable of transforming global education. Because of the current bandwidth limitation and the lack of effective three-dimensional displays, the virtual environment provided today through routine Web access does not yet fully compete with "being there," but this is expected to change by the second decade of this century when visual-auditory virtual reality environments will be in full immersion, very high resolution, and very convincing. By then, most schools and universities will follow MIT's lead as students at any age, from toddlers to adults, will increasingly attend classes—available for all grade levels in many languages—virtually to have access to the best education in the world at any time and from any place. Such virtual environments will provide high-quality virtual laboratories where experiments can be conducted in biology, chemistry, physics or any other scientific field. And students will be able to interact with a virtual Albert Einstein or Kazi Nazrul Islam or even "become" a virtual Kazi Nazrul Islam.

For one thing, the realization that today's best teachers can become global celebrities is going to boost the caliber of those who teach. For the first time in many years it's possible to imagine ambitious, brilliant 18-year-olds putting "teacher" at the top of their career choice list. Indeed the very definition of a "great teacher" will likely expand, as numerous others outside the profession with the ability to communicate important ideas find a new incentive to make that talent available to the world. Additionally, every existing teacher can greatly amplify his or her own abilities by inviting into their classroom, on video, the world's greatest scientists, visionaries and tutors. (Can a teacher inspire over video? Absolutely. We hear jaw-dropping stories of this every day.)

Now think about this from the students' perspective. In the past, everyone's success has depended on whether they were lucky enough to have a great mentor or teacher in their neighborhood. The vast majority have not been so fortunate. But a young girl born in Bangladesh today will probably have access in 10-20 years' time to a cell phone with a high-resolution screen, a web connection, and more power than the computer you own today. We can imagine her obtaining live insight and encouragement from her choice of the world's great teachers. She will get a chance to be what she can be. And she might just end up being the person who saves the planet for our grandchildren. For students in Bangladesh and around the world, this utopian world may in the next decade become the real world, too, thanks to the following trends and developments:

- Interactive textbooks: Various publishers are developing web-based interactive e-books with links to tutorials, simulations, quizzes, animations, virtual labs, discussion boards, and video clips. (These are not yesterday's e-textbooks.)
- Customizability: Instructors, and regional instructor networks, will be able to rearrange the content, delete unwanted material, and add (or link to) materials pertinent to their students' worlds and their own course goals.

- Affordability: Students will pay for course access tied to their names. With no hard copy book production and shipping, and no used books, publishers will stay afloat with a much smaller fee paid by many more students, or via a site license.
- Student accountability: Instructors will track their students' engagement in advance of class sessions, thus freeing more class time for discussion.
- Expanding broadband access: Thanks partly to a number of pilot initiatives, access to the internet is becoming possible at many schools, colleges and universities in Bangladesh. Case in point: US-based Vicki Davis' 10th grade Computer Science class at Westwood Schools in Camilla, Georgia and Julie Lindsay's grade 11 ITGS class at International School Dhaka (ISD) in Bangladesh conducted over the internet back in 2007 a two-week collaborative project to discuss topics from Thomas Friedman's 2005 book, *The World is Flat: A Brief History of the Twenty-first Century*.

2.4 The evolving transformative roles of the mobile phone

It's a question that makes economists scratch their heads: How did the mobile phone that just a few years ago was regarded as a yuppie plaything become the single most transformative tool for development? It turns out that a number of developments came together to make mobile phones more accessible to poorer people and trigger the rapid growth over the past few years. The spread of mobile phones in the developed world, together with the emergence of two main technology standards, led to economies of scale in both network equipment and handsets. The resulting lower prices brought mobile phones within reach of the wealthiest people in the developing world. That allowed the first mobile networks in developing countries to be set up, though prices were still high.

The next big step was the introduction of prepaid billing systems, which allow people to load up their phones with calling credit and then talk until the credit runs out. When mobile phones first came in, subscribers everywhere talked first and paid later (a model known as postpaid), so they had to be creditworthy. Prepaid billing spares operators the trouble and cost of sending out bills and chasing up debts. For example, it helped the spread of mobile phones among teenagers in Europe in the late 1990s because it offered parents a way of preventing their children from running up huge bills. More importantly, it dramatically expanded the market for mobile phones in poor countries.

Once the switch to prepaid was made, the biggest barrier to broader mobile access became the cost of a handset, which was still an expensive item in the late 1990s. But the price of a basic model steadily fell, from around US $250 in 1997 to around US $20 (or even US $10 for a remanufactured unit) in 2010. As handset-makers became aware of the scale of the opportunity in the developing world, they turned their minds to producing low-cost models. And for those who still could not afford their own handsets, help was at hand in the form of microfinance popularized by Grameen Bank in Bangladesh.

Iqbal Quadir, a Bangladeshi who moved to the US after completing high school and became an investment banker, looked at this model and had an epiphany: "A cellphone could be a cow." In 1997 the resulting effort to combine microfinance and mobile phones created GrameenPhone, a joint venture between Grameen Telecom and Telenor, a Norwegian telecoms firm, which recently floated in the Dhaka Stock Exchange with a hugely oversubscribed Initial Public Offering (IPO). Grameen Telecom pioneered the idea of the "telephone lady," extending loans to women in rural villages to enable them to buy a GrameenPhone mobile handset, an antenna and a large battery so they could sell calls to other villagers. Taking a small cut on each call, they were able to pay off the loan and thereafter use the proceeds to pay for health care and education for their children and to develop other businesses. Soon this "village phone" model quickly extended mobile coverage to thousands of villages in Bangladesh.

With prices continuing to fall, the vast majority of mobile users in Bangladesh and elsewhere in the developing world now have their own handsets. Still, demand for shared phones has not dried up completely. Calling from a village phone costs less than buying a top-up, so even people with their own handsets may sometimes make calls from shared phones if they have run out of credit.

Prepaid billing and affordable handsets on their own are not enough to ensure a rapid adoption of mobile phones. Another vital factor has been the liberalization of the telecoms markets and the issuing of licenses to rival operators. As those operators compete for customers and try to recoup the cost of building their networks, calling charges fall and mobile adoption increases.

Mobile phones also unlock entrepreneurship: porters, carpenters and other self-employed workers can advertise their services on lampposts and notice boards and ask potential clients to get in touch with them. Iqbal Quadir likes to tell the story of a barber in Bangladesh who could not afford the rent for a shop, so he bought a mobile phone and a motorbike instead, scheduling appointments by phone and going to his clients' homes. This was more convenient for them and he was able to serve a larger area and charge higher fees.

Globally, such micro-entrepreneurs account for 50-60% of all businesses, and in Bangladesh their share is believed to be as high as 90%. Mobile phones make micro-entrepreneurs vastly more productive: a plumber no longer has to return to his shop to pick up messages from clients, for example. As Grameen Bank founder Professor Yunus once put it: "When you get a mobile phone, it is almost like having a card to get out of poverty in a couple of years." Emerging markets also thrive on unique services such as the micro-payment plans; "torch phones" that feature multiple LED lights for users who live in areas with little or no regular electricity service; multiple phone books for users who share their handsets with family members; or solar device chargers for use in Bangladesh and sunny Africa.

Farmers in Uganda have been using Farmer's Friend, an agricultural-information service, to get farming tips. Rice farmers who have trouble with aphids can text for advice and receive a message telling them how to make a pesticide using soap and paraffin. A farmer with blighted tomato plants can learn how to control the problem by spraying the plants with a milk-based mixture. The Farmer's Friend service accepts text-message queries such as "rice aphids", "tomato blight" or "how to plant bananas" and dispenses relevant advice from a database compiled by local partners. More complicated questions (e.g., what to do when "my chicken's eyes are bulging") are relayed to human experts, who either call back within 15 minutes or, with particularly difficult problems, promise to provide an answer within four days.

These answers are then used to improve the database. Farmer's Friend is one of a range of phone-based services launched in June, 2009 by MTN, Google and the Grameen Foundation's "Application

Laboratory", or AppLab. As well as disseminating advice in agriculture, provided by the Busoga Rural Open Source and Development Initiative, the new services also provide health and market information.

Tata Consultancy Services, an Indian operator, offers a service called mKrishi which is similar to Farmer's Friend, allowing farmers to send queries and receive personalized advice. There have been lots of pilot schemes in the past, but commercial offerings are now beginning to gain ground as the rural population is increasingly willing to pay substantial subscription fees to get this information multiple times a day.

Nokia, the Finnish multinational handset-maker, launched its own information service, Nokia Life Tools, in India in June, 2009. In addition to education and entertainment, it provides agricultural information, such as prices, weather data and farming tips, which can be called up from special menus on some Nokia handsets. The basic service costs 30 rupees a month, and a premium service, which provides detailed local crop prices in ten states, is available at twice that price. Again, these are just a few anecdotal examples, but they illustrate the myriad unseen ways in which mobile phones are improving people's lives in the developing world. Experts point out that once poor countries have established comprehensive mobile coverage, and a reasonable proportion of the population own a handset, they have a platform from which new services, such as farming advice and mobile money, can be launched. This second wave of mobile-driven benefits, however, will reach its full potential only if access can be extended even further. That, in turn, will require mobile operators in developing countries to find new ways to cut the cost of ownership even more.

It turns out that as people shift from holding a mobile phone to their ears to holding it in their hands, it opens the door to information services. CellBazaar provides a text-based classified-ads service in Bangladesh. Of course, it's often not quite as elaborate as the World Wide Web, but it's a web of services that can be offered on mobile devices. Offering agricultural and health information is more difficult than offering a phone service, however, because such information must be localized and must take cultural differences into account. The best answer is to work closely with local partners. The Grameen Foundation is also experimenting with the idea of "community knowledge workers," that is, local people who can help others get access to mobile services, reading, translating and explaining text messages where necessary, just as village-phone operators provide access to basic mobile communications.

Grameen's collaboration with MTN and Google in Uganda is just one of dozens of services across the developing world that offers agricultural, market and health information via mobile phones. In India, for example, farmers can sign up for Reuters Market Lite, a text-based service that is available in parts of India. Its 125,000 users pay 200 rupees (US $4.20) for a three-month subscription, which provides them with local weather and price information four or five times a day. Many farmers say that their profits have gone up as a result.

These new services have become feasible because mobile phones are increasingly ubiquitous. Experts believe that we are now in a new phase where we are seeing the network effects of so many people using mobile phones. Although there's a lot of talk about what one could do with more-sophisticated digital devices, but it's much more compelling when one focuses on the devices that people have in their hands today and make the most of them.

Virtual banking with mobile money

Most experts believe that the mobile service which is delivering the most obvious economic benefits is money transfer, otherwise known as mobile banking (though often for technical and regulatory reasons it is not, strictly speaking, banking). Interestingly enough, it has grown out of the widespread custom of using prepaid calling credit as an informal currency. In some countries, where airtime can be transferred directly from one phone to another by text message, the process is even simpler: load credit onto your phone and send it to someone who in return gives cash to your intended recipient.

Some mobile-money schemes also allow international remittances; others issue participants with debit cards linked to their mobile-money accounts. Since there are many more mobile phones and sellers of mobile airtime than there are cash machines and bank branches in much of the developing world, mobile money is well-positioned to bring financial services within the reach of billions of "unbanked" people without access to such services.

It is now expected that extending mobile money to other poor countries, particularly in Africa and Asia, would have a huge impact.

It is a faster, cheaper and safer way to transfer money than the alternatives, such as slow, costly transfers via banks and "snail mails" through post offices, or handing an envelope of cash to a bus driver. Rather than spend a day travelling by bus to the nearest bank, recipients in rural areas can spend their time doing more productive things. The incomes of Kenyan households using M-PESA, a mobile phone-based money-transfer service, have increased by 5-30% since they started mobile banking, according to a 2009 study.

Mobile money also provides a stepping stone to formal financial services for the billions of people who lack access to savings accounts, credit and insurance. Although for regulatory reasons, M-PESA accounts do not pay interest, the service is used by some people as a savings account. Having even a small cushion of savings to fall back on allows poor people to deal with unexpected expenses, such as medical treatment, without having to sell a cow or take a child out of school. Mobile banking is safer than storing wealth in the form of cattle (which can become diseased and die), gold (which can be stolen), in neighborhood savings schemes (which may be fraudulent) or by stuffing banknotes into a mattress.

Given all of its benefits, why is mobile money not more widespread? Thus far, its progress has been impeded by banks, which fear that mobile operators will eat their lunch, and by regulators, who worry that mobile-money schemes will be abused by fraudsters and money-launderers. In many countries mobile money has been blocked because operators do not have banking licenses and their networks of corner-shop retailers do not meet the strict criteria for formal bank branches. And some mobile-money schemes that have been launched, such as one in Tanzania, failed to catch on. As recently as a year ago, people wondered whether M-PESA's success was a fluke.

However, in 2009 there have been some more hopeful signs. Kenya's success story has demonstrated mobile money's potential, and its benefits are starting to be more widely appreciated. More enlightened regulators are no longer insisting that these services meet the rigid rules for formal banking. Some banks, meanwhile, have come to see mobile money not as a threat but as an opportunity, and are teaming up with operators. Phone companies have been watching Kenya closely to learn how to establish and market a successful mobile-money scheme. Recently MTN has launched a mobile-money service in Uganda in conjunction with Standard Bank and it appears to be doing well. MTN is reportedly fine-tuning its service in Uganda before rolling it out across Africa.

We believe that banks and regulators in Bangladesh should take note. Instead of lobbying against mobile money, banks should see it as an exciting chance to exploit the telecom firms' vast retail networks and powerful brands to reach new customers. Tie-ups between banks and operators will help reassure regulators. But they, too, need to be prepared to be more flexible. People who want to sign up for mobile-money services should not, for example, have to jump through all the hoops required to open a bank account.

Concerns about money-laundering can be dealt with by imposing limits (typically US $100) on the size of mobile-money transactions, and on the maximum balance. In addition inflexible rules governing the types of establishments where cash can be paid in and taken out ought to be relaxed.

Prompt delivery of workers' remittances, at affordable costs, to recipients in rural areas away from bank branches has for long remained a challenge for banks in Bangladesh. Remitters and recipients not well-served by banks have often been lured by fast acting "hundi" channels diverting the foreign exchange inflows to illegal capital flight, tax evasion and crime/terrorism financing.

The good news is that thanks to a few recent initiatives by Bangladesh Bank (BB), mobile banking will soon be coming to the doors of the masses in Bangladesh. BB is encouraging partnerships between banks and mobile phone networks, a number of such BB-approved partnerships are already active. Recently, BB has strengthened its monitoring and supervision activities on agricultural and SME loans with the help of the existing countrywide mobile network and is keeping record of cell phone numbers of farmers and small entrepreneurs.

Another piece of good news is that the ongoing automation of the country's banking sector is expected to gear up the economic growth by at least 1 percent upon its completion by 2012. Bangladesh Bank is carrying out an integrated automation program with assistance from the UK-based Department for International Development (DFID) and World Bank under which two major components of the banking services will come under cyber technology in 2011. Under the program, all transactions like bill payment, fund transfer, tax payment and payments for online shopping will only be a click away. It is expected that this system would be in place by 2011, offering a speedy fund transfer, and thereby stimulating further economic activities.

A digital doctor on the watch 24/7

Given the risk-averse culture of the health systems of the rich world, experts suggest that some great advances could emerge as leapfrogging innovations in the poor world. As it happens, the next great technology revolution in health care is bubbling up from the villages of Africa and may in time benefit the rich world too. It is built on the astounding success of the most famous of all leapfrog technologies: mobile phones.

The most promising applications of mobile health technologies (also known as mHealth) are public-health messaging, stitching together smart medical grids, extending the reach of scarce health workers and establishing surveillance networks for infectious diseases. The use of the technology is spreading: a recent report funded by the UN Foundation and the Vodafone Foundation, two charities, documented more than four dozen projects across the developing world.

In Uganda, for example, Text to Change uses an SMS-based quiz to raise awareness amongst phone users about HIV/AIDS that brought a 40% increase in the number of people getting tested. A 2007 study in Thailand showed that compliance with a drug regimen to tackle tuberculosis jumped to over 90% when patients were sent daily text reminders to take their pills on time.

Another promising application of mHealth involves integrating mobiles into Electronic Health Records (EHRs) and software for clinical-decision support. In Western Kenya a new counselling and HIV testing project allows rural health-care surveyors to set up EHRs from patients' homes by putting their data into mobile phones. Developed by a team led by Kenya's Moi University, this system aims to establish EHRs for some 2 million patients. Public-health officials think this will help them identify and treat HIV patients and improve continuing patient care.

One lesson emerging from these various experiments is that the visible face of any mHealth or e-health scheme, regardless of where it operates, needs to be as simple and user-friendly as possible. The hidden back-end can and should use sophisticated software and hardware.

The mobile-based technology provided to Rwandan health workers by Voxiva, an American firm, should make users even in rich countries jealous. Local officials in Rwanda now have mobile phones loaded with software that allows them to enter and transmit health data back to their base so they can access information on potential outbreaks, shortages of medicines and so on in real time. They also use mobile phones to order medicines, send public-health alerts and download medical guidelines.

Another area in which mHealth could make a big difference is in helping to get the most out of the inadequate staff of health-care systems in the developing world. While some critics maintain that what Africa needs most is more money for doctors, not fancy technology, we argue that even with extra money for medical training Africa cannot realistically hope to have enough doctors in rural areas in the near future. Training doctors takes time, and many of them do not want to work in remote areas. Therefore, one option is to ensure that community health workers are trained to perform many of the simpler medical tasks currently done by doctors. This service model should work well in Bangladesh, too.

This new sort of remote medicine is gaining currency. The US-based Council on Foreign Relations has come up with a concept it calls "doc in a box," which is a standard cargo container fitted up to serve as a basic rural health clinic. The box, which costs a few thousand dollars to make, allows trained villagers to offer many services, such as vaccinations and basic malaria treatment, which would otherwise require a trip to a faraway clinic. The units are linked by mobile phone to fully trained professionals.

Another success story comes from Mexico where a for-profit mHealth firm, called Medicall Home, serves some 4.5 million Mexicans. It provides unlimited consultations by mobile phone with doctors for a flat fee of about US $5 a month. This works because many Mexicans lack health insurance or live in remote areas far from hospitals, but almost always have mobile phones. The firm is working with Voxiva, a privately owned, global provider of mobile-centric information solutions in the health sector, to offer more mHealth services and to extend them across Latin America. With funding from Fundación Carso, a charity funded by Carlos Slim, a Mexican telecoms magnate, the group hopes to mine its data to benefit both patients and public-health officials.

GE Healthcare (GEHC), an arm of US-based General Electric, plans to revolutionize rural health services in maternal care in countries like India and Bangladesh "the same way as cellphones did," according to Syed Omar Ishrak, Bangladesh origin President and CEO of GEHC clinical systems. In Bangladesh, GEHC is also taking help of microfinancing from the Grameen Bank. "If we succeed in the maternal care in Grameen health program, we can translate that to cardiac care and other ailments," says Mr. Ishrak.

GE is expected to commit US $2 billion of financing over the next six years to drive healthcare information technology and health in rural and underserved areas, plus US $1 billion for partnerships, content and services. As part of its Healthymagination initiative, GE has committed to expand its maternal infant care product offerings by 35 percent and expand its work with Grameen-like projects to 10 countries by 2015. The joint goal is now to create a sustainable rural health model that reduces maternal and infant mortality by more than 20 percent. Recently GE introduced three new innovations targeted at the huge unmet clinical needs in Bangladesh: the MAC 400, a portable electrocardiograph (ECG); GE's Lullaby Baby Warmer, which helps reduce infant deaths from hypothermia and asphyxia; and the LOGIQ P3, a portable ultrasound imaging system.

How far can this technology go? Experts at Google believe that a combination of mobile telephony and information technologies, deployed in a robust global surveillance system, can catch the next SARS or HIV long before it turns into a global pandemic. The key is "early detection and effective early response."

One relatively new tool in the box is digital detection. Researchers at Google, MIT's Media Lab, IBM and other outfits are applying sophisticated software tools to try to predict outbreaks of disease. For example, software can "crawl" the web and look for press reports in many languages that point to the outbreak of an unusual disease. In a study published in *Nature* in February, 2009, Google demonstrated how this technique was able to predict flu outbreaks in the US a week or more before the government's Centers for Disease Control and Prevention did.

One promising mHealth technology is Frontline SMS, a free application that allows health officials to analyze a huge flood of text messages without the need for central servers or internet access. Some experts argue that rich-world solutions simply won't work in places with constrained resources and intermittent connectivity. For a global surveillance system to be robust, it must provide the people closest to the trouble with the information and authority they need to act swiftly. InSTEDD, a California-based not-for-profit software development firm, has created an open-source application that puts together data from disparate mobile sources and combines it with maps and other data to be used by field workers to act on a warning.

The Rockefeller Foundation, along with the UN Foundation and others, is encouraging such mobile innovators to agree on best practices and common standards to allow the most promising ideas to spread easily, quickly and widely. Indeed, if the internet is humanity's planetary nervous system, we are now building our planetary digital immune system. Indeed, this is one more case of what can happen when we're able to bundle digital hardware, software and "humanware" into "everyware" in order to make healthcare accessible to all.

Mobile phones or netbooks—a false choice?

There's been a long-running debate within the digital technology community about the relative merits of computers and mobile phones as tools to promote development. Leading the computer camp is Nicholas Negroponte of the Massachussetts Institute of Technology (MIT), the man behind the US $100 laptop. He and his followers argue that bringing down the cost of laptops, and persuading governments in developing countries to buy and distribute millions of them could have enormous educational and economic benefits.

Critics of his scheme argue that it makes more sense to spend US $100 on a schoolhouse, or textbooks, or teacher training, rather than on a laptop. And advocates of mobile phones, including Iqbal Quadir, who has sparred with Negroponte on the subject, point out that mobile phones provide immediate economic benefits, which enable them to spread in a self-sustaining, bottom-up way, without the need for massive government funding. Negroponte responds that mobile phones are not much use for education; Quadir replies that thanks to economic development driven by mobile phones, parents can afford to educate their children. The good news is that the back-and-forth argument, having rumbled on for years, has now ended in compromise.

As of 2011, however, it appears that those in the mobile camp seem to have won since mobile phones are now seen as a vital tool of development, whereas Negroponte's laptop project has failed to meet its ambitious goals. But although his engineers have so far only managed to get the cost of their elegant laptop down to about US $150, they have shown what is possible with a low-cost design, and helped create today's vibrant netbook market.

If Netbooks do indeed become the preferred devices to access the internet in the developing world, Negroponte will have the last laugh. But if those netbooks turn out to be, in effect, large mobile phones with keyboards that access the internet via mobile networks, as also seems likely, Quadir and his camp can claim to have won the day. Technological progress in devices and networks seem to have rendered the debate moot: the important thing is that internet access will be on its way to becoming as widespread as mobile phones.

Obstacles remain even to universal mobile access, and beyond that to universal internet access. One problem has been a lack of backbone links. As international links improve and network equipment becomes cheaper and more effective, it will not be difficult to provide a low-cost mobile-broadband service, according to experts. The main challenge will be to reduce the price of access devices until we come up with a mobile-data device that costs US $60-80 maximum.

In the meantime, the Grameen Foundation is promoting the internet equivalent of the village-phone model that could provide a stepping stone to wider internet access in the poorest areas of the world, just as village phones did for telephony. The Grameen Foundation has already experimented by giving netbooks to a few village-phone operators in Uganda so that they can sell internet access as well as telephony. Despite the relatively slow connection provided by Uganda's 2G mobile networks, demand for the service proved to be stronger than expected, and revenues were double the level required to make the service self-sustaining (as of 2010).

Recent research shows that access to the internet can provide an even bigger boost to economic growth than access to mobile phones. But to make the most of the internet, users have to have a certain level of education and literacy. Its effect on development may be greater in the long term, but is unlikely to be as sudden and dramatic as that of the spread of mobile phones in the first decade of the 21st century.

In the grand scheme of telecoms history, however, mobile phones have made a bigger difference to the lives of more people, more quickly, than any previous technology. They have spread the fastest and proved the easiest and cheapest to adopt. It is now clear that the long process of connecting everyone on Earth to a global telecommunications network, which began with the invention of the telegraph in 1791, is on the verge of being completed. Mobile phones will have done more than anything else to advance the democratization of telecoms, and all the advantages that are associated with it.

2.5 Building on what works in Bangladesh and beyond

We could cite many more case examples of initiatives from around the world that have proven to work in transforming banking, healthcare, education and democratic participation, thanks to the broadening adoption of digital technologies. Indeed, we hope to be able to share and celebrate more exciting case examples as they become available at our website: www.goingdigitalbook.com. The important point is that Bangladesh can take advantage of the lessons learned from the uses of digital technologies in other countries, build on what works elsewhere and steer clear of services or business models that simply do not work.

Mention "apps for democracy" and people are likely to cite the recent historic transformations in Egypt and Tunisia (among others) that were organized via Facebook and Twitter. However, there's a different angle to the concept of "Apps for Democracy" (http://www.appsfordemocracy.org/), a Washington DC-based initiative that leveraged public contests to develop web-based government services. In the spirit of bringing the ethos of openness, participation, and collaboration, the Apps for Democracy initiative encouraged contestants to tap into the city-wide data warehouse to invent new apps. The experiment produced 47 internet, iPhone and Facebook apps in 30 days, delivering US $2.3 million in value to the city at a total cost of only US $50,000, including the prize money for the winning teams.

> "Automation started by amplifying the power of our muscles and in recent times has been amplifying the power of our minds. So for the past two centuries, automation has been eliminating jobs at the bottom of the skill ladder while creating new and better-paying jobs at the top of the skill ladder."
> – Ray Kurzweil (b. 1948)

Among the world's most effective crisis-mapping platforms is Ushahidi, which means "testimony" in Swahili (http://www.ushahidi.com/). It started out as a small Kenyan-born organization that enables users to submit eye-witness accounts and other relevant information in a disaster situation via e-mail, text, or Twitter, and then visualize the frequency and distribution of these events on a map. The credit for this idea goes to Ory Okolloh, a prominent Kenyan lawyer and blogger, who needed to document the ongoing events when violence erupted in the aftermath of Kenya's disputed election in 2008.

Since then Ushahidi has gone global and the crisis-mapping site sprang into action when a devastating magnitude 7.0 earthquake struck Haiti in 2010. Thanks to emergency responders who were closely monitoring the interactive crisis-mapping site, a text message sent from a cell phone in Port-au-Prince, the epicenter of the earthquake, was translated from Creole into English and posted on Ushahidi.com, it became clear that the text was a cry for help from a survivor from beneath the rubble of one of Haiti's largest supermarkets. After a search-and-rescue team pulled a body from the rubble, it turned to be that of a deeply shaken and barely alive seven-year-old girl who managed to survive on a small ration of leathery fruit snacks in the supermarket wreckage.

Tired of tons of rubbish scattered across illegal dumping sites around Dhaka and elsewhere in Bangladesh? Why not do what the citizens of Estonia did in 2008? When concerned Estonians decided that the time had come to clean up thousands and thousands of tons of rubbish abandoned since they regained independence from the former Soviet Union in 1991, they turned not to the government, but to tens of thousands of their peers. Using a combination of global positioning systems and Google Maps, two entrepreneurs (Skype guru Ahti Heinla and Microlink founder Rainer Nolvak) enlisted volunteers to plot the locations of over ten thousand illegal dump sites, including detailed descriptions and photos.

Phase 2 of their cleanup initiative was, even by their own admission, rather ambitious: Clean up all of the illegal sites in one day using mass collaboration! So, on May 3rd, 2008, over 50,000 volunteers scoured fields, streets, forests, and riverbanks across Estonia, picking up everything from tractor batteries to paint cans. Now the question remains, if 50,000 Estonians can clean up their entire country (albeit a relatively small one of only 45,000 sq. km, which amounts to about 30% of the area of Bangladesh), what could Digital Bangladeshis do to clean up the country from the ground up? Even if we can't finish the job in three days, couldn't we get it done in a week? Of course, to garner the same level of citizen participation as in Estonia, Bangladesh will need to mobilize some 6.3 million people for the cleanup campaign (based on the total population size of Estonia at 1.3 million vs. Bangladesh's 164 million). Perhaps a better, if not more optimistic, way of looking at this situation may be that we'll need only about 170,000 people to do the job, given the geographic area of Bangladesh vs. Estonia!

Users of e-government services rank improved transactional efficiency (as reflected in a reduced number of visits and less waiting time), reduced corruption, and better quality of service (such as reduced error rates and increased convenience) as most important. Nondiscriminatory treatment and effective complaint handling system are also desired features. Indeed, successful e-government projects have reduced transaction costs and processing time and increased government revenues. For example, the e-Customs System in Ghana (GCNet) increased customs revenues by 49% in its first 18 months of operation and reduced clearance times from three weeks to two days. An e-procurement system in Brazil cost only US $1.6 million, yet it enabled savings of US $107 million for the state in 2004 alone as a result of improved process efficiency and lower prices for goods and services procured. The fully automated tendering process launched as part of the same system in Brazil saved suppliers an estimated US $35 million.

Some e-government projects have also improved governance by reducing corruption and abuse of discretion, thereby making vital contributions to development. In India, a survey found that fewer users were required to pay bribes to accelerate service delivery under e-government projects than under manual systems, and that the frequency of paying bribes to service officials had fallen. For example, the land registration system in the state of Karnataka in India is estimated to have cut bribes by US $18 million annually. Furthermore, an overwhelming number of supervisors sense that abuse of discretionary power through means such as denying services to citizens has narrowed. They are also more aware of the need to comply with service standards specified in citizen charters.

The potential to access public services at home or at a local center also empowers women and minorities. For example, among the users of e-government services, women are usually in charge of dealing with public administration at the household level. The delivery of e-government services translates to easier access and less time than traveling to or queuing up at government agencies. For minorities, ICT facilitates access to relevant public information on rights and benefits, inheritance and family laws, health care, and housing, allowing the public to make informed decisions on issues of importance.

Professor Muhammad Yunus recounts great examples illustrating how many Grameen phone ladies have successfully used the power of direct access to their governments. Thanks to Grameen's telephone ladies program, each time a woman launches a mobile phone business, she is given a list of important telephone numbers, including the number of the local Member of Parliament, the head of the local government administration, the Police Chief, the local health service facilities, and other relevant officials—up to and including the Prime Minister of Bangladesh. She is told that these numbers are for her use whenever she or the people of her village have a problem and need government help.

Professor Yunus acknowledges that it's a symbolic gesture, but also a very real indication of the power that being connected electronically can bring to individual people. His favorite story involves a phone lady in a village where a crime had occurred—an assault on a local person by an unknown stranger who quickly escaped from the crime scene. When the people of the village became angry and distraught since the local police chief remained totally indifferent to the situation, the phone lady said, "Don't worry. I'll call the Police Chief." She promptly rang him up and said, "People in our village are really getting very angry because you refuse to respond to our calls. I request you to send some police to our village right away to investigate this crime. Otherwise, I am going to call the Prime Minister's Office—I have her number right here!" The result: The police arrived in one hour.

Mobile phones can also be used to root out corruption in more direct ways. For example, Zubair Bhatti, a Pakistani bureaucrat, asked all clerks in the Jhang district who handled land transfers to submit a daily list of transactions, giving the amount paid and the mobile-phone numbers of the buyer and the seller. He explained that he would be calling buyers and sellers at random to find out whether they had been asked to pay any extra bribes or commissions. When charges were subsequently brought against a clerk who had asked for a bribe, the others realized that Mr. Bhatti meant business, and buyers and sellers reported a sudden improvement in service. Mr. Bhatti extended the scheme to other areas, such as cracking down on veterinarians who demanded bribes from farmers, and has proposed that the Jhang model, as it is now known, be adopted in other districts. There is even talk of institutionalizing the Jhang model with call centers across Pakistan.

Another great example of the power of ICT in strengthening democracy by providing a platform for citizen activism comes from India. Back in 2001, two young journalists filmed an apparent case of bribery using a cleverly concealed video camera in which a government official was seen accepting a wad of cash amounting to INR 100,000 (about US $2,000) in exchange for a defense contract. When they posted the film on the Web at a news site called Tehelka.com, the whole country was so outraged that the Defense Minister and several of his colleagues had to resign immediately to stave off a complete collapse of the then ruling government of India. The lesson to be learned from this example is that while most Indians assume that millions of dollars' worth of bribes change hands behind closed government doors every year, actually seeing US $2,000 being exchanged can have an incredible impact on public opinion, which can drive dramatic and positive change in governance at all levels.

Claiming your US $80-trillion bonanza

Readers: Your bribery stories above just reminded me of your offer of the US $80 trillion "prize" for reading and understanding this chapter. Now that we're near the end of the chapter, I'm ready to collect my prize!

Authors: The prize actually resides in taking stock of the fact that stock prices reflect the conventional wisdom of a buyer-seller market, which happens to be based on the shortsighted linear intuitive assumption that most people share regarding future economic growth. If you've understood our "digital big bang theory" outlined in this chapter, you should realize that the conventional wisdom severely understates digital deflation and the acceleration of economic growth because the rate of digital technological progress will continue to accelerate, a la the Moore's Law. If we replace the linear outlook with the more appropriate exponential perspective, the Discounted Cash Flow (DCF) models that take into account the time value of money will need to reflect the accelerated returns. It turns out that if present values were to grow (compared to current expectations based on the linear intuitive assumptions) by an annual compounded rate of as little as 2% and we're able to use an annual discount rate of 6% (and assuming that the discount rate does not increase due to the perception of accelerated future growth), then the present values resulting from only 20 years of compounded and discounted future (additional) growth will be three times that of today's global market capitalization. Thus, the present values of the equity markets (conservatively pegged at US $40 trillion) should triple over the next 20 years, amounting to US $80 trillion in additional wealth for all of you.

Readers: But you said that I would get that money.

Authors: Well, we said you would get the money and we simply could not succumb to any kind of favoritism by picking one reader over another. Given that the English word "you" can be singular or plural, we actually meant it in the sense of "all of you" readers from anywhere in the whole world. That's why we suggested reading the sentence carefully!

Readers: But not everyone will read this chapter.

Authors: We sure hope that everyone would get the message one way or another. So if all of you "get it," this will add to your stock of new intellectual capital. Whether you're able to monetize this intellectual capital into US $80 trillion will depend on how readily you can predict which specific technologies or competitors will prevail in the marketplace, or how well you can stage your investments to capitalize on the dynamics of market and technology developments. In fact, a whole new discipline has sprung up around what's called real options valuation for dealing with such staged investments—similar to the concept of Bridge One and Bridge Two for building the digital infrastructure in Bangladesh as we discussed in Chapter Zero—which, by the way, are related but different from purely speculative financial options! A real option is the right—but not the obligation—to undertake some real-life decision, e.g., the option to make, abandon, or scale up or down the size of a capital investment. For example, the opportunity to invest in the expansion of a firm's factory, or alternatively to sell the factory, is a real "call" or "put" option, respectively. A financial option, on the other hand, is a derivative financial instrument that establishes a contract between two parties concerning the buying or selling of an asset at a reference price. The buyer of the option gains the right, but not the obligation, to engage in some specific transaction on the asset, while the seller incurs the obligation to fulfill the transaction if so requested by the buyer. In any event, your new understanding of exponential growth in both the price-performance of technology and the rate of economic activity will help you reset your perception of increased future equity values, and thus set the discount rates for the DCF models appropriately. For example, one thousand dollars of computation today is far more powerful than one thousand dollars of computing only ten years ago (in fact, by a factor of more than one thousand!).

Readers: Do you have any examples outside the computational realm?

Authors: Even when economists conclude that we always get one dollar of products and services for a dollar by assuming "a car is a car," they greatly understate the major upgrades in safety, reliability, and comfort features. The fact is that we get much more for that dollar. For example, BP's cost for finding oil in 2000 was less than one dollar per barrel, down from nearly ten dollars in 1991. Processing an internet transaction costs a US bank one penny, compared to more *than one dollar using a human teller. (Of course, the absolute cost structure of a Bangladeshi bank will be quite different from that of its US counterpart, but the relative costs of fully automated vs. human-mediated operations of both should be similar.) University of Chicago professor Pete Klenow and University of Rochester professor Mark Bils estimate that the economic value, i.e., the surplus in constant dollars captured by consumers from the "new and improved" versions of existing goods has been increasing at 1.5% per year for the past twenty years because of qualitative improvements in products and services.*

Reader: Hmm, interesting. As a global investor, I wonder if I should invest in Bangladesh today as it readies itself for the digital world with its Digital Bangladesh initiative.

Authors: We're glad you're thinking of investing in the future of Bangladesh since we happen to believe that the country is hugely undervalued by investors today. In fact, in the following chapters of this book we provide glimpses of specific investment opportunities related to building robust digital platforms in Bangladesh so that investors and entrepreneurs can actively participate in creating wealth through collaborative innovation on a global scale by 2021. To this end, the next chapter deals with the challenges and opportunities in creating an investment-friendly environment in Bangladesh through reforms and policy innovations at all levels of the government.

The new math of digital network economics

If economics was never your cup of tea in high school or college, don't worry. Most economists didn't know much about network economics either, until very recently. Besides, the network is the key concept here and crucial to understanding the economics of it. Applied to economics as well as business, a network effect (also called network externality) is the impact that one user of a good or service has on the value of that product to other people. The classic example is the phone (fixed or mobile). The more people own phones, the more valuable the phone is to each owner. This creates a positive externality because a user may purchase their phone without intending to create value for other users, but does so in any case. Over time, positive network effects can create a bandwagon effect as the network becomes more valuable and more people join, in a reinforcing feedback loop.

Network effects become significant after a certain critical mass has been achieved. At that point, the value obtained from the good or service is greater than or equal to the price paid for the good or service. As the value of the good is determined by the user base, this implies that after a certain number of people have subscribed to the service or purchased the good, additional people will subscribe to the service or purchase the good due to the positive utility/price ratio, or "the bigger bang for the buck." This is indeed one additional phenomenon—besides the Moore's Law—that underlies our "digital big bang theory."

Chapter 3

Creating the Roadmaps and Policy Instruments to Enable Inclusive Economic Prosperity

"A reform is a correction of abuses; a revolution is a transfer of power."
— *Edward Bulwer-Lytton (1803-1873)*

There are two takeaways from this chapter:

What kind of goals should we target? Well, if you want to make it to the other side of a chasm, then small, tentative jumps won't do. In fact, they would be lethal. To clear such a divide, one must make a grand leap. In other words, our goals should be as big as the chasm is wide.

What would it take for us to leap across such a big chasm from the LIC to the MIC status for Bangladesh? It turns out that if we can recommit ourselves to the roadmaps towards Digital Bangladesh and uphold the essential policy instruments, Bangladesh will soon be equipped to make such leaps through her globe-circumscribing 25,000-mile long legs, that is, the country's ever-expanding broadband digital infrastructure.

Today's national and global economies owe their health, if not their existence, partly to rapid transportation, but more importantly to rapid distance-bridging communication, notably talking on the phone and communicating online over the internet. When you talk on the phone, give advice, make requests or place orders, things happen on the other end, thousands of miles away. Sales are made, relationships are formed, and the participants manage to create wealth in the process. It's magic!

Yet, the ICT evolution that makes it all possible has been less than fifty years in the making. What this means is that half-a-century ago no country in the world had any regulatory or policy framework for ICTs.

In comparison to the timescale of legal and governance evolution that spans several millennia, this time period is a blip. But in this blink of an eye, so to speak, the global business practices and rules for governance have morphed into completely new regimes.

3.1 The regulatory and policy landscape for ICTs

If truly a Rip van Winkle lawyer went to sleep in 1961 and woke up 50 years later in 2011 he would be completely at a loss in the new legal paradigms anywhere in the world. In those fifty years, forty of which as a sovereign existence, Bangladesh also adopted many regulatory and policy mandates in the context of ICTs. Let us now try to chart out that regulatory and policy evolution.

Bangladesh Computer Council Act – 1990

Bangladesh Computer Council (BCC) was formed in 1990 through an act of the Parliament for promotion of computer usage and literacy particularly in government agencies and generally in all spheres of national activities. According to Colonel (Retd) Azizur Rahman, the brains behind the setting up of the BCC, it was modeled after the Singapore National Computer Board. The BCC Act allows wide dispensation to the council in promoting the effective use of information technology including the charter for opening commercial subsidiaries for providing professional IT services. Dr. Rofiquzzaman, an expat Bangladeshi and a professor of electrical and computer engineering at the California Polytechnic Institute at Pomona, was appointed the first Vice-Chairman, while, the President of the Republic chaired the council.

However, this arrangement did not survive long as the Presidential form of government came to an end with the ouster of the-then President, General (Retd) H M Ershad in December 1990. Under the parliamentary form of government since 1991, the BCC is chaired by the Minister in charge of the Science and Technology Ministry of the government. This ministry has been renamed as the 'Science & ICT' Ministry in 2002. However, with the change of government in 1991, BCC not only lost its stature but also its founder executive director (ED is the executive head of BCC) Col. (Retd) Azizur Rahman, who had great visions for the BCC and tremendous passion for IT but turned out to be a weak administrator. Since his ouster BCC has been run mostly by government bureaucrats, many of whom literally took it as punishment posting (as it was outside of the corridors of power so to speak) and one particular BCC ED gained notoriety for his eccentric remark that computers are 'devil's boxes'.

The BCC Act mandates the organization to recruit computer professionals to run its affairs. In reality, close to half the senior organizational positions are occupied by civil servants who are basically "parked" in BCC due to lack of positions in the capital city. The situation is further aggravated by direct administrative controls exercised by the Science and ICT ministry on the affairs of the BCC. There is a reform measure under way which, if implemented, will put all IT professionals working for the government under the management of the BCC and if that happens then the BCC may free itself from such unwarranted bureaucratic interventions.

The JRC report on boosting software export – 1997

On 28 May 1997, the Commerce Ministry instituted a 14-member committee, headed by Professor Jamilur Reza Choudhury of the Bangladesh University of Engineering and Technology (BUET), to examine the obstacles in the way of establishing a software export industry in Bangladesh.

Four members of this committee travelled to India and visited several software parks and establishments in Bangalore, Mumbai and Kolkata and submitted a report on 14 September 1997 containing 45 recommendations for creating an enabling environment for a flourishing software industry. This was the first formal policy-level exercise of the government for the ICT industry. The recommendations were taken up in due earnest by the Commerce Ministry under the leadership of the-then Commerce and Industries minister, Mr. Tofael Ahmed who instituted a monitoring committee headed by the Vice-Chairman and CEO of the Export Promotion Bureau (EPB) to oversee the implementation of the recommendations. Professor J R Choudhury was appointed adviser to this committee. However, after around two years of continuous efforts, this committee could only see to the full or partial implementation of only a handful of the recommendations and as per the advice of the committee adviser Professor J R Choudhury, the committee was abolished in favor of a much higher-level IT Task Force in the year 2000 which is headed by the executive head of the government, i.e., the Prime Minister.

The National Telecom Policy – 1998

The telecom policy of 1998 was the first national level policy document for the ICT industry which subsequently paved the way for the Bangladesh Telecom Regulatory Commission (BTRC) Act and the gradual deregulation and licensing of private landline, cellular, internet and call centre operators. Although some of the cellular telecom and internet service licenses predate the BTRC Act, the regulatory field for the telecom industry has been brought under a common and systematic framework under the Act passed in 2004.

The Copyright Amendment Act – 2000 and 2002

The intellectual property rights (IPR) laws of Bangladesh have a long history dating back to early part of the twentieth century. These laws remained largely unchanged over the decades although IPR types and propagation technologies changed dramatically since the latter half of the last century. IPR involve three types of IP's – copyrights, patents and trademarks. The software and IT services industry desperately needed the copyright law to be amended to recognize software copyrights. This was one of the first five charter demands of the software industry after the formation of the industry association in late 1997 named Bangladesh Association of Software and Information Services (BASIS). The association, since its inception, worked closely with the Bangladesh Computer Council, Bangladesh Law Commission and the Copyrights Registrar under the government's Ministry of Cultural Affairs to effect the necessary amendments to the copyrights law of 1913. The amendment was finally passed by the parliament in July 2000 but some drafting errors in the act required another amendment in 2002 to make the act enforceable. It must be mentioned here that the copyright act amendment process started a few years before BASIS was formed but the final push came from the software industry through BASIS.

ICT Task Force – 2000, and Digital Bangladesh Task Force – 2010

In line with the recommendations of the Jamilur Reza Choudhury report of September 1997, an ICT Task Force was formed in 2000 with the Prime Minister as the chair. Due to political exigencies the task force was able to meet a total of 5 times in eight years till 2008. In 2009 the task force was renamed as 'Digital Bangladesh Task Force' in line with the election pledges of the Awami League led coalition in government today. The renamed task force has met once in the last two years. This is the highest policy-making and monitoring body of the nation for ICT affairs comprising four Cabinet Members, six Secretaries to the government, heads of BTRC and BCC, Computer Science Chairs of selected universities and heads of ICT industry associations. The task force wanted to emulate their counterpart in India that bulldozed through great many regulatory and administrative reforms, as well as fast-tracked strategic infrastructure investments (such as for software technology parks) there to facilitate the unfettered growth of the Indian software industry. However, the exercise has not yielded similar results here as the pace of positive interventions for the industry from the task force has so far lacked speed, direction and ownership.

The National ICT Policy – 2002

A national ICT policy draft was under preparation since late 1999 which took its final shape by early 2001. The policy document was primarily put together by the Bangladesh Computer Council (BBC) under the direction of the Ministry of Science and ICT. However, the Federation of Bangladesh Chamber of Commerce and Industries (FBCCI) took an initiative in early 2002 to put together an ICT policy recommendation in consultation with the ICT industry associations namely BASIS, BCS and ISPAB. The policy recommendation was formally handed over to the Science and ICT Ministry in March 2002. The national ICT policy 2002 was formally approved by the cabinet in September of that year, however, it borrowed little from the industry recommendation. Despite that the policy at least formally outlined the goals and aspirations of the nation around ICTs for the first time and set some milestones for the development of the ICT sector. The ICT Policy 2002, however, lacked a cohesive structure; dozens of actionable items were strewn across the document lumped together with policy directives and strategic objectives.

The BTRC Act – 2004

Since the licensing of the three private mobile operators in 1996-97 ending the monopoly of Citycell that had been the sole operator since 1990, there had been demands for setting up a regulatory authority to ensure a level playing field for all operators. The Telecom Policy 1998 also foresaw the need for enacting the relevant laws in this area for the smooth development of the telecom sector. The landline teledensity of the nation was languishing at below 1%. Today due to the healthy growth of the mobile sector Bangladesh enjoys a teledensity of more than 50%.

The BTRC was set up in 2004 after passage of the BTRC Act in that year. Initially the commission was besotted to the Bangladesh Telephone and Telex Board (BTTB) and was manned by BTTB officers either after retirement or on deputation. The mobile telecom operators clamored that the BTRC lacked latest telecom expertise and open market orientation and were hobbled with bureaucrats with little knowledge of the industry. The situation improved with the appointment of telecom professionals as chairs of BTRC since 2007 and induction of industry experts as consultants. However, just as BTRC was gaining respectability as a regulator, the government curtailed BTRC's authority by vesting its complete administrative control with the Post and Telecom Ministry in late 2010. The Post and Telecom Ministry with little or no knowledge of the telecom industry may hinder fast-paced development of the industry in future according to most industry observers including the authors of this book.

> "Risk is innovation's middle name."
> – Bilal Kaafarani
> (b. 1959)

The ICT Act – 2006 and 2009

The legal infrastructure for ICTs in Bangladesh only five years ago lacked laws for electronic transactions, privacy rights, cyber crimes, digital security, and other legal aspects of a digital lifestyle. These concerns have been partially addressed by the ICT Act of 2006 which is based on a model electronic transactions law provided by the UNCITRAL (United Nations Commission on International Trade Law)—a UN body providing expert assistance on legal and regulatory framework to member countries. The act primarily encompasses the laws and regulations to enable digital transactions and signatures through the secure mechanism of Public Key Infrastructure (PKI). The act also addresses some aspects of data privacy, computer hacking and cyber security. The act required framing of rules and enforcement of the legal provisions within 180 days of passing of the law. However, in the politically charged environment of 2006 the government machinery was at a virtual standstill. In 2009 the ICT Act was amended to allow more time for the framing of rules and enabling digital transactions which are yet to come.

Access to Information (A2I) Project, Prime Minister's Office

UNDP set up the A2I project at the PMO in September 2006 to help the government with their e-government agenda. The project in its current shape runs through June 2011. UNDP and the government are expected to extend the project in view of the momentum it has gathered in mobilizing support for e-government initiatives during its present tenure. During 2007-2008 the A2I project came out with the Horizon Scan Report on the e-government readiness and a list of highest priority e-government initiatives to be taken up by each division of the government called the 'Quick Wins'. The project mobilized digital innovation fairs nationally and in each divisional headquarters to bring visibility to e-government programs. Currently the A2I project is preparing a 'Digital Bangladesh Strategy Report' due to come out in 2011.

The National ICT Policy – 2009

The ICT Policy 2009 (a copy of which is available at www.GoingDigitalBook.com) is a fresh policy document supplanting the earlier policy document from 2002. The new policy hinges on a singular vision of transforming the country through leveraging ICT's into a middle-income country by 2021 and a high-income country in 30 years while ensuring equitable development of all sections of the society. It cuts across all socio-economic fields of importance by enumerating 10 core objectives ranging from access to connectivity to climate change, education, health and industrial productivity. The policy document is structured as a pyramid with 56 strategic themes below the core objectives and 306 action programs at the bottom. The ICT Policy is a veritable guide for the implementation of the visions of "Digital Bangladesh" and has mandated provisions of annual reviews for the action programs and periodic reviews of the strategic themes and the policy document itself. It also classified the action programs into short, medium and long terms for planning purposes.

3.2 Rounding out the missing links

Despite significant progress made to date in terms of policy articulation and capacity building for the implementation of action items toward realizing the dreams of a Digital Bangladesh by 2021, we fall short in a few areas that need immediate attention. Outlined below are several such "missing links" in our digitization roadmaps and policy instruments.

Amendment of patents and trademarks laws

Although the copyrights law has been amended in 2000 to recognize IPR in electronic form such as software and digitally recorded audio and video, Bangladesh's laws for patents and trademarks are completely out of sync with the times. The Registrar of Patents and Trademarks, administered by the Ministry of Industries, is working on the necessary amendments with assistance from the Law Commission and World Intellectual Property Organization (WIPO)—a UN body that promotes IPR best practices around the globe. However, simply amending the relevant laws will not suffice as the registrar will also need capacity development in terms ICT infrastructure and expertise in order to safeguard the electronic patents and trademarks. The government also needs to bring IPR administration under a single institution as opposed to having two ministries administering two registrars – one for copyrights and one for patents and trademarks.

Data privacy and electronic security laws

The present ICT Act (of 2006) does not address data privacy and cyber security matters. With cyber social and e-commerce networks enveloping the globe (facebook.com has more members than people in the North American continent, groupon.com operates in dozens of countries), all countries need appropriate data privacy laws to safeguard the interests of their citizens. In the same vein the country needs national security measures to counter both internal and external cyber threats that are all too real. Such security provisions need to be under a legal framework and statutory cover of a law.

Convergence roadmap for ICT regulations—Infocomm Authority

The regulatory landscape for ICTs is populated currently by a number of regulatory authorities, namely, Bangladesh Telecom Regulatory

Commission (BTRC) for telecoms and spectrum, Controller of Certifying Authorities (CCA) for digital certificates and broadcasting regulatory authority (not yet there—in their absence the Information Ministry administers such regulatory dispensations). With the convergence and integration of broadcasting, telecommunications and information technologies the regulatory needs of these industries are finding a lot of commonalities. In some countries the technology convergences have already given way to regulatory convergence. The earliest example (2003) is OfCom in the UK. Singapore, South Korea and Zambia have also followed suit. Bangladesh also needs to move in the direction of regulatory convergence which is inevitable.

Mandated computer literacy and internet access

Computers are ubiquitous and are used in every facet of modern human life. Just as literacy and access to books were the rallying cry of the pre-modern era, in today's society computer literacy and access to internet are essential tools of modern living. Many countries have mandated these under public service obligations. By ensuring computer literacy and internet access to all citizens a nation can avoid the ignominy of a 'digital divide'. In developed countries such a divide is primarily due to generation gaps but in developing countries the divide is more prevalent due to poverty. Special measures are thus necessary to impart computer literacy and spread internet access to all sections of the society irrespective of income levels and geographical location. The present government's initiative to set up computer labs with internet access to all schools in the country can do wonders to mitigate the digital divide in the country. To ensure continuity of the program and sustained funding for it, necessary legal provisions should be incorporated in the constitution. Right to education for all must include computer literacy and the rights to communications infrastructure must include telecom and internet access as basic rights. Given the country's paucity of resources, there can be a binding timeline for rollout of such facilities throughout the country with specific financial allocations made for the period. The growth impetus this would provide will more than pay for the investments in this regard. The social and psychological boost this would entail would be priceless.

> "Innovation fuels the engine of growth. Leadership delivers the fuel."
> – Jane Stevenson (b. 1959)

3.3 How to bridge the gaps in regulatory and policy landscape

Although Bangladesh has several regulatory institutions and policy instruments for ICTs, the overarching vision of a digital nation can only be realized through a well-coordinated and well-heeled regulatory and administrative setup. Given below is a set of narrowed-down top-level recommendations that borrows from the proven and tested ways of making ICTs central to the economic development of many developing nations such as India, Kenya, Pakistan and the Philippines.

An elevated and emboldened ICT Ministry

In Bangladesh information technology related affairs traditionally have been put under the care of the Ministry of Science and Technology which was once a division under the Ministry of Education. Although the Bangladesh Computer Council (BCC) was formed in 1990 as a statutory quasi-government body, it was placed under the Science and Technology division of the Ministry of Education in 1991. The Education Minister was the ex-officio Chairman and the State Minister for Science and Technology was the ex-officio Vice-Chairman of the BCC. Soon afterwards the Science & Technology Division was put under a separate Ministry.

In 2002 this ministry was renamed as "Science & ICT" though there was no discernible change in business allocation. To this day it has remained a "junior ministry" (bottom quintile of all ministries in terms of "pecking order" and importance in the hierarchy) with a State Minister in charge. For ICT's to have a central role in uplifting the socio-economic well-being of the nation (as envisioned in the ICT Policy 2009 and "Digital Bangladesh" manifesto), the Science & ICT Ministry (or simply the ICT ministry, when the present Prime Minister's directive to carve out a separate Ministry for ICT is carried out) needs to be upgraded to a top quintile ministry having an ICT visionary in charge of it. The ICT Minister needs to have sufficient authority and his stature must have the requisite clout to effect the necessary changes in procedures (under business process re-engineering or BPR) as well as drive the Digital Bangladesh initiative with a missionary zeal. He must be an IT evangelist and a task master rolled into one.

An ICT adviser to the Digital Bangladesh Task Force

The "Digital Bangladesh Task Force" is the highest executive body for implementation of ICT policy mandates and coordination of interagency activities in this regard. Steering the task force to achieve tangible goals within meaningful timeframes necessitates an ICT-savvy advisor for overseeing the agenda and follow-up actions of decisions reached.

Ideally there should be a full-time adviser at the Prime Minister's Office for the purpose. At present these tasks are done on a piecemeal basis by the Principal Secretary of the Prime Minister's Office, (Chief) Private Secretary to the Prime Minister and Secretary Ministry of Science & ICT. This splintered management of the Digital Bangladesh task force is not only confusing to the stakeholders but also counter-productive at times. The ICT adviser's position would be able to channel the authoritative powers of the PMO in a meaningful fashion to energize the digital transformation of the government and the nation. The adviser should be of a cabinet rank and work closely with the ICT minister in a complementary role.

A roving ICT ambassador for the global Fortune 500

Bangladesh needs to aggressively market its potential as a global sourcing destination for ICT services on the strength of its large population and the emphasis on English language in its education system. One must not forget that the outsourcing market is primarily supply-driven (supplier-induced rather than demand-driven). In the absence of state-level marketing and branding of IT services, Bangladesh is barely visible in the global hubs of IT services. Only one Fortune 500 company is known to have an offshore development center in the country (Samsung Corp has started a development center in Dhaka for mobile applications and content in late 2010 having around a hundred developers).

To systematically target and entice Fortune 500 global corporations to locate their IT services centers in Bangladesh is a full-time evangelistic job. Bringing such high-profile IT services clients to the country not only creates large numbers of IT services jobs but it also signals to the world that the country is a serious contender for providing IT services. The growth multiplies fast and the race to become a digital nation is given a new impetus with the IT services export revenues fueling a global market expansion. In the absence of such an evangelist roaming the globe to bring home the top-flight consumers of world IT services, Bangladesh is losing out to well-heeled marketers of IT services outsourcing such as Kenya, Philippines and Vietnam. With a full-time roving ICT ambassador, the country can effectively market itself and clinch a hard-fought beach-head in the highly lucrative global IT sourcing industry. With the global IT services and IT-enabled Business Process Outsourcing (BPO) market approaching a thousand billion (US) dollars, we can certainly snare a 1% share of this market giving us a 10 billion dollar add-on to our export basket.

Enacting laws mandating the provisions of ICT Policy – 2009

The ICT Policy 2009 is exactly what it says it is—a policy document with no means to enforce its mandates. To give it teeth and enforcing authority the nation needs to promulgate a 'Digital Bangladesh Act' (DBA) which can mandate the provisions of the ICT Policy 2009 in a statutory manner. The DBA actually will be a set of laws dealing with the legal, regulatory, administrative and targeted implementation aspects of the provisions of the ICT Policy 2009 that will subsume the provisions of other acts in this context such as the ICT Act of 2006 which only deals with electronic signatures and transactions security for example. Such special purpose acts are not uncommon either in Bangladesh or elsewhere. In legal lingo such acts are sometimes referred to as special purpose vehicle (SPV) acts. A recent incidence of a SPV act is the Special Economic Zones Act of 2010.

> "There are two ways to slide easily through life: To believe in everything or to doubt everything. Both ways save us from thinking."
>
> – Alfred Korzybski (1879 -1950)

3.4 Upholding the BRIDGE to a Digital Bangladesh for all

We introduced the concept of "Bridge One" in the "why this book" section as a metaphor for what we need to do right now to catapult Bangladesh into the status of a digital nation by 2021 and thus earn the right to build Bridge Two, which will enable us to enjoy the full flowering of digital technologies by 2031. We also introduced the notion of a bridge to explain the "Bangladesh paradox" in Chapter 1. Given the fecundity of the concept of a bridge as a metaphor, we thought it would be entirely appropriate to propose a framework to guide our national policies and individual actions going forward and call it BRIDGE, which stands for the following core principles:

B – Bangladesh comes first

R – Reforms that work for the good of everyone

I – Imagination cultivated as the ultimate renewable resource for an innovation-driven economy

D – Digital infrastructure as our new national backbone/platform for development

G – Growth along economic, cultural and social dimensions by firing on all cylinders of our economic engine

E – Entrepreneurship as the new fuel/driver of more inclusive growth through equal opportunity for wealth creation by all

Although selling the iconic Brooklyn Bridge in New York City has become an urban legend (whereby a great swindler would sell it and the perfect sucker would fall for the scam), the point must be made that we cannot afford to put our BRIDGE principles up for sale! It turns out that the BRIDGE framework cannot be built and protected until we manage to bridge the perception gaps that exist out there about corruption and inefficiency in both the public and private sectors. By going digital, we believe, we can capitalize on a once-in-a-lifetime opportunity to create government as a platform for inclusive social achievement where the private sector is fully engaged to create economic prosperity for all.

> "Few people think more than two or three times a year. I have made an international reputation for myself by thinking once or twice a week."
> – George Bernard Shaw (1856–1950)

Of course, there are legends galore about public-sector kleptocracies ranging from the full-fledged kind—where the government is built around theft—to budding kleptocracies—where corruption is rampant, tolerated and expected but some legal and even democratic norms exist alongside it. The difference between full-fledged and budding kleptocracy is best illustrated by the old joke they like to tell around the World Bank about Asian and African Ministers of Infrastructure who exchange visits to one another's countries.

First the African visits the Asian Minister in his country, and at the end of the day the Asian takes the African to his home for dinner. The Asian Minister lives in an absolutely palatial residence. So the African minister asks his Asian counterpart, "Wow, how can you afford such a home on your salary?" The Asian Minister takes the African over to a big bay window and points to a new bridge in the distance. "You see that bridge over there?" the Asian Minister asks the African. "Yes, I see it," the African says. Then the Asian Minister points a finger to himself and whispers: "10 percent," signaling 10% of the cost of the bridge went into his pocket.

Well, a year later the Asian went to visit the African Minister in his country. "Wow, how can you afford such a home on your salary?" the Asian asked the African. The African pulled his Asian counterpart over to the big bay window in his living room and pointed out to the horizon. "Do you see that bridge over there? The African asked the Asian. "No, there is no bridge there," answered the Asian. "That's right," the African minister said, pointing to himself: "100 percent."

Levity aside, this often-told anecdote highlights the importance of "zero tolerance" for kleptocracy in Bangladesh. In fact, kleptocracy and democracy are a dangerous combination that creates a toxic brew that is fatal to trust-based productive collaboration, which is absolutely necessary to get anything done in an efficient and effective manner. Without a fundamental commitment to meritocracy at all levels of our society, we will remain severely handicapped in our ability to leapfrog as Digital Bangladesh. After all, investors and entrepreneurs cannot thrive in an environment where corruption breeds cynicism and honest hard work is only a fool's errand.

But honesty is always the best policy when it comes to pitching ideas to investors. The next chapter introduces the pros and cons of the various sources of capital for productive investment in Bangladesh and provides some guidance to entrepreneurs and policymakers alike as they weigh the options and policies to attract the right investors to specific projects.

Chapter 4

Tapping into the Various Sources of Capital for Productive Investment

"Money is the most popular labor-saving device."
— *Evan Esar (1899-1995)*

There are three takeaways from this chapter:

How should entrepreneurs go about pitching their venture plans to the capital providers? Given that money is the "oxygen of business," entrepreneurs must learn how to tap into the different sources of investment capital, and structure the terms of the investment that's appropriate for the venture or project under consideration. In other words, they need to be savvy about "sweat equity," private equity, venture capital, mutual funds, and debt financing, amongst others.

What are the various forms and institutions of investment capital? There are at least six different "faces" of capital (or capitalists). It pays to tap into the right sources of capital to suit an entrepreneur's venture plan and the amount of capital needed.

How should investors view Bangladesh as an investment destination and assess the business plans from Bangladeshi entrepreneurs? Each investor will look at investment opportunities to meet their risk and return requirements. We provide a list of institutions, organization and funds that span the spectrum of risk-return profiles.

Capital—as money that serves as a "factor of production" that is not wanted for itself but for its ability to help production and delivery of other goods and services—can be best viewed as the oxygen of business. The hard truth is that lack of capital can kill even a good business in practically no time, while having it available when needed will likely help a business expand and grow faster. We expect the Digital Bangladesh initiative to create lots of great business opportunities for both investors and entrepreneurs in Bangladesh and abroad. Large infrastructure projects like IT parks and new airports would need very large institutional funding from governmental, banking and multilateral organizations. At the other end of the spectrum, startups, SMMEs (small, micro and medium size enterprises) will need family, private or venture capital funding, compatible with taking higher risks for the upside potential of very high returns on the investment.

Clearly, we're talking about the sources of productive—not speculative—investment in this chapter. The speculative kind is exemplified by the relentless focus on "buy low and sell high" investment philosophy, e.g., to take advantage of the booms and busts in the housing/real estate markets. Also not included here is any discussion of "conspicuous consumption" in the guise of "investments" in unproductive assets, such as big and expensive houses or villas to impress, or just to keep up or socially compete with friends and neighbors. Our productive investment philosophy is built on the premise that attractive returns result from profitable growth sustained by delivering innovative products and services that the people of Bangladesh truly need and are willing to pay for.

Let's take the case of a venture named *Healthy Yet So Tasty* (or HYST for short) food catering service (a sanitized case) that wants to develop a portal that allows businesses to order healthy lunches for employees throughout Dhaka (and subsequently throughout Bangladesh). To open this portal, HYST needs some financial resources in addition to market researchers to investigate whether there is a market for this idea. To attract the needed financial resources, the entrepreneurs of the venture decided to approach a local community SMME focused bank to see if the bank is interested in their idea.

After a few meetings, the entrepreneurs are successful in convincing the bank to take a look in the feasibility of the idea. The bank decides to put a few experts for investigation. After two weeks, the bank decides not to invest since it came to the conclusion that the risk of losing the investment is around 66%, which is too high a risk for the bank.

Another venture—let's call it *As Good As New Inc* (another sanitized case)—takes a different route. First, it approached an NGO that supports environmental sustainability and promotes recycling. The NGO was able to provide credible market research and competitive assessment of the reconditioned/remanufactured goods business in Bangladesh. So when the entrepreneurs approached a bank to provide financing for this startup, they were able to present lists of potential customers along with the current and potential market sizes for reconditioned automotive parts and electronic goods, including rechargeable batteries. They even provided plans to build a web portal for tapping into export opportunities based on data from the US National Center for Remanufacturing and Resource Recovery (NCR3) at Rochester Institute of Technology in upstate New York, which supports extensive research on remanufacturing processes, including testing standards for remanufactured products. Within a week, the bank was able to approve the funding for this startup.

Fortunately, there is a broad range of funding sources available with varying terms. For example, startups usually avoid debt financing and prefer equity financing instead. That's because equity investments allow ownership in the form of shares (of various types) as legal claims on the excess cash or profit generated by the venture. In turn, the venture is able to use the invested capital to grow the business and generate more profits. If successful, the venture may sell shares in the public stock market through an Initial Public Offering (IPO), which allow company founders and early investors to achieve massive return on their investments, typically making the founders millionaires or even billionaires. For example, Larry Page and Sergey Brin, the co-founders of Google, are now worth over US $15 billion each as Google is valued at US $202 billion (as of February 2011).

Instead of IPOs, a venture may become attractive to a larger company that may decide to acquire the venture by buying all its shares. This is just another way of achieving high returns for the entrepreneurs and investors who can then go start or fund other/new ventures or companies. This spiral of innovation, investment, exit, followed by another startup continues and is the cornerstone of an entrepreneurial economy. The famous Silicon Valley, an area around San Francisco in the US, has been able to sustain this spiral of innovation for several decades while spawning entrepreneurial companies like Apple, Facebook, Google, HP, Oracle, Seagate, Twitter, and VMWare in the process.

We also believe that the Government of Bangladesh has an important role to play in order to attract investments and nurture an innovation culture. Firstly, the government must embrace the culture of innovation and entrepreneurship and provide leadership through deployment of digital technologies at a rapid pace at various levels of governmental functions and citizenry services. Secondly, it should adopt new policies that are conducive to venture capital investments from foreign or domestic sources. Finally, the government needs to be proactive in soliciting both domestic and foreign direct investments. Catalytic events to this end should include one yearly seminar on "Bangladesh as an attractive destination for FDI" by the Prime Minister in a high-profile venue, e.g., New York City, San Francisco or London, and a national event—e.g., NRB Summit—in Dhaka to make a pitch to NRB's for considering the serious investment opportunities available in Bangladesh today.

We hope an entrepreneurial culture equipped to deliver radically innovative products, services and business models tailored to the needs of consumers and citizens of Bangladesh will become the cornerstone of a digitally rebuilt Bangladesh, since we must make for the lost time in missed opportunities with economic development. Of course, innovation and entrepreneurial finance are huge topics that could easily take up entire books to cover at any depth. In this short chapter, we can do justice only to a small sliver of the various sources of capital for productive investment necessary for executing the plans of technology delivery, infrastructure improvement, broadband delivery expansion, WiMax and 4G connectivity network buildups, nationwide fiber deployment, and the like.

The best way to avoid being strapped for cash is to plan ahead in terms of where the investment funds will come from and in what time frame. The smart entrepreneurs do not want to start thinking about raising funds when they're already short of cash since fundraising efforts take time to materialize, often as much as six months.

4.1 Start with a bankable idea

The first task is to come up with an excellent idea or concept that can be turned into a sustaining business. In other words, your product or service must be in demand and people or companies must be willing to pay for it enough such that you can recover the cost and make some profit. The second task is to assemble a few other individuals who like your idea and are willing to participate and start the company as a team. The third task is to write a simple, short but well thought-out business plan that will be your guide to building the company. This will also be the document that you present to prospective investors when you want to seek outside funding. In between these stages, the founding team and early employees will work very hard to build the proof-of-concept of the company. People may work at this

> "An investment in knowledge pays the best interest."
> – *Benjamin Franklin*
> *(1706-1790)*

early stage without, or at a bare minimum, salary. The equity one builds during this phase of the business without putting much hard cash into the venture is what's known as "sweat equity."

With the founding team in place, the idea fleshed out in a business plan and some early prototype of your product or service ready for demonstration, you are ready to pitch it to potential investors. Indeed, several IT and technology companies have recently received sizeable investments. Some recent fund raising success cases are as follows:

- Grameen Solutions Ltd, Dhaka, Bangladesh raised BDT 10 crore additional capital from two new Bangladeshi private investors who invested BDT 5 crore each in October, 2010.
- In December, 2010, SEAF Bangladesh Ventures LLC (SEAF BV) invested in Systems Solutions & Development Technologies Ltd. (SSD), a leading software solutions developer in Bangladesh. The size of the deal was not disclosed but US $0.5 million is the typical investment size for SEAF BV, which amounts to BDT 3.5 crore.
- VIPB invested in OidipIT (an animation company), Devnet (Bangladesh's leading enterprise content management software company), and MNHsIT (a software company that produces such e-newspapers as eDailyStar, and eProthomAlo) during 2009-2010.
- www.BDeshTV.com, an NRB founded company in the USA, has raised seed money from its founders in USA and are in the process of raising another US $1 million (BDT 7 crore) from investors for its first round from investors in the USA and Bangladesh.

What follows is a brief overview of the types of sources/sponsors of investment capital that entrepreneurs in Bangladesh should keep in mind as they plan their "road shows" with potential investors.

Personal, family, relatives and friends-level investment

Personal funds are the money the founders provide to the venture when a company is formed or a project is launched. Family members, relatives, friends and colleagues who believe in the entrepreneur's vision may provide additional capital as equity or debt investment in the form of loans.

Angel funding

Angels represent high-networth individuals who have become wealthy and like to invest in companies that operate in areas they have expertise in. Angels may invest alone or in syndication with other angels to share the risks. Angel funding tends to range from BDT 5 lakh to 20 lakh.

Venture capital

Venture capitalists (VCs) are professionally run partnerships that make large, highly calculated investments in young companies that may become tomorrow's stars dominating a segment of business. These are almost always equity investments and can be in the ranges from US $ 2 million to 50 million in the US. We expect VC investments in Bangladesh to range from BDT 50 lakh to BDT 50 crore.

Private equity

These are like venture capital companies but are willing to invest even more money than VCs in later rounds of investments. Brummer & Partners, a Swedish hedge fund, has recently launched a private equity fund in Bangladesh, which is managed by Mr. Khalid Quadir. US-based Warburg Pincus has a big presence in India and may find Bangladesh to be an attractive place to invest as well. KKR, Bain Capital, Silverlake Partners, the Carlyle Group are some of the well-known global private equity firms.

Government-backed Entrepreneurs Equity Fund

Due to lack of domestic sources of venture capital and private equity funds, Bangladesh government started a government-backed Entrepreneurs Equity Fund (EEF) in 1998. It now amounts to a size of BDT 100 crore (US $16.5 million). IT, agribusiness and thrust-sector companies are eligible for this EEF capital. Individual EEF investments can range from BDT 50 lakh to BDT 5 crore. The bank providing the EEF fund holds equity in the company, which is surrendered to the company when the investment is paid back in a period ranging from three to five years. BASIS in concert with Bangladesh Bank and a private bank coordinates and identifies the companies that should receive EEF fund from those who apply.

Public-private partnership (PPP)

PPPs are the newest and most vibrant form of investment in the South Asian region. Bangladesh, India, and Sri Lanka have offered concrete plans and procedures to initiate a huge pool of money for investing in very large infrastructure projects like laying new submarine cables, elevated expressways, regional airports, IT parks and the like. The Government of Bangladesh allocated BDT 3,000 core in its 2010 national budget to support a PPP fund. Private banks and multilateral organizations can match the PPP funds by manifolds. India is building a nationwide highway system using huge PPP funds. For example, the new Bangalore International Airport was built using PPP model in the shortest time. Recently Bangladesh approved a US $1.2 billion PPP project for an elevated expressway to be built by a consortium led by a Thai firm (Ital-Thai) that will own 73% while the government will retain 27% of the project.

Capital management funds

These are mutual funds that operate under strict guidelines by the National Regulatory Authorities and are managed by professional money managers to buy large chunk of stocks in public companies from the stock market or through private placements. Small portions of mutual fund assets may be placed in private equity to seek higher return. Retail investors can buy shares in these capital management funds, just like any other listed companies, and earn returns through dividend and share price appreciation. Currently, this is a very active sector in Bangladesh with Brummer & Partners, RACE Asset Management, VIPB, AIMS of Bangladesh, Asian Tiger Capital Management among the pioneers.

Social business funds

Initiated by Nobel laureate Dr. Muhammad Yunus of Bangladesh, the concept of social business represents a different funding model for companies operating in a free-market economy. In this model, no dividend is paid to the investors who are entitled to only the original investment money. Instead, all the surplus profit from the social business is reinvested into the company. The primary goal of a social business is to serve the community instead of maximizing profit, which is a core business principle of the current capitalistic system. Several social business funds have emerged in Bangladesh and globally. For example, the Grameen Bank has created SAF (Social Access Fund) and is in the process of creating three other social funds with Monaco, the Islamic Development Bank, and the Credit Agricole Fund of France.

Microcredit

Thanks to the Grameen Bank and many other financing organizations designed to help the poor without collateral, the micro-credit principle has now taken root in all the villages of Bangladesh and has expanded worldwide via the Grameen Trust. By providing loans ranging from BDT 500 to 1 million to people who are not otherwise creditworthy by normal banks or institutions, this form of financing allows borrowers to start self-sustaining businesses instead of looking for jobs that do not exist.

Bank financing

Traditional banks provide financing to businesses that are creditworthy. In this financing model, businesses take loans from the banks and pay it back with interests within a well-defined period of time.

Debt financing

A form of debt financing is created when a creditor or investor agrees to lend a sum of assets to a debtor. Typically, the money taken as a loan comes from private equity firms or individual investors. The debt is paid back with agreed-upon interest rates and payment terms. Profitable companies can issue corporate bonds to obtain debt and use debt as part of their overall capital structure.

Multilateral financial institutions

The World Bank, International Monetary Fund (IMF), Asian Development Bank (ADB), and European Union Development Fund provide country-level sovereign loans and grants for large infrastructure projects. Commercial companies can partner with sovereign governments to design and implement these projects and thus tap into these multilateral sources of large funds.

Big charities and foundations

The Bill & Melinda Gates Foundation, Google Foundation, Azim Premji Foundation, Grameen Foundation, BRAC Foundation, MacArthur Foundation, Ford Foundation and similarly large well known foundations fund targeted areas that are aligned with their strategic priorities. For example, the Bill & Melinda Gates Foundation's focus is health and immunization, while Google's is innovation. Azim Premji Foundation's priority is improving education in India drastically. Entrepreneurs can apply for funding from these foundations with concrete proposals to support their philanthropic goals.

4.2 Funding organizations active in Bangladesh today

- Brummer Fund
  Brummer & Partners Asset Management Bangladesh Ltd
  Khalid Quadir, CEO
  khalid.quadir@gmail.com
  Dhaka, Bangladesh

  With $7 billion of assets under management, Brummer & Partners, the largest Scandinavian hedge-fund manager, has set up Brummer Fund to invest up to $100 million in Bangladesh, "the world's next low-cost labor hub."

- Venture Investment Partners Bangladesh Ltd
  Zia Ahmed, PhD
  Chairman
  Shamsuddin Mansion, 4th Floor
  41 Gulshan North C/A
  Gulshan Circle 2
  Dhaka 1212, Bangladesh
  Tel: +880-2-986-1346, +880-2-986-1362
  http://www.vipblimited.com

  VIPB provides various direct equity and quasi-equity funding schemes, ranging from as low as BDT 300,000 and above to the under-served SME ventures throughout the country. The advisory arm of VIPB provides different types of business and technical assistance to help the clients meet the financial and business objectives. Interested entrepreneurs are encouraged to check out the link for more information.

- SEAF Bangladesh Ventures
  Fahim Ahmed, Managing Director
  Zia Ahmed, Managing Director
  41 Gulshan North C/A
  Gulshan Circle 2
  Dhaka, Bangladesh
  Tel: +880-2-986-1346
  Email: fahim.ahmed@seaf.com

- SEAF Headquarters
  Bert van der Vaart, Executive Chairman
  1050 17th Street NW, Suite 1150
  Washington, DC, 20036 USA
  Tel: +1 (202) 737-8463
  Fax: +1 (202) 737-5536
  E-mail: contactus@seaf.com
  http://www.seaf.com

  Founded in 1989, Small Enterprise Assistance Funds (SEAF) is an investment management group that provides growth capital and business assistance to small and medium enterprises (SMEs) in emerging and transition markets underserved by traditional sources of capital. SEAF Bangladesh Ventures LLC (SEAF BV) is a permanent capital vehicle, registered in Delaware USA, that invests in medium-sized businesses in Bangladesh. SEAF BV was launched in June 2010 with an equity investment from the International Finance Corporation (IFC) and Small Enterprise Assistance Funds (SEAF), and is managed by SEAF Ventures Management LLC, a subsidiary of SEAF. SEAF BV seeks to provide long-term capital combined with strategic advisory support to growing businesses in Bangladesh. The target investment size for SEAF BV ranges around US $0.5 million, with scope for follow-on investments.

- US-Bangladesh Investment Group
  8106 Meadow Springs Ct.
  Vienna, VA 22182, USA
  Tel: +1-703-448-8106

  US-Bangladesh Investment Group promotes investment primarily from US-based non-resident Bangladeshis into Bangladesh.

- RACE Management, PLC
  Hasan Imam, PhD
  CEO & Managing Director
  ceo@racebd.com
  Tel: +880-2-9883479
  Akram Tower, Suite 03, 7th Floor
  199 Shahid Syed Nazrul Islam Sarani
  Dhaka 1000, Bangladesh
  www.racebd.com

  Incorporated in March, 2008, under the Companies Act 1994 of Bangladesh, RACE Management seeks to bring world-class asset management expertise to the Bangladeshi capital markets.

- Asian Tiger Capital Partners Limited
  Ifty Islam
  Managing Partner
  ifty.islam@at-capital.com
  This e-mail address is being protected from spam bots, you need JavaScript enabled to view it UTC Building, Level 16
  8 Panthapath, Dhaka-1215, Bangladesh. This e-mail address is being protected from spam bots, you need JavaScript enabled to view it
  Tel: +(8802) 8155144 begin_of_the_skype_highlighting +(8802) 8155144 end_of_the_skype_highlighting, 8110345, 8110375
  Fax +(8802) 9118582

  Driven by a vision that Bangladesh can emulate the growth of China, India, Vietnam and Malaysia among other economic success stories in the region, Asian Tiger Capital Partners (aka "AT Capital") believes that Bangladesh has the potential to be one of the next Asian Tigers. It brings a global advisory, research and investment team and their access to leading market participants.

- Grameen Fund
  Shaikh Abdud Daiyan
  Managing Director
  Grameen Bank Tower
  Mirpur-2, Dhaka 1216,
  Bangladesh
  gfundmd@grameen.net
  Tel: +880-2-9005349
  www.grameen.com

A not-for-profit company in Bangladesh established by Professor Muhammad Yunus, Grameen Fund provides risk capital to small and medium enterprises (SMEs) beyond the scope of Grameen Bank's objectives of providing microcredit to the very poor. Its lending capital is provided by Grameen Bank and other institutions like Calvert Foundation.

- Warburg Pincus LLC
  450 Lexington Ave
  New York, NY 10017
  United States
  Phone: +1 (212) 878-0600
  Fax: +1 (212) 878-9351
  http://www.warburgpincus.com

  Warburg Pincus invested $85 million in Mumbai-based Metropolis Healthcare Ltd in January, 2010. Metropolis Healthcare offers a range of services including laboratory medicine, radiology and imaging services, hospital laboratory management and remote pathology testing services. It has 55 labs spread across India, Sri Lanka, UAE, South Africa, Bangladesh and Seychelles.

- Asian Development Bank
  Thevakumar Kandiah
  Country Director
  Email: tkandiah@adb.org
  Plot No. E-31
  Sher-e-Bangla Nagar, Agargaon
  Dhaka 1207, Bangladesh
  Tel: +880 2 815 6000-8, 815 6009-16
  Fax: +880 2 815 6018-19
  http://www.adb.org/Bangladesh/main.asp

  Headquartered in Manila and established in 1966, ADB is owned and financed by its 67 member countries, of which 48 are from the region and 19 are from other parts of the globe. ADB is an international development finance institution whose mission is to help its developing member countries reduce poverty and improve the quality of life of their people.

- World Bank
  Public contact: Ms. Mehrin A. Mahbub
  Plot E 32 Sher-e-Bangla Nagar, Agargaon
  Dhaka 1207, Bangladesh
  (Opposite Bangladesh Betar)

Tel: (880-2) 8159001, 8159015
Fax: (880-2) 8159029
Email: bangladeshinfo@worldbank.org
http://www.worldbank.org.bd

Billed as a vital source of financial and technical assistance to developing countries around the world, the World Bank's mission is to fight poverty and to help people help themselves and their environment by providing resources, sharing knowledge, building capacity and forging partnerships in the public and private sectors. It's not a bank in the usual sense since it's made up of two unique development institutions owned by the 187 member countries: the International Bank for Reconstruction and Development (IBRD), which aims to reduce poverty in middle-income and creditworthy poorer countries, and the International Development Association (IDA), which focuses on the world's poorest countries. Its work is complemented by that of the International Finance Corporation (IFC), Multilateral Investment Guarantee Agency (MIGA) and the International Centre for the Settlement of Investment Disputes (ICSID).

4.3 Surveying the broader investment landscape

Of course, investors will look for the highest risk-adjusted returns from their investments while entrepreneurs want the best term structure that provides them the maximum flexibility to operate/execute their ventures/projects. Truth be told, however, getting funded is too often an occupational hazard for entrepreneurs with a great idea. Overly preoccupied with the moment-to-moment thinking of how to secure the needed funds as soon as possible, they often gloss over the really important task of assessing the pluses and minuses associated with the individual sources of financing, be that in the form of equity, debt, leasing or grants.

Especially when caught in a cash crunch, they ignore the fact that the built-in expectations of the providers of capital today may constrain the decisions they'll be able to make down the road. This could be a big mistake. That's because the very process of getting the money sends many entrepreneurs on a march toward failure unless they can ensure that the capital providers' expectations of the venture's performance in terms of growth and profitability will allow them to correctly make the decisions that will lead to success. For example, traditional venture capitalists (VCs) may be impatient for revenue growth when investing in nascent ventures, while leveraged buyout (LBO) players investing in mature enterprises tend to be patient for growth but impatient for profit and cash flow.

Most entrepreneurs would agree with George Bernard Shaw who once remarked that "lack of money is the root of all evil." Indeed, lack of funding is the number one reason given for the failure of so many promising ventures. Even those engaged in mature businesses soon realize that not much, if anything, happens without money to keep things going. However, if money makes the world go around, private equity is the "smart money" that makes it go the extra mile to create and capture more economic value. Indeed, private equity's role in fueling today's entrepreneurial successes is unparalleled. It plays a disproportionate role in catalyzing wealth creation by entrepreneurial individuals as well as nations.

> "Knowledge has an important property. When you give it away, you don't lose it."
> – Raj Reddy (b. 1937)

Private equity, especially of the traditional VC (i.e., venture capital) type, did not really begin to take off until a couple of little-known events came together in the US, the first being the advent of modern portfolio theory, which dictated that large pools of capital could enhance their returns by diversifying their investments over a variety of asset classes. Clearly, investments solely or primarily into early-stage ventures might be deemed too risky for a traditionally conservative pension fund manager.

However, the portfolio theorists revealed that, if the manager were to take the discrete pools of capital and allocate certain percentage to bonds, another percentage to publicly traded stock, and the remainder to so-called alternative investments, e.g., real estate and private equity (i.e., buyouts and VCs), superior returns would result, all other things being equal. Coincidentally, as the modern portfolio theory was gaining in popularity as an asset management imperative, the US Department of Labor enacted in 1979 the Plan Asset Regulation, which released pension fund managers from strict application of the so-called "prudent man rule" and protected them from liability if they were to invest capital in professionally managed VC and LBO funds.

Today, private equity is a "mature" industry and many of the key players are looking for growth through new business models, e.g., transitioning from an early-stage/startup fund to a later-stage investor, and expansion in new geographies, e.g., Europe and Asia. In this context, perhaps the burning question is this: Is this world of high finance (i.e., private equity) completely out of reach for Bangladeshi entrepreneurs? Well, we do not think so. This is illustrated in the list of local and global investors listed earlier in this chapter.

However, given the different financing options and sourcing possibilities potentially available to those rare entrepreneurs with patently bankable ideas, they'll need to be savvy enough not to get stuck with the short end of the bargaining stick during deal structuring. In other words, entrepreneurs—who want to start a new venture or dramatically improve the performance of an existing one—need to know how best to structure a private equity fund to their advantage.

The good news is that as competition for the great money-making deals intensify in the world's developed economies, the major private equity firms are confronted with the reality that their domestic growth options are limited. As a result, many are now looking abroad and stepping up their efforts to invest in developing countries.

The hands-on style of active ownership of private equity in vestors—as opposed to the arm's length relationship of public equity investors—allows greater control on aspects of corporate governance, which enable the investors to be a constructive and value-adding participant.

It is well known in the investor community that in order to start, let alone flourish, private equity needs a relatively stable government, an independent judiciary, constitutional guarantees of free inquiry and the ownership of property. With these institutional frameworks absent, private equity is unlikely to prosper because, by its nature, the process involves high-risk/high-return investing by the providers of both financial capital and the so-called "sweat equity" (by those entrepreneurs who invest their talents at suboptimal pay in anticipation of significant returns via appreciation of their equity holdings).

To position Bangladesh as a preferred destination for private equity investments, we'll need to cast aside the mindset of the proverbial elephants who continue to be tethered to the "baby stakes" even after they have grown up. As the story goes, when the elephants were small, they tried to pull off the small stakes and invariably failed; so they grow up believing that the stakes are unshakable and never try again! We must keep in mind that what's at stake (pun intended!) here is the future prosperity, if not the economic viability, of Bangladesh and that we'll have to go for what we're fully capable of, and not limit ourselves by what we have been in the past.

4.4 Reading the mindsets of various investor types

While no amount of money will make a bad venture successful, for many businesses, especially the ones that are seriously underperforming or financially distressed or are in the early stages of development before profits become predictable, traditional sources of capital, e.g., banks and credit unions, are simply unavailable. Given that success today hinges not only on providing a quality and timely product or service but also on knowing how to finance the enterprise, it pays to recognize that not all sources of entrepreneurial finance are created equal and nor do they have the same expectations of returns. One can think of at least six different—admittedly somewhat caricatured— "faces" or mindsets of private equity, namely *venture (i.e., buildup) vs. vulture (i.e., cleanup) capital, virtuous (autocatalytic or self-sustaining) vs. vicious (self-destructive or toxic) capital,* and *virtual (liquid) vs. viscous (illiquid) capital*. This is the primary reason that entrepreneurs need to consider the pros and cons of the various sources of capital with their eyes wide open.

Traditional *venture capitalists* (VCs), for example, invest in new, unproven enterprises that conventional financial institutions ignore. In addition to the traditional venture capital firms, such as Asian Tiger Capital Partners (Bangladesh), Azione Capital (Singapore), Bain Capital Ventures (US), Bessemer Venture Partners (US), Insight Venture Partners (US), Khosla Ventures (US), Small Enterprise Assistance Fund (SEAF) Bangladesh Ventures LLC, Venture Investment Partners Bangladesh Ltd and the like, these groups include successful serial entrepreneurs and wealthy individuals (often dubbed "angel investors") who often wish to get in on the ground floor of a new or expanding enterprise. Instead of lending money, they exchange capital for an equity or ownership stake in the companies they finance.

These traditional VCs are active investors and are integrally involved in the creation of young companies. In addition, most venture capital investment takes place in syndicates involving two or more venture capital firms. This process referred to as co-investing enables venture capitalists to pool expertise, diversify their investment portfolios and share risk. VCs actively cultivate networks comprised of financial institutions, universities, large corporations, entrepreneurial companies and other organizations. These networks and the information flow at their disposal enable them to reduce many of the risks associated with new enterprise formation and thus to overcome many of the barriers that hold back innovation. In other words, the traditional VCs are in the buildup mode and a lot of the new VC money is also contingent on startups' meeting certain goals, such as revenue targets.

In the past when selling a company, VCs had tried to get their investment back in full, and then everyone else had divided up what remained. Today, however, many VCs are insisting that they get several times their investment back before anyone else - including the founder(s) - gets any money. Here are some daunting statistics stacked against entrepreneurs when soliciting VC funds in the U.S. (needless to say, the hurdles are likely to be even higher for entrepreneurs in Bangladesh):

- Traditional VCs generally finance only six out of every 1,000 business plans they receive each year
- Fewer than 20%, and more like one in ten, of funded startups go public through Initial Public Offerings (IPOs)
- About 60% of high-tech companies that get VC funding go bankrupt, and another 30% end up in mergers or liquidations. VCs generally own about 60% of the equity in software-based startups by the time they go public
- Founder-CEOs generally own less than 4% of their ventures after the IPO, an amount usually worth about $6.5 million on average

Critics may argue that many VCs have become so greedy that they often act more like *vulture capitalists*. There is, however, another type of vulture capitalists, who, despite their obvious image problem, carry out an important role of scavenging or cleaning up by consolidating highly fragmented industries to improve performance or turning around financially distressed or dying businesses. The traditional LBO firms have been playing this role over the past two decades in the US and more recently in Europe, and many are now venturing into Asia.

4.5 Capitalizing on the disciplining effect of debt

The beauty—albeit it's in the eye of the beholder—of the LBO-style vulture capitalism is that it often combines the financial discipline of operating management accruing from the high debt level (also known as "leverage") in the capital structure of a business with the unlimited upside potential of capital gains or appreciation of the equity investment's value. By shrinking the equity investment required, it allows managers of modest means to become owners. The key to high equity gains is the recognition that top-line or revenue growth is not necessary for value creation. The leveraged financing allows reforms in management—sometimes radical, sometimes no more than mundane operational "blocking and tackling"—to be converted into capital gains.

To see how this works in its simplest form, imagine an all-equity company that is bought for $10 million. Before the acquisition, the business generates $1 million in cash flows, just enough to give shareholders a 10% return. The acquisition is financed with $9 million in debt and $1 million in equity. The company is then able, through improved operations, superior asset utilization, and disciplined capital investment, to increase cash flows from $1 million to $2 million per year, without either increasing or decreasing the value of the assets. By paying no dividends and using this $2 million in cash flow strictly for debt service, this company can pay down the $9 million of debt (say, at an interest rate of 10%) in about 6 years. At the end of that period, the company would still be worth $10 million, but it would now be all equity. In other words, the original $1 million equity investment has been transformed into one worth $10 million, for a 47% compounded annual rate of return! This is how financial leverage concentrates ownership in fewer hands and substantially amplifies the returns to the new owners.

> "If you have an apple and I have an apple and we exchange these apples, then you and I still have one apple each. But if you have an idea and I have an idea and we exchange these ideas, then each of us will have two ideas."
>
> – George Bernard Shaw (1856-1950)

The third facet of entrepreneurial finance, *virtuous capitalists* may offer only a modicum of capital (often requiring matching funds from the founders themselves), but they bring mountains of goodwill. Another distinguishing feature is that they often—if not always—care more about promotion of societal values and job creation than economic value creation (i.e., monetary returns) alone. Included in this group are friends and relatives, philanthropic foundations, charitable organizations, non-governmental organizations (NGOs) funded by donor agencies, government-subsidized investment companies, and government grants. By way of promoting "finance with a conscience," many virtuous capitalists seek to advance the cause of balancing temporal value (i.e., making money) with timeless values (i.e., creating a better society).

Vicious capitalists include the modern-day Luddites or anti-technologists, extreme environmentalists, and the enemies of open societies and liberalized economies. They support subsidies and other protectionist measures for uncompetitive businesses or sectors in closed economic systems. Their idea of business is the continuation of politics by other means. As a result, these investors tend to become parasitically dependent on government subsidies/handouts since they cannot carry their own weight by earning their cost of capital—for mature businesses, the going rate being about 10%, which is the weighted average of the interest on debt and expected rate of return on equity capital—they end up destroying economic value and thus become unsustainable in the long run.

> "Modernity needs to understand that being rich and becoming rich are not mathematically, personally, socially, and ethically the same thing."
> – Nassim Nicholas Taleb (b. 1960)

Virtual capitalists are the globe-trotters who are always looking for arbitrage opportunities to invest their "knowledge capital" as much as their monies in liquid (i.e., easily tradable) markets. Adept at parceling out venture-specific risks, they are the equivalents of hedge funds and certain financial derivatives traders, thus moving the private equity world as close to the theoretical "efficiency" of the public capital markets as possible. Examples of virtual capitalists include corporate venture capital funds (e.g., those sponsored by 3M, BASF, DuPont, GE, and Merck, amongst others) and the emerging new category of intellectual capital-intensive enterprises, e.g., IP Group plc (UK) and Innovaro Inc (US), which work with top-notch universities and research institutes to turn patented or proprietary research findings into profitable business ventures.

Viscous capitalists are those who are willing to take the risk of getting their capital "stuck in the mud" (perhaps for a long time) and are not in a rush to pull out their investments (or cannot do so without significant penalties). For assuming the risk of illiquidity, they naturally expect higher returns. Equipment leasing firms and vendors who self-finance the sale to customers when traditional financing is unavailable or unattractive to their financially strapped customers belong in this category. However, many of these are probably endangered species in today's world of high-velocity finance.

As counterparties to the investment decision process, however, the different types of investors caricatured above have to assess not only the track records of the entrepreneurs, but also the operating environments of the ventures/projects. Currently, there appear to be at least two major barriers to creating a VC-friendly environment in Bangladesh, namely lack of exit strategy (through IPO or sale to a bigger company, for example) and limited rights of minority shareholders like VCs.

Dreaming of investing in Bangladesh Inc.

Once upon a time—not long ago—a business executive was watching the news on TV about the sector-specific strategic priorities and the enabling environment designed to realize the dreams of a Digital Bangladesh by 2021. Inspired by the promises of a digitally inclusive Bangladesh, he wanted to invest in the major domestic sectors likely to be revitalized by broadband connectivity, but was having second thoughts about the "country risk" associated with Bangladesh. As he was dozing off, he wondered, "What if Bangladesh was run as a world-class citizen-centric business organization?" Suddenly he saw the TV broadcast interrupted by this breaking news: "Buy Bangladesh, hold India, and sell China." The rest of the broadcast scrolled off the TV screen as follows:

In compliance with an order from the Supreme Court, the nation's largest corporation Keystone Digital Ltd (KDL) announced today that it will be acquiring the Government of Bangladesh as Bangladesh Inc for an undisclosed sum. "It's actually a logical extension of our planned growth," said Nurul Alam, chief executive officer (CEO) of KDL. "It's really going to be a positive arrangement for everyone."

KDL representatives held a briefing and assured members of the press that organizational changes will be "minimal." Bangladesh Inc will be managed as a wholly owned division of KDL and the Government of Bangladesh is expected to be profitable by "the 4th quarter of this year at the latest," according to Mr. Alam.

Mr. Alam went on to say that Jatiya Sangsad, the unicameral parliament, would "of course" be abolished. "KDL isn't a democracy," he observed, and "look how well we're doing." When asked if the rumored attendant acquisition of Myanmar (Burma) was proceeding, Mr. Alam said, "We don't deny that discussions are taking place." KDL representatives closed the press conference by stating that Bangladeshi citizens will be able to pay lower taxes, and enjoy increases in government services and discounts on all KDL products.

About KDL

Founded in 2001 on March 26, the Independence Day of Bangladesh, KDL is the country's top digital systems and services provider, which raised 7.0 billion dollars through the IPO sale of 6.9 billion shares in early 2011. KDL also raised the same amount from institutional investors. It says the money will be spent on mobile network expansion and developing its information technology infrastructure.

Securities and Exchange Commission chief hailed the IPO as a "watershed event," saying it would bring "depth and maturity" to the country's share market. "The KDL IPO will bring qualitative change to the market. I think the move will instill confidence in other major companies to follow suit. It will make the stock market more stable and the centre of our economic activity," he said.

About Bangladesh, Inc.

Founded in 1971, Bangladesh is the seventh most populous country and among the most densely populated countries in the world with a high poverty rate. However, per-capita (inflation-adjusted) GDP has more than doubled since 1975, and the poverty rate has fallen by 20% since the early 1990s. The country is listed among the "Next Eleven" economies. Dhaka and other urban centers have been the driving force behind this growth. Headquartered in Dhaka, Bangladesh Inc is now a wholly owned subsidiary of KDL.

(*Disclaimer: This is a parody of an original spoof of Microsoft acquiring the Federal Government of the United States that appeared on the internet in 1997. Any resemblance of this light-hearted spoof from an investor's dreamland with any real-life events and personalities in Bangladesh and beyond is entirely coincidental, and any defense of its authenticity—legal or otherwise—is hereby deemed unnecessary.)

Chapter 5

Bridging the Knowing-Doing Gap Through Disciplined Implementation

"We think in generalities, we live in detail."
– *Alfred North Whitehead (1861-1947)*

There are three takeaways from this chapter:

How do we make the visions of Digital Bangladesh happen? The strategic priorities of the Digital Bangladesh initiative as outlined by the Access to Information (A2I) Program of the Prime Minister's Office (PMO) can be implemented in concrete well-defined steps with milestones to measure success along the execution path as outlined in this chapter.

How can the priorities of Digital Bangladesh initiative be implemented? The implementation or execution process is described in detail. The discussion will continue at this book's site at www.goingdigitalbook.com where you can join to offer your voice.

How much will the implementation likely cost? The estimated levels of investments required is US $5-7 billion for 15 years (2009-2023), which may come from a combination of private investments, government grants, loans and public-private partnerships (PPPs).

Implementation or execution is often described as the missing link between aspirations and results. We prefer to define implementation as the discipline of bridging the knowing-doing gap since the visions and roadmaps correspond to knowing the "what" and "why" of an initiative while the implementation framework must address the "how to do it" and "who will actually carry it out." Since the previous chapters of the book outlined the "what" and "why" of going digital as part of the Digital Bangladesh initiative, this one will focus on the "how," "who" and a bit of "when" and "where" of implementation. In short, this chapter is meant to be the missing how-to guide for the Digital Bangladesh initiative.

Implementing the Digital Bangladesh initiative will generally follow the goals and targets established in the ICT Policy adopted by the Government of Bangladesh in 2009. Chapter 3 provides the background on the roadmaps and other policy instruments to drive the implementation process. In this chapter we emphasize the key steps needed to achieve these policy goals and address how to execute the implementation mechanism.

In the spirit of practicing what we are "preaching" in this book, we're inviting all our readers to collaborate with us on how we should make Digital Bangladesh happen. To this end, we'll be tracking the progress of the key projects and initiatives mentioned in this chapter and others that may be introduced in the coming years. You can help by providing updates and feedback and also learn from others about the status of the various projects that interest you. Let the dialogue begin by joining us at www.goingdigitalbook.com.

The good news is that the Access to Information (A2I) Program of the Prime Minister's Office in Bangladesh has recently outlined the "Strategic Priorities of Digital Bangladesh" along with the strengths and addressable risks associated with the individual initiatives. Our proposed implementation framework is a technology-driven model with minimal bureaucratic interference and we believe this need to be the general mode of implementation for the Digital Bangladesh initiative. In addition, we must take rapid-paced and private-sector driven approaches to reach the cherished goal. In other words, it must *not* be like the Rooppur nuclear power plant project, which has been in planning/vision stage for 45 years; a Memorandum of Understanding (MoU) has only recently been signed with a Russian contractor for it to build a 2000MW fission-reactor power plant. This is not acceptable in the world of digital technologies where three or more generations of change can take place in those 45 years! We believe the technology-driven mission of the Digital Bangladesh initiative must be implemented in a much faster timeline to reap the planned benefits.

5.1 Acknowledging the political context of Bangladesh

We recognize the concerns that government bureaucratic slowdown or indecision to be the biggest challenge that can keep the vision of Digital Bangladesh from coming to fruition. However, we think that even if Bangladesh follows a free-enterprise economic model, the large structural and directional initiatives must come from the government. In other words, the major steps needed, such as funding and prioritization of different Ministries under which many of the processes have to be approved even if they are implemented by the private sector, have to be set at the top of the government decision-making hierarchy, i.e., the powerful Prime Minister's Office. Thus a strong 'political will' at the top of the government will be critical in sustaining the momentum of the Digital Bangladesh implementation process that will likely have wide socioeconomic impacts.

We sense that the current government has the political will and Prime Minister Sheikh Hasina has bet her new government's success and her party's future on setting the country on a course toward realizing a good portion of the visions of Digital Bangladesh in her current term of five years. Given the mass appeal of the Digital Bangladesh concept, we anticipate that BNP (Bangladesh Nationalist Party), the current opposition party, or any other party that comes to political power in the near future, will embrace a similar ICT-driven nation building approach even if their branding changes. All in all, the goals and efforts toward building a digitally inclusive Bangladesh are unlikely to be much different under any future party in power.

In some sense, the increasingly globalized world has forced the digitization mandate on Bangladesh. That's because no developing country can achieve rapid economic growth without the infrastructures in place for a digital economy. We commend a critical mass of enlightened politicians for correctly sensing this need for structural and policy reforms toward building a "government of the people, by the people and for the people" who are digitally connected. Prior to the December 29, 2008 national election, both major political parties adopted the high-profile ICT infrastructure plans in their manifestoes. The Bangladesh Awami League (AL) led grand alliance seized this momentous opportunity more by making the visions of "Digital Bangladesh" a major pillar of their election manifesto. It is generally recognized that this helped AL garner significant support from the younger generation that is especially receptive to the visions of digital technologies as platforms for job opportunities and service delivery. Perhaps in this dimension, the youths of Bangladesh may not be any different from those in Egypt and Tunisia who managed to overthrow the authoritarian governments in their countries. The Facebook nation, the Twitter nation is upon us everywhere.

Let's first visualize how digital service delivery picture will look when the visions of Digital Bangladesh vision come to fruition in different stages. The schematic diagram below shows how citizens can access contents from upazila, district or national data centers with devices ranging from cell phones, smart phones, tablets, personal computers or information kiosks. These accesses should be available by the close of the current government's first five-year plan in 2013.

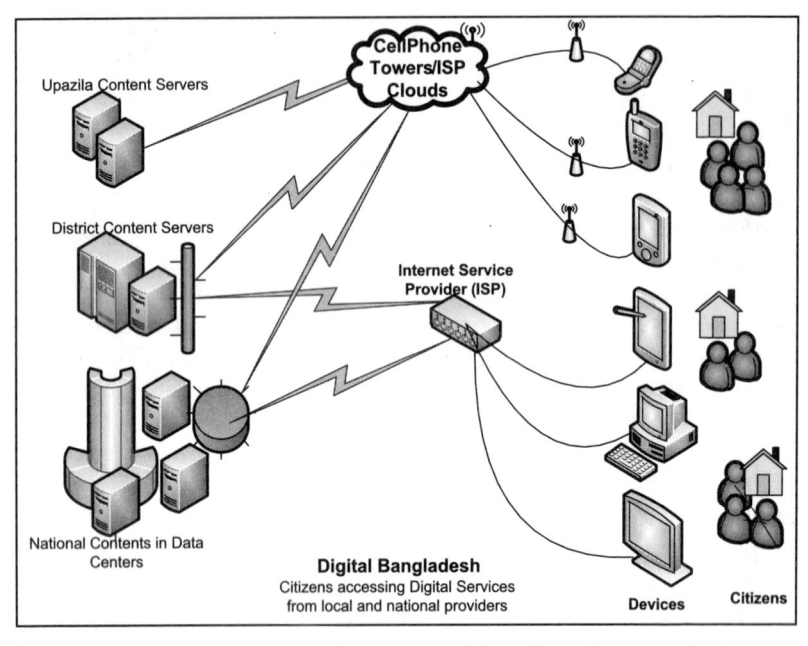

Digital Bangladesh
Citizens accessing Digital Services from local and national providers

We propose a few key milestones and benchmarks to track success toward realizing dreams of Digital Bangladesh:

- Deploy 50,000 Village Kiosks by the end of 2012
- Open the high-tech/IT park at Kaliakoir near Dhaka by 2013
- Complete the fiber-optic backbone, nationwide broadband and country-wide internet access by 2013
- Add two more submarine cables and two terrestrial links to neighboring countries to the existing internet backbone to add capacity and avoid network outage by 2015
- Build technology parks in Chittagong, Khulna, Rajshahi and Sylhet by 2016

- Build at least 10 Entrepreneurial Development Centers (EDCs) around the 10 key universities of the country—Asian University for Women in Chittagong, Barisal BM College & University, BRAC University, BUET, Chittagong University, Dhaka University, Khulna University, North-South University, SUST in Sylhet, and Rajshahi University by 2014
- Take deliberate steps to make the Chittagong region the "Silicon Valley" of Bangladesh
- Expand the entrepreneurial culture and sound risk-taking business climate for the country's population, especially among the youth, the "Facebook generation"
- Develop a venture capital investment culture to nurture small startups and turn Bangladesh into a knowledge-intensive innovation destination similar to Taiwan known for electronics design and PC manufacturing
- Nurture and plan to have 20 successful (global-scale) high-tech and IT-centric companies that are headquartered in Bangladesh by 2013. This number can be expanded to 100 companies in the next 5 years (2014-2018), and 300 companies in 2019-2023, to deliver the services and technologies consistent with the visions of Digital Bangladesh
- Boost public confidence in the capital market through reforms, e.g., by creating the Dhaka Exchange Next (DENext) to be US NASDAQ or EuroNext like stock exchanges for SMEs and bringing transparency through financial disclosure rules for Initial Public Offering (IPO) transactions

5.2 Key steps in the implementation process

Arguably, the implementation of the visions of Digital Bangladesh began in June 1996 when broadband connectivity was introduced into Bangladesh via VSAT (Very Small Aperture Terminal) satellite and more fully in 2006 when SEA-ME-WE 4 submarine cable based terrestrial fiber-optic link was established between Cox's Bazaar and Singapore. Thanks to this initiative, today there are over 170 registered internet service providers (ISPs) nationwide, which makes the case for the proverbial saying, "If you build it, they will come." In that spirit, we believe the following key areas have to be addressed to ensure that the goals of Digital Bangladesh are achieved by 2021.

Wire the nation and create a fiber-optic backbone

Reliable digital service delivery to all the citizens of Bangladesh would require a nationwide high-capacity network that can move data, voice and video. This means laying out new generation, high-capacity underground cables countrywide creating a high-speed data transmission backbone. The fact is that the old voice and data network operated by BTCL (Bangladesh Telecommunications Company Limited, formerly Bangladesh Telegraph and Telephone Board) is mostly copper-wire from the voice/telephony era through which high-speed digital service delivery to users is simply not possible. Fortunately, our government planners have understood this limitation not a moment too soon. As a result, BTRC (Bangladesh Telecommunications Regulatory Commission) embraced a nationwide new fiber-optic expansion plan and issued a nationwide NNTN (New Nationwide Transmission Network) license to a domestic new private company, Fiber@Home (www.fiberathome.net), on January 7, 2009 to build a countrywide high-speed fiber-optic network, which will eventually become the major backbone for all kinds of telecommunications and electronic entertainment services. In December, 2009, BTRC issued a second nationwide fiber-optic layout license to a second private sector vendor, Summit Communications Limited by BTRC to have redundancy, price competition and add to nationwide backbone data network capacity.

Financed by local investors, Fiber@Home proved to be well-equipped to build a network up to the upazila headquarters of the country. In fact, the company managed to complete its three-year target of nationwide transmission network, mandated by the government, in just six months. By January 2010, the company's network reached Dhaka, Khulna, Rajshahi, Sylhet, Chittagong, Bogra, Pabna, Kushtia, Jessore, Comilla, Gazipur, Tangail, Natore, Jhenidah, Narayanganj, Feni, Narsingdi, Brahmanbaria, Habiganj and Moulvibazar. These areas will have the latest services of telecommunications via SDA, MPLS and other hi-tech telecommunication links from Fiber@Home Ltd.

Fiber@Home has been laying out fiber throughout Dhaka by creating rings around the city and reaching into residential houses, apartments and office buildings. What has been connected so far by Fiber@Home is impressive with the following accomplishments as of 2010:
- Long-haul transmission network: Deployed 1200 km
- Metro ring network: Deployed 120 km
- FTTx network: Deployed 180 km
- Network presence in 23 districts and 90 upazilas

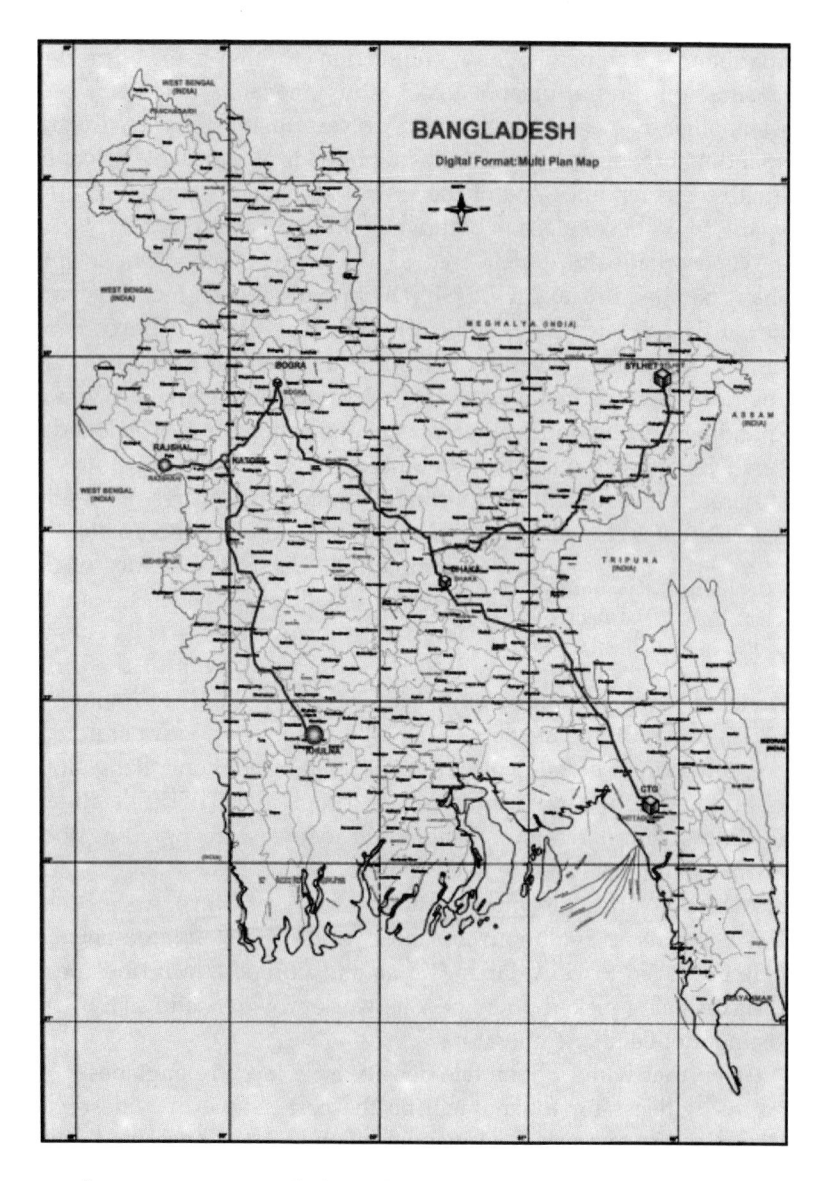

Bridging the Knowing-Doing Gap Through Disciplined Implementation 123

Above is a map of the Fiber@Home nationwide transmission network laid out by the end of 2010 (red lines indicate the completed underground fiber lines). Graph courtesy of Fiber@Home.

Expand broadband connectivity

Broadband—technically, any connection to the user with data transmission rates at or above 0.25 Mbps (megabits per second)—is just another name for "high-speed" access to the internet. Clearly, expanding broadband connectivity nationwide at affordable prices for all citizens constitutes one of the visions of Digital Bangladesh. This expansion will take place in both wired and wireless forms.

Wired broadband is delivered to a home or office via fiber optic cable, coax line of cable TV, DSL (Digital Subscriber Line) telephone line or ISDN telephone line. For example, BTCL, Fiber@Home, Summit Telecommunications and other telecom network operators provide wired broadband access and are laying out new wired links or expanding existing cables to offer faster and better wired broadband to users who are within reach of their network.

Wireless broadband is the fury of modern always-on digital lifestyles that include 24/7 access to Google, Facebook and Twitter, for example. Of course, the beauty of the wireless broadband is that it can be accessed from anywhere—be it at home, office, on the road or out at the farm! Wireless broadband can be built with 2G, 2.5G, 3G, 4G technologies. 2G, 2.5G and 3G are data networks built by mobile phone operators in and around their mobile voice networks. GrameenPhone, Banglalink, Robi (old AKTel), Airtel (old Warid), CityCell and BTCL Teletalk are the six mobile operators of Bangladesh today, each upgrading their network to offer 3G service to customers.

> "Genius is 1% inspiration and 99% perspiration."
> – *Thomas Edison (1847-1931)*

WiMax (Worldwide Interoperability for Microwave Access) and LTE (Long Term Evolution) are the two key 4G standards and are being deployed in USA, Japan, Korea and Europe at a furious pace. WiMax is being picked up by new network providers and LTE by the existing mobile phone operators.

Given that wired phone tele-density is so low in Bangladesh, 3G and 4G wireless broadband will be the cornerstone of widespread internet access to reach its large population in every home and office across cities and villages. BTRC has already pushed the mobile operators to build and deploy 2.5G, 3G mobile networks, allocating them the frequency spectrums necessary.

Mobile phone operators are expected to use LTE when they build their 4G network. The authors believe that it may be prudent for BTRC to influence operators to skip 3G and implement 4G directly. BTRC can do it by offering wider 4G license bids and discouraging issuance of 2.5G/3G licenses.

For 4G WiMax, BTRC has provisioned that only new non-mobilephone operators will be allowed and has issued license to five new network operators after an open competitive bidding. BanglaLion is one of this WiMax licensee and has already started offering WiMax service in Dhaka (full Dhaka coverage available by 2010) to be followed by countrywide access by 2011. Other WiMax operators are to follow as they are bound by agreement to bring service within a stipulated period of 3 years. After all, each of these WiMax operators paid BDT 300 crore (US $43 million) to get the WiMax operator license and they should have all the incentives to build the network quickly to recoup their large investment.

> "Insanity is doing the same thing over and over again and expecting different results."
> – Albert Einstein (1879-1955)

Currently widespread wireless broadband internet access is being offered to populations based in cities, upazilas and villages using 2G and 2.5G mobile phone networks. For example, 98% of all populated areas of Bangladesh are covered by the GrameenPhone network, the largest mobile phone operator of the country. WiMax, a 4G technology, recently introduced in the country by BanglaLion, has started the journey along the 4G road. Other 4G core technology access is soon to follow. It is expected that with 2G, 3G, 4G access will reach every point in the country by 2013, thus fulfilling a key vision of Digital Bangladesh!

Expand the submarine cable coverage

Since 2006 Bangladesh has been precariously dependent on the SEA-E-ME-4 submarine cable link from Cox's Bazar to Singapore with only 10 Gbps (Gigabits per second) capacity. Bangladesh's portion of the cable is owned by the government-owned national telecom company, BTCL. Currently, it is used to pass internet traffic to and from the outside world and also to transmit voice telephone and mobile calls on the international trunk. Although there are some additional 64–256Kbps VSAT satellite links used as redundant links in case the submarine cable goes down, these VSAT links are expensive and not suitable for the high-speed internet connection. So Bangladesh needs to add more submarine cables and terrestrial land links to acquire adequate internet data bandwidth capacities required for offering myriad digital services like call centers to the rest of the world.

At least two more submarine cables and two additional land-based terrestrial links must be established. The submarine cables could either be all privately owned, or one owned by the government and the other one by the private sector. One of the land-based terrestrial links could connect to Kolkata, India and the other one to Myanmar. The land links would allow low-cost access to high-bandwidths available from the neighboring countries. With these five, the country would have 10+20+20+10+10 = 70 Gbps data bandwidth available to connect to the outside world, which should be adequate for several years. In fact, we believe Bangladesh should plan on adding additional capacity of 20 Gbps every 3 years on a periodic basis as the data bandwidth usage grows on its way toward becoming a middle-income country over the next decade.

Build high-tech/IT parks

Best-performing IT parks and technology centers are typically built as part of a satellite city around a major city. Kaliakoir – with 232 acres of land already allocated for building an IT park—could be such a satellite city, since it is only 40 km from Dhaka and 25 km from Dhaka's international airport. The government has formed a 'Hi-Tech Park Authority' to administer the current and future technology parks.

South Korea is helping Bangladesh in establishing IT training centers at Bangladesh Computer Council (BCC) in Dhaka and other National facilities. Given that South Korea has turned itself into a digitally connected nation, it can be a very good model for Bangladesh to learn from.

These satellite cities would have people work, live and play in a modern green environment. For example, Gurgaon near Delhi and Salt Lake Electronics City near Kolkata have thrived on this satellite city model. Gurgaon is considered the "call-center capital of the world" as it houses support centers of global giants like GE (General Electric) of USA and British Telecom. China's rapid IT and electronics satellite city growth is another successful model Bangladesh can learn from.

Companies from South Korea, Singapore and Malaysia can be the government's partner, as these companies have successfully built IT parks in their own countries and in India. Recently Malaysia's Hi-tech park authority for Multimedia Development Center (MDC) located outside of Kuala Lumpur has shown interest in building a park and submitted a report to MOSICT (Ministry of Science & ICT). Bangladesh Computer Council, an organ of the MOSICT, is driving the IT park planning efforts and needs to expedite the process of selecting a prime contracting company for building the IT Park. It probably needs to be built by a private company to ensure operational excellence with high global standards. Ascendas (www.ascendas.com) is such a renowned private-sector company that has built IT parks in China, Singapore, India, Vietnam, Malaysia, Thailand and Oman. Alternatively, the park can be a private-public partnership venture where the land and basic infrastructure are provided by the public sector and the rest comes from the private sector. Bangladesh's first software park was established in 2003 in Dhaka. Named ICT Incubator it houses around 40 IT service firms. A second software park is under construction near the first one.

Learn from other IT parks in India, Malaysia, and China

India built eight STPs (Software Technology Parks) in the 1980s to provide the basic IT infrastructure for companies interested in IT development and export from India. These parks have performed

Shown above is the International Technology Park, Bangalore, India

Depicted above is a schematic model of Malaysia's Multimedia Super Corridor (MSC)

remarkably well and now there are entire IT cities being built to house IT and high-tech workers and companies. International Tech Park Bangalore (http://itpbangalore.com/home.html), is the most prominent of the IT parks in Bangalore. It is managed by Ascendas, but the Bangalore Tech Park is a joint venture between India and Singapore.

Similarly, Malaysia embarked on the development of its bold Multimedia Super Corridor (MSC) technology media city on the outskirts of Kuala Lumpur in 1996. Designed to leapfrog Malaysia into the information and knowledge age, it includes an area of approximately 15x50 squared kilometres (km^2) which stretches from the Petronas Twin Towers to the Kuala Lumpur International Airport and also includes the towns of Putrajaya and Cyberjaya. Although it reportedly cost about US $1 billion to complete, the site now provides world-class physical and information infrastructure, allows unrestricted employment of local and foreign knowledge workers, ensure freedom of ownership by exempting companies with MSC Malaysia Status from local ownership requirements, and provides competitive financial incentives, including no income tax for up to 10 years or an investment tax allowance, and no duties on import of multimedia equipment.

Shown above is an aerial photo of China's Dalian Software Park

There are estimated 30 to 50 city-level, province-level and national-level software parks in China today. The Dalian Software Park is an industrial zone created in 1998 in the Western Suburbs of Dalian City in Liaoning Province of China, where many of the world's large and medium-sized IT-related companies have set up shop to do software development and provide information services. While American and European companies typically have gone to Bangalore and other cities in India because of India's superior English language capability, the Japanese companies have gone to Dalian and other cities in China due to the Japanese language capability available there. Dalian is one of China's eleven "National Software Industry Bases" and one of five "National Software Export Bases." Currently, more than 300 companies, including 32 *Global 500* companies (according to Fortune's global ranking), have offices in the park.

Establish technology parks

Bangladesh needs to establish technology parks at Chittagong, Khulna, Rajshahi and Sylhet. A good location for an Electronic Park is Chittagong where it can be modeled after BEPZA (Bangladesh Export Processing Zone Authority) for providing the infrastructure for various high-tech products and electronic goods manufacturing in Bangladesh. Khulna, Rajshahi and Sylhet can house the technology parks in and around a major university of the regions. Being close to the Sundarbans, Khulna can create an industrial engineering, shipping and eco-friendly technology regions. Already being the host of the country's pisciculture and natural silk research center, Rajshahi can house the agro-biotech and genomics engineering park while Sylhet can house the Science and Computing Technology Park close to the Shahjalal University of Science and Technology (SUST).

These technology parks can house the new digital services and technology companies that will serve the needs of the local region while being digitally connected to the rest of the country and the wider world via the high speed internet links. For internet access, we believe that there would actually be big cost advantages for locating companies in these division-level technology parks rather than in Dhaka. Government should also give direct income tax incentives, like much lower taxes, for domestic and foreign companies to locate their facilities in these technology parks rather than in and around Dhaka city. Needless to say, these division-level technology parks should help by evenly distributing the digital expansion of the country while relieving Dhaka of the tremendous population growth pressures and the all-too-familiar traffic congestions.

A 'Software Technology Park' under-construction in Dhaka

Nurture entrepreneurial culture at universities

We recommend that the government of Bangladesh establish Entrepreneurial Development Centers (EDC) in PPP model around major universities of the country. The eleven possible universities located at different regions throughout the country that can house the EDC are: BUET (Bangladesh University of Engineering and Technology), North-South University, Dhaka; BRAC University, Dhaka; Islamic University of Technology, Tongi; SUST, Sylhet; Chittagong University; Asian University for Women, Chittagong; Rajshahi University; Khulna University; Barisal BM College & University; and Rangpur Carmichael College & University.

> "Leadership is the art of getting someone else to do something you want done because he wants to do it."
>
> – Dwight D. Eisenhower (1890-1969)

We believe that ten-year roadmaps should be developed for these 10 EDCs and funds be allocated in the national annual budget to implement the plans. Not only will these centers create countrywide regional research and development activities and drive job growth in small entrepreneurial companies, they will also be the pride of the nation when implemented. The National Science Foundation (NSF) in the US drives these types of science-driven research programs with allocations from the Federal government's budget supporting innovation centers and departments in various colleges and universities. In Bangladesh, we'll need to focus on practical research and development projects done at these EDCs to create technology and patents that can be leveraged to build innovative products and services to first meet local needs and then sell globally as opportunities develop.

Clearly, Digital Bangladesh will need to tap into the energy and creativity of scientists, engineers and technology-savvy mangers. It is from these development centers where these talents will emerge. In addition, the EDCs can inculcate the spirit of entrepreneurship, culture of innovation, modern business skills, management and creative thinking so that students and participants develop the flair for independent thinking and the entrepreneurial mindset.

Given that Bangladeshis naturally put high value on education and learning, there is no reason why Bangladesh cannot emulate science- and innovation-based success models of the United States. If the EDCs can turn university research into practical products and solutions, they could help us realize the dreams of Digital Bangladesh soon becoming a research-based inventive country, as well.

Build Bangladesh's Silicon Valley in Chittagong

If done right, any of the EDCs at these ten Universities located around the country's six administrative divisions could become the incubators of technology-based startups, much like the famed Silicon Valley which also grew in the shadow of two renowned universities, namely Stanford University and the University of California at Berkeley. Perhaps the most advantageous in this regard is the port city of Chittagong with its beautiful beaches, hills, international airport, moderate climate and moderate cost of living to attract and retain the young talents. It can house software, IT, fabless chip design companies of the country. The world's longest sea beach at nearby Cox's Bazaar will be an additional draw. Given that the country's submarine cable for internet connectivity lands at Cox's Bazaar and is then fiber optic linked via fiber-optic cables to Chittagong and Dhaka over terrestrial land lines, Chittagong will always have lots of digital network capacity to house data centers, telecom nodes and cloud computer hubs, making it the ideal location to be the country's Silicon Valley.

Deploy village kiosks throughout Bangladesh

While large cross sections of the urban and professional classes in Bangladesh have access to the internet and digital services via mobile phones, smart phones, computers and internet cafés, the question remains, how can we reach the vast majority of the poor and underprivileged population living in the villages? The answer is village kiosks, which can serve as digital access points and learning centers to spread awareness of e-services, much like the telephone ladies of GrameenPhone helped to spread the use of mobile phones to the rural masses.

The good news is that government efforts have begun to create some 50,000 kiosks in all parts of the country with round-the-clock fast internet connectivity and access to all digital public services being readied by the government, e.g., license registration and renewal, passport application, agricultural commodity procurement prices established by the government, crop subsidies, land record management, and access to various public forms.

The government has announced the timely and noteworthy goal of deploying all of 50,000 village kiosks throughout the country by 2011 Once they are deployed, building the learning centers around them can take place over the next three years (2011-2013). We believe that these learning centers can provide various educational, developmental and health-related training programs and seminars to the general population, and the village youth in particular on how to access the various digital services, and help them learn new vocational skills via training materials available on the internet.

Solve the electric power generation shortage

The government must allow sufficient private sector participation to add power generation capacity and bring market competition to this mission-critical sector. The current regime of regulated and massively subsidized prices for electricity is quite visibly not working. We believe that allowing the market to set prices through the privately generated electricity producers and consumers who are willing to pay higher prices for uninterrupted/outage-free electricity would help solve the power generation problem. Now that agreement has been signed with Russia to build the Rooppur nuclear power plant near Isswardi in Pabna, the government must expedite the process to complete the project within the next five years, which will certainly ease the power shortage problem by adding 2,000 megawatt electrical power to the national grid.

Provide e-services through computers & mobile devices

The UNDP-funded A2I (Access to Information) program is currently well on its way to making the services of various government ministries and utility service organizations via web portals. Introduction of digital payment services for electric, gas and telephone bills, digital tax returns will be a huge relief for the country's general population since the government as well the utility companies have been notoriously inefficient in bill payment processes. Although the mobile phone is increasingly the primary delivery vehicle for digital services, we believe that the government and NGOs should continue promotion and distribution of low-cost desktops, laptops and netbooks, especially to colleges and universities.

Introduce e-learning to modernize and expand education

With the biggest online libraries like GoogleBooks, encyclopedias like the Wikipedia, and millions of sites that offer text and multimedia content searchable through powerful search engines like Google or Bing, the internet is the by far the largest knowledge repository of the world. Awareness of these resources can provide self-paced e-learning opportunities that could revolutionize education in Bangladesh. If the government or NGOs can provide free or low-cost internet access, students in primary (elementary) schools, high schools and colleges could take advantage of this new world of learning and knowledge sharing. In addition, internet access could awaken the sleeping giant of a nation by moving on a path toward achieving its target of 100% literacy rate by 2021.

Launch e-health initiatives

Access to health services can be expanded by leveraging telemedicine technologies and improving access to health information and doctors over the internet. When the 50,000 village kiosks and the learning centers around them are equipped with high-resolution web cameras needed to view patients and provide medical diagnosis and advice from doctors located in any part of the country or even overseas, we should see significant improvement in awareness of good hygiene and health practices. We would also be aware of what it takes to maintain good health through preventive medicine and healthy lifestyle choices, e.g., quitting smoking and promoting healthy eating habits.

Make government a big buyer of IT services

It is almost axiomatic that a nation that does not use IT services cannot be an exporter of it. We believe that the realization of this axiom by the government of Bangladesh will help us overcome the single biggest hurdle in achieving the expected economic growth and prosperity for the nation. As a champion of the visions of Digital Bangladesh, the government has to be a big buyer of digital products and services not only to instill confidence in the population about the benefits of going digital but also to steer the private as well as the public sector to adopt modern digital technologies for efficiency and to improve the speed of service and workforce productivity. This will catalyze the virtuous cycle of expansion of demand for computers, software, IT services, electronic goods, mobile phones, smart phones, broadband network, internet services providers and technology-savy work force—essentially building what is called a "positive feedback loop" in electrical engineering parlance.

We believe any future government of Bangladesh, be it led by Bangladesh Nationalist Party (BNP), Awami League (AL) or any other party is not likely to dramatically change the course we're currently on toward building a digital ICT-driven nation. Sure, the branding may change a little. But the dreams of a digitally inclusive Bangladesh are fully aligned with where the wider world is headed and a young country like Bangladesh cannot afford to pass up the opportunity to leapfrog a few decades of technology stagnation and economic growth by implementing the visions of a digital future—and to carry it out fast in internet time.

Enable private sector-led e-commerce for domestic growth

With a large population of about 160 million and younger demographics (70% of the population under the age of 30), Bangladesh stands to benefit from e-commerce-driven growth since the younger population is likely to adopt and adapt to the digital world at the fastest rate. At this time, we need to promote development of e-commerce sites and web services and encourage consumers to use the web to buy and sell goods and services. Of course, some basic rules and guidelines have to be put in place for the execution of web-based commerce.

Making various bill payments over the web can cut down road traffic as people will prefer to access service from their homes and offices without having to travel by road to reach the stores or offices. Telecommuting, working from home via access to office computers via secure VPN (virtual private network) can reduce traffic jams in big cities and reduce migration to urban centers as people can work from anywhere as long as a computer connected to the internet is available. Computer-based money transfer can also speed up transactions and lower the costs of money transfers and payments. Credit and debit card service providers will grow, adding a new economic engine of growth for the country.

Expand mobile banking

Mobile banking can redefine banking, trading, finance and commerce in Bangladesh as there is widespread use of mobile phones which can be readily leveraged executing mobile banking transactions. Money transfer from the country's 8,500 postal offices is a new service that began in 2010, allowing fast and quick money transfer using SMS messaging through any mobile phone.

Bangladesh's central bank estimates that the automated check handling (ACH) facility it introduced into the country in late 2009 will add about 1.2% GDP growth to the country in 2010. Thus both e-commerce and mobile banking will benefit from the GDP-accelerator effect of the ACH service offered by banks, stores, commercial companies and government and public sector organizations.

Boost the performance of call centers

As places from where customer support, product order taking, airline reservations, ticket purchases, bill payments, payment collections, outbound sales calls and such other modern services are provided via live human agents, call centers have become a new business opportunity for Bangladeshi entrepreneurs. With expanded telecom, broadband and internet services, Bangladesh is now ready to offer first-class low-cost call center services to customers in any part of the world.

Interestingly, the country's demand for call center services from domestic companies and domestic customers are already showing impressive growth. A case in point is the support requirements of GrameenPhone, the country's biggest mobile phone operator. With roughly a 43% share of the mobile market in Bangladesh, GrameenPhone has greatly expanded its own call centers to serve its customers numbering over 34 million. Plus the country's upwardly mobile (economically) customers are expecting higher quality in customer support for answers to basic questions about service features, as for example. This has prompted its competitors to establish modern call centers to service its domestic customer base.

Modern call centers serving overseas customers have also emerged in Bangladesh and can be the single most promising export-growth sector in IT services for Bangladesh if it can strengthen its English language proficiency, since English is the most commonly used language amongst the call center customers. The good news is that English is taught as a mandatory language from primary level in Bangladesh's education system today. As a result, Bangladesh can boast of being potentially one of the most populated country conversant in English (after USA, India, and UK). Plus the younger population (70% of which is below the age of 30) can be trained relatively fast to develop the English fluency levels needed. Given the low labor costs in Bangladesh, the pay rates at the call centers are such that these jobs are considered high-paying by the younger generation.

What's more, the wage rates for call center jobs in neighboring India is increasing, providing good labor-rate-arbitrage opportunities for call centers based in Bangladesh. Indeed, the business opportunities in call centers can have an effect like what the country has seen in the successful garment export business. In fact, many of the garment export houses, with large accumulated capital, have been seen to be seeking to diversify into the call center export market. With all these factors in its favor, Bangladesh needs to seize this historic opportunity quickly and aggressively.

> "Good leaders have the confidence to dream big dreams and the ability to get others to make those dreams a reality."
> – Dale Morrison (b. 1950)

Embrace the new cloud-based digital services

New or emerging digital technologies often open up good opportunities for a "new entrant" like Bangladesh to get into areas where there may not be as much competition compared to the mature areas. One such new and emerging technology goes by the moniker "cloud computing" and it is redefining computing and IT service delivery models worldwide, thanks to the availability of inexpensive servers, massive data-storage capacity, high-speed networks and the internet. In case you're wondering about the nature of this new beast, rest assured that cloud computing (also known as utility computing) has nothing to do with the clouds floating in the sky. Instead, it is a new way of delivering computing power, data storage and applications from one data center location over an internet grid to thousands or millions of users.

The general or mainstream kind of cloud, for example, online services provided by Amazon EC2, Google Apps and Salesforce.com, are known as "public" cloud because any business or individual can subscribe to this utility. Designed to make web-scale computing easier for developers, Amazon EC2 (which stands for Elastic Compute Cloud) is a web service that provides resizable compute capacity in the cloud.

Private cloud computing is a different take on the mainstream version, in that the smaller cloudlike IT systems within a firewall offer similar services, but to a closed network which may include corporate offices, other companies that are also business partners, raw-material suppliers, resellers, production-chain entities and other organizations are intimately connected with a corporate entity.

Industry observers are expecting big things from cloud computing. Gartner analysts estimated that global cloud services revenues moved beyond US $56 billion in 2009—from US $46 billion in 2008—and could grow to US $150 billion in 2013. Another market research firm, IDC (International Data Corporation), is more conservative in its projections, calling for worldwide spending on cloud services to reach US $42 billion by 2012.

So, why all the fuss about cloud computing? Well, with the advent of the cloud computing paradigm, large-scale computing without one's own data centers is now possible. One can use the public cloud to deploy applications and services like Facebook, Twitter, Google, Google +, Gmail, and YouTube. The good news is that these large data centers can be housed in Bangladesh with its growing telecom and broadband capacity at a low cost with IT educated workforce that can maintain the cloud data centers.

Since cloud computing allows the creation of lots of or as many servers as one wants out of a single physical real server, IBM Z-systems mainframes can now create over one thousand Linux virtual machines (VM) with high-level of security and availability. Intel/AMD CPU-based x86 platforms can create hundreds of VMs in a single large server. This virtualization and scalability provides enormous computing and storage power for building massive cloud computing centers at modest costs.

As we understand it, the goal of the current government of Bangladesh as part of the Digital Bangladesh initiative is to create four large data centers, thus consolidating IT centers scattered throughout its many agencies across the country. Since these new data centers will offer Web-based services to citizens and will be available from any internet browsers and servers acting in a web-portal form, these data centers can be categorized as the government's (or public sectors) cloud.

If you've been using Facebook, Google (search), Yahoo Mail, Hotmail, Flickr (photo storage), Apple iTunes, internet backups, or Salesforce.com, then you are already a beneficiary of cloud computing.

That's because these services are provided to you from cloud computers (i.e., computers that are not in your office or home).

Increasingly, cloud computing is being opened up as a public cloud where you or a company can rent the computing, storage or IT service it needs on dynamic utility-modeled pay-what-you-use-based pricing models. Amazon's EC2 is reportedly the first grand public cloud computing initiative. Microsoft's Azure platform based on Windows servers is its cloud offering that has been available since January 1st, 2010, while Google offers its cloud computing as "Google Engine."

Create well-paying jobs

It has been estimated that implementation of the Digital Bangladesh initiative could create around 500,000 new jobs in 2010-2013. So where are these well-paying jobs going to come from? Although it's hard to pin down the exact scale and scope of the newly created employment opportunities, our good-faith effort suggests the following:

- Thousands of new jobs for the web portals, contents, digital service conversion, scanning images for digital access, etc.;
- A significant number of high-paying jobs related to building and maintaining the four new data centers for the government of Bangladesh;
- Thousands of new jobs at call centers for the generally educated population with possibly some focused training to improve English fluency;
- New jobs from the expected high growth in the software exports market;
- New IT jobs in the Chittagong region if Bangladesh is able to attract a global player in cloud computing (e.g., Amazon, Google, Microsoft, IBM or Salesforce.com) by offering excellent broadband connectivity through the gigabit-scale submarine cable from Cox's Bazaar (this is entirely plausible since geography is increasingly becoming less important as cloud computers can reside anywhere as long there's fast internet access);
- 50,000 short-term jobs for the creation, deployment, and training to support village kiosks, and additional 250,000 new permanent jobs related to operation and maintenance of the kiosks (estimates based on 5 jobs per kiosk);

- Conducting skill seminars at the village kiosks to create a better-skilled workforce;
- Overseeing youth science project activities in all high schools and other educational institutions.

Expand exports

We believe there are huge untapped opportunities to expand exports of IT services and IT-enabled services from Bangladesh. Here's our shortlist:

- Minimally capture US $100 million in ICT exports revenue by 2014, which amounts to 3 times the level achieved in 2010 (as per the roadmap developed by BASIS);
- Focus on export of services through call centers to seize the high-growth segments of this market;
- Expand into BPO (business process outsourcing) services to engage the low-cost, but skilled/trained labor of the country in professions other than IT, such as legal documentation, medical transcription, security camera monitoring and corporate back-office operations;
- Attract selected assemblers or manufacturers of labor-intensive electronic goods and allied high-tech products who currently operate in China, South Korea, Malaysia and Taiwan to the industrial park in Chittagong operated as an EPZ.

5.3 What would it cost to build a Digital Bangladesh?

We estimate that the investment required to deliver on the promises of Digital Bangladesh would amount to about one billion US dollars in the 2009-2013 time period. The required investments for the next five years (2014-2018) should add up to two billion dollars, to be followed by four billion dollars for the 2019-2023 period. Thus, the overall investment for these 15 years of digital development in Bangladesh is pegged at about seven billion US dollars.

E-government is the most cited and high-profile of all ICT applications, given its importance in underpinning the broad range of development efforts not just in Bangladesh but across the developing world. China has itself earmarked on major initiatives in this area since

1999. Total e-government spending is estimated to have increased to more than US $10 billion in 2008, from US $7 billion in 2006. India is also planning large investments. For example, its e-Government Program will receive US $5.5 billion in funding between 2007 and 2012. Bangladesh needs to invest at least US $0.4 billion (in nominal dollars; or about Tk. 2,800 crore) during the same period for its purely GDP-based parity with India's e-Government Program.

To ensure smart use of this large sum of money, we must leverage the best of both the resident talents in Bangladesh and the non-resident Bangladeshi (NRB) community living abroad. It is estimated that there are about 10 million NRBs living in various countries of the world today. As people of Bangladeshi origin who have settled abroad or are working overseas on a work related visa, the NRBs represent an under-tapped, if not completely untapped, resource for Bangladesh. Given that they are often in the higher income brackets than most resident Bangladeshis, they are likely to have more disposable income for investments. Besides, having seen and lived in digitally connected parts of the world, they have ideas and expertise that should be transferrable to Bangladesh. In some cases, they can provide insight and guidance to new companies in Bangladesh on how to globalize their market presence, or how to partner with foreign companies that may be looking to expand their base in Bangladesh. In other words, the NRBs could be the veritable bridge for the most effective transfer of market insight as well as investment funds.

Like the NRIs (Non-Resident Indians), NRBs will have a significant role to play in realizing the dreams of a digital bonanza for Bangladesh. Likewise, the NRCs (Non-Resident Chinese) have successfully catalyzed the rapid development of China, Hong Kong and Taiwan. The good news is that the key role of NRBs have already been acknowledged by all the major political parties of Bangladesh. To this end NRBs have been assigned in key planning and implementation phases of various projects within and outside the government. It needs to be continued and further expanded to propel Bangladesh onto a trajectory of faster growth while generating the highest returns for the investments by leveraging their diverse creative experience from living in various countries of the world. This can only help Bangladesh toward reaching the goal of becoming a middle-income country by 2021, if not sooner.

Resetting targets with changes in technology and context

It's worth reminding ourselves that the implementation plan outlined in this book must be updated periodically based on the progress made against the milestones and to take advantage of the rapid pace digital technologies as per Moore's law, for example. So we recommend that the implementation plan be reviewed at least on an annual basis for actual progress and the plans updated every two years by a high-level national taskforce consisting of MIST, BCC, BASIS, BCS, and BOI. The Digital Bangladesh Task Force headed by the Prime Minister is one such powerful organ and should be reformed and empowered to monitor this vital national mandate.

Suggested online implementation resources to tap

Resource	Internet Links
Fiber@Home	www.fiberathome.net
BanglaLion – WiMax provider	www.banglalionwimax.com
BTRC	www.btrc.gov.bd
Bangladesh e-government projects	www.a2i.pmo.gov.bd
Bangladesh Computer Council	www.bcc.net.bd
Kaliakoir HighTech Park	www.htpbd.org.bd
Bangladesh government web sites	www.bcc.net.bd/html/webdir.php
National Information search site	www.infokosh.bangladesh.gov.bd
Global IT park operator Ascendas	www.ascendas.com/english
Economic news portal	www.bangladesh-economy.org
24-hour Online TV by NRBs	www.BDeshTV.com
Board of Investment (BOI)	www.boi.gov.bd
Bangladesh government portal	www.bangladesh.gov.bd

Given the enormity of the challenges ahead for committing to ushering in a new era of digital transformation for Bangladesh, it may seem at times that uphill battles may constantly be fought on multiple fronts. In those moments, one needs to be reminded that we can afford to lose a few battles as long as we're winning, the war against poverty and against the lack of opportunity especially for the aspiring youth throughout the country. When confronted with Goliath, David refused to hide behind protective armor. Instead, he accepted the challenge to beat Goliath at his own game with only his sling and five stones chosen in a brook. How did he do it?

Contrary to many of the popular TV versions of this epic story, here's how it went: David and Goliath confront each other, Goliath with his armor and shield, David with his staff and sling. David hurls a stone from his sling with all his might, and hits Goliath in the center of his forehead. The rest, as they say, is history!

Of course, the point of this story is that focus and confidence can take on the mightiest of obstacles. It turns out that to muster such apparently super human confidence, it often helps to get a glimpse of what a win will produce in the end. To this end, we've managed to dream up what Bangladesh looks like and feels like in 2021 by boarding a time machine of sorts to experience for ourselves what it's like to be "back to the future" as it relates to Digital Bangladesh. We earnestly ask for your indulgence as we report some of our findings in the next chapter.

Chapter 6

The New Face of Bangladesh Looking Back from 2021

> "The best way to predict the future is to create it."
> – Peter F. Drucker (1909-2005)

There are four takeaways from this chapter:

How has the internet itself changed by 2021 and what has been its impact on the learning- and creativity-driven reforms in the various economic, social and government sectors of Bangladesh 2021? Something called cloud computing back in 2010 fundamentally changed how people interact with the internet. Introduction of apps for everything and the "internet of things" made the internet so pervasive that computers are now largely invisible and people do not talk hardware and software anymore since the focus now is more on "humanware" interfacing with "everyware." The interactive social media has made everyone feel so connected that people think of only "six pixels of separation" with anyone else on the planet.

How has the day-to-day life in Bangladesh 2021 changed as it emerged on the other side of the digital tipping point, i.e., with more than 50% of its population having transitioned from being vintage Bangladeshis (or BDs) to self-styled "Digital Deshis" (or DDs)? Most adult DDs spend the majority of their time acquiring new skills and knowledge. Most learning is accomplished through handheld displays. Paper books and documents are rarely used since most of them have been scanned and are available through wireless networks. Digital health monitors built into watches, jewelry and clothing, which diagnose both acute and chronic health conditions. These monitors can also provide a range of remedial recommendations and interventions.

How are people dealing with issues like privacy, piracy, safety, and exposure or even addiction to various questionable online activities? Since the virtually constant use of digital communication technologies leaves behind a highly detailed trail of every person's every move, privacy has emerged as a charged political issue, especially for the vintage BDs. However, the DDs are increasingly willing to trade off some level of privacy for accessibility via social media. There is also growing tolerance for the diversity of views and lifestyles among the DDs, much to the chagrin (or envy) of the vintage BDs.

What were the things that surprised Mr. Rip Van Winkle@Bangladesh 2021 the most about the DD livelihoods and lifestyles? Perhaps the most surprising occurence was how quickly DDs were beginning to develop "virtual" relationships with online personalities (as teachers and companions) and even close friendships with digital avatars.

Imagine capturing a glimpse of the kaleidoscopic image of a dynamic ensemble of thousands of buzzing villages and hundreds of bustling towns that is Bangladesh today whose complexion and complexity you can see only once (that's, after all, how a kaleidoscope works). How about composing a clear picture of the country in 2021? Needless to say, this requires nothing less than the audacity of our collective imagination. At this point, we the authors of this book can offer only a few pixels worth of a coarse-grained image and would like to invite you, the reader, to use your own creative imagination to compose the "megapixel" version in your own mind. The pixels we provide here in this chapter are meant to be just thought-starters. We hope they're provocative enough to ignite your imagination and propel you forward on a proverbial time machine. Welcome aboard and get set for a virtual trip to Bangladesh 2021!

Let's start with a brief sketch of how the internet itself has changed by 2021 before we get into how it has transformed the lives of everyone, especially for the Digital Deshis (DDs) among us in Bangladesh and beyond. Here's a quick summary of where things stand today in 2021:

- The mobile device has become the primary internet connectivity tool for most people worldwide, voice recognition and touch user-interfaces with the internet are now more prevalent and widely accepted than ever before.
- Those working to prevent piracy by enforcing intellectual property laws and copyright protection are engaged in a continuing "arms race" since the "crackers" continue to find ways to copy and share content without permission and payment.

- The divisions between personal time and work time and between physical and virtual reality have been further erased for everyone who is connected, and the results have been mixed in terms of social relations.
- Despite the increased transparency of organizations in both the public and private sectors, the expected improvement in personal integrity, social tolerance or forgiveness has yet to materialize.
- The "next generation" engineering of the World Wide Web (WWW) to improve the current internet architecture is under way instead of an effort to rebuild the network architecture from scratch.

Well, we've come a long way since the "stone ages" of the digital era of the 1990s when Sun Microsystems introduced the catchy marketing slogan, "The Network Is the Computer." Back then the concept of the network being the computer was meaningless to most people since at the time the PC on our desk was our computer. By 2010, however, the network has become the computer because the different technologies

> "If you see the future as an obstacle, you are walking in the wrong direction."
>
> – *Rolf Jensen (b. 1942)*

that used to be isolated in the closed box of the PC (i.e. the hard drive for storing information, the microchip for processing information, and the software applications for manipulating information) can now be dispersed throughout the world, integrated through the internet, and accessed/shared by everyone across the globe. As a result, we've stopped going out and buying new software programs and installing them on our hard drives. Instead, we've started using the internet itself as our computer, tapping into the vast quantities of software and data flowing through the network. In short, the World Wide Web (WWW) has now turned into the World Wide Computer (WWC).

6.1 The occupational hazard of a forecaster

The irony is that IBM Chairman Thomas Watson became the laughing stock for predicting in 1943 that "I think there is a world market for maybe five computers," and thus completely missing out on the PC revolution of the 1980s and 1990s with hundreds of millions of desktops and laptops being used by people as their "personal computers." Thanks to the second coming of the internet—dubbed

Web 2.0—each of us with access to the internet in 2010 has the ability to program a supercomputer, that is, the WWC, with a virtually unlimited store of data and software, at our fingertips. Hence the new verdict on Mr. Watson's misjudgment is that he actually overestimated the global market size for computers by four! Well, such is the occupational hazard of predicting the future scale and scope of technologies in general and digital technologies in particular. Taking cues from Mr. Watson, we the authors of this book will refrain from making such predictions about the new face of Bangladesh 2021. Instead, we'll nudge you in the right direction during this virtual tour across time, spanning an enormously critical period during which Bangladesh emerges as a middle-income country with tens of millions of Bangladeshis (BDs) rising to the challenge of crossing the proverbial digital divide and transforming into bona fide "Digital Deshis" (DDs).

In any event, what Mr. Watson stood for in the mainframe computer era of the 1940s, Bill Gates of Microsoft was in the more recent PC era. So we need to pay a short visit with Mr. Gates as he wrestles with the competitive dynamics of the new WWC era. Anticipating the shape of things to come with the full flowering of the digital age, Mr. Gates penned an extraordinary memorandum in 2005 with the prophetic words, "The next sea of change is upon us." Sent to Microsoft's top managers and engineers, the memo read, "The broad and rich foundation of the internet will unleash a 'services wave' of applications and experiences available instantly....Services designed to scale to tens or hundreds of millions [of users] which will dramatically change the nature and cost of solutions deliverable to enterprises or small businesses." Although the memo was blandly titled "Internet Software Services," it was intended to sound an alarm, to warn the company's rank and file that the rise of something called "cloud computing" threatened to destroy its traditional business. This new wave, Gates concluded, "will be very disruptive."

6.2 What Google's strategy taught Bangladesh

While Microsoft was in the process of repositioning itself in the emerging new era of cloud computing, Google geared up quickly to seize the "attacker's advantage" during the first decade of the twenty-first century. Google invested heavily to build a database that would become a copy of virtually the entire internet! How? Well, it scanned the contents of the billions of pages it discovered and continually updated the database by "spidering" software that crawled through the Web, link by link.

Designed by some of the best minds in computer science, its data centers—comprising of dozens of "server farms" in covert locations around the world—contained one or more "clusters" of custom-built server computers constructed from cheap commodity microprocessors and hard drives that Google purchased in bulk, directly from their manufacturers. Each computer received its electricity through a power-supply unit invented by Google engineers to minimize energy consumption, and the machines ran a version of the free Linux operating system tweaked by Google's programmers, which also had the effect of undermining Microsoft's lock on the Operating System (OS) market, especially for servers.

As soon as a person entered a keyword into Google's search engine, the software routed the search to one of the clusters, where it was reviewed simultaneously by hundreds or thousands of servers. Although the typical search required, according to Google engineers, "tens of billions of [microprocessor] cycles" and the reading of "hundreds of megabytes of data," the whole process was completed in a fraction of a second. And this was something only Google could do. Thus, Google managed to eclipse Microsoft with its search engine and a highly successful business model that relies on revenues from targeted ads during online search.

Furthermore, no corporate computing system, not even the ones operated by very large businesses, could match the efficiency, speed, and flexibility of Google's system. One analyst estimated that Google could carry out a computing task for one-tenth of what it would cost a typical company. In other words, if other companies choose to do what Google has already done with its central stations—aka "server farms"—to fulfill all or most of their computing requirements, they'll be able to slash the money they spend on their own hardware and software—and all the dollars saved are the ones that would have gone into buying the stuff from Microsoft and the other tech giants.

Why is the Google story relevant for Bangladesh? You see, the power of Google's strategy in capturing the full disruptive potential of cloud computing became clear when people realized that Google did not need the traditional vendors, since it built its own computers and used free (Open Source) software. By 2021 it became clear that Bangladesh was smart in taking its cues from Google as the country invested heavily to build its digital infrastructure to successfully leapfrog onto the cloud computing paradigm.

6.3 An underdog's chance to leapfrog

Back in 2010, the question was, could the disruptive strategy adopted by Google be adapted by a technology "underdog" like Bangladesh? The answer turned out to be yes, and Google (and others like it, e.g., Amazon Web Services in hardware virtualization) was part of the answer, too. As Google expanded its reach in the cloud computing space, it was able to rapidly introduce new services as well as acquire ones developed by other companies. Although many of these services, from the Google Earth mapping tool, to the YouTube video-hosting site to the Blogger weblog publisher, were aimed mainly at consumers, in addition, Google also began to muscle into the business market.

> "The future enters into us in order to transform itself in us long before it happens."
> – Rainer Maria Rilke (1875 -1926)

As for example, Google launched a popular package of services, called Google Apps, that competed directly with one of Microsoft's biggest moneymakers, the Office suite. Google Apps included word processing, spreadsheets, email, calendar, instant messaging, and Web-site design and hosting. It cost as little as US$50 (in 2010 dollars) per employee per year—and the basic version, with advertisements, was available for free. Using the programs required nothing more than a cheap PC and a browser. Already, many small companies could satisfy most of their everyday computing needs with the software running in Google's data centers. As Google continued to grow, many more businesses fell into that category.

What did this rise of what the cognoscenti called "cloud computing" mean for investors and entrepreneurs looking for opportunities in Bangladesh for technology investments? There were some who realized that what was happening to computers in the early years of this century mirrored what happened to electric power generation at the start of the twentieth century. For example, through the end of the nineteenth century, if you wanted to run a machine in a factory or a home in the US, one had no choice but to generate the power needed to run it.

But as soon as the alternating-current electric grid was built, people and businesses stopped producing their own power. Instead, they just plugged their machines and appliances into the new network. Ironically enough, given the shortage of power generation capacity in Bangladesh even during the first decade of this century, we were lagging the US and other developed economies by about a hundred years since many Bangladeshi factories and homes had no choice but to install "backup" power-generating equipment to ensure uninterrupted power supply. Nevertheless, affordable electricity brought about an epochal transformation—with electric light altering the rhythms of daily life, electric assembly lines redefining work in the factory, and electric appliances bringing the "Industrial Revolution" into the home.

What's important to realize is that what happened to the generation of power a century ago was happening to the processing of information. Private computer systems, built and operated by individual companies, were being supplanted by services over a common grid—the internet—by centralized data-processing plants, that is, extensive networks of "server farms," run by Amazon, Google, Microsoft, Yahoo and others. In this age of cloud computing, a broad range of "web services", including Software as a Service (SaaS), were increasingly available to anyone with access to the internet. When broadband access in Bangladesh became as affordable—even if not as reliable—as electricity, the resident and non-resident Bangladeshis all over the world logged on to BanglaDISH, our own version of Facebook and YouTube rolled into one channel for social networking and mass collaboration over the internet.

6.4 The rites of passage for a Bangladeshi blogger

Many of us started programming this worldwide supercomputer, often without knowing it. Let's take the case of Sneha, a young woman in Dhaka, who happened to be an aficionado of Rabindranath Tagore's poetry. Back in 2002, she decided to share her passion with others by putting together a Website. She had to register a domain name, sign up for an account with a local Internet Service Provider (ISP), and buy an expensive Web-design program called Dreamweaver. Her site was a bare-bones production—pages of text interspersed with some photographs, a couple of tables, and a handful of links to other Tagore-related sites—but it took her a long time to get it looking good and

> "Everyone takes the limits of his own vision for the limits of the world."
> – *Arthur Schopenhauer*
> *(1788-1860)*

operating correctly. As changing or adding content was a hassle, she found that she rarely updated the pages. Not surprisingly, the site drew few visitors. After a few months, she got bored and abandoned her creation on the Web.

Around 2010, though, Sneha decided to give it another shot. But instead of building a traditional site, she started a blog. Launching it was a snap. Using the browser on her PC, she signed up at the blog-publishing site WordPress. Her blog was automatically set up on one WordPress's servers and assigned its own Web address. Sneha wrote her blog entries in a browser window using WordPress's software, which was running on computers owned by Automatic, the company that operated the WordPress service. Every time Sneha completed an entry about Tagore's poetry, she clicked the "publish" button in her browser, and the software saved the entry on WordPress's computers, formatted it according to Sneha's instructions, and published it on her blog.

Then Sneha decided not to limit her blog to text. Using her cameraphone, she had recently made a short video of a big Tagore poetry festival, and she wanted her blog's visitors to be able to watch it. So she transferred the video onto her PC and, again using her browser, uploaded a copy to the YouTube video-hosting service. YouTube translated the file into a format viewable by any computer, and it provided Sneha with a simple cut-and-paste code for adding the video to her blog. Although the video was stored on YouTube's computers, it played through a window on Sneha's site.

Sneha had also taken some photographs of Tagore's birthplace—the Jorasanko mansion—and other historic sites in and around Shantiniketan during her recent trip to Kolkata, India, with her digital camera. Willing to share them as well, she uploaded copies to the Flickr photo-sharing service. She noticed, however, that the colors looked washed out on the screen. To tweak them, she went to another site, called Phixr, and launched its online photo-editing software. Her photos were transferred from Flickr to Phixr automatically, and she used the Phixr tools to boost their color saturation and make a few other adjustments. She saved the changes, sending the enhanced photos back to Flickr. At this point, Flickr provided Sneha with another simple code that let her add a photo frame to her blog. The Flickr service fed a new picture into the frame every few seconds. As with the YouTube videos, the photos remained stored on Flickr's computers, though they appeared on Sneha's pages. Sneha also noticed that a lot of other people had uploaded photos of Tagore memorabilia to the Flickr site. She instructed Flickr to randomly insert some of these photos into her blog as well.

However, she wasn't done yet. A fan of Tagore songs, Sneha decided she'd like to let visitors see what Tagore music she had been listening to lately. So she signed up for an account with Last.fm, an online service that monitors the songs its members play on their computers and creates a customized online radio station tailored to each member's tastes. Sneha instructed Last.fm to keep the Top 10 of her most-played Tagore songs and to show the list in a box, or "widget," in a column at the side of her blog. Last.fm updated the list every time Sneha played a new Tagore song.

Sneha also wanted to let her readers know who else was reading her blog. She signed up with MyBlogLog for a service that kept track of her blog's visitors and listed their names—and even their pictures—in another widget. Finally, she wanted to allow her readers to subscribe to her writings, so she set up an account with Feedburner, which provided her with a "subscribe" button to add to her blog. Using the syndication technology known as RSS, Feedburner alerted subscribers whenever Sneha posted a new article, and it let Sneha know how many people had signed up.

Sneha's work, which only took her a few hours, gives a sense of how simple it became to draw data and services from various utility suppliers and to combine them into a single Web page. What's remarkable is that she didn't need to install any software or store any data on her PC—other than, temporarily, the original video and photo files. The various software applications, and all the data, resided on the utility companies' systems. Using simple tools, she programmed—yes, this is the new kind of programming in the age of cloud computing—all these far-flung machines to create a multimedia experience for her readers. What's even more remarkable is that Sneha didn't pay anything for the software, the storage, the computing power, except for the broadband connection through which all the data traveled. Everything else was free.

In fact, Sneha was able to make a little money from her blog by opening up an account with Google's AdSense service. Google automatically placed text advertisements on her pages, gearing the ads to the interests of Tagore fans. Any time a reader clicked on an ad,

Google shared the advertising revenue with Sneha. While she was at it, Sneha also signed up for a free account with Google Analytics, which monitored her traffic and provided her with detailed reports on who was visiting her blog, what pages they were looking at, and how long they were spending on each page. Sneha was tapping into Google's vast data centers and enormously complex algorithms—again at no cost to her.

Admittedly, the tools for programming the World Wide Computer were in an early stage of development in 2010. While it was not difficult for Sneha to construct her blog, she did have to go to many different sites and copy codes manually. By 2021, the programming tools have got easier to use even as they became more powerful because that's what always happens with software. To this end, Yahoo gave us a preview of what's to come when in 2007 it introduced its Pipes programming service. Pipes allows anyone to create a custom Web service by combining and filtering the contents of different internet databases from a single browser window. Sneha, for example, could use Pipes to construct a service that monitored her favorite information sources—newspapers, magazines, blogs, wikis—and spotted any new mention of Tagore. Every morning, the service would publish a fresh list of headlines on her blog, with links to the full stories.

However, back in 2010, Sneha was becoming a forerunner amongst the Digital Deshis (DDs) who eventually made up more than 50% of her generation by 2021. But, most people were rather slow to realize how the internet offered a profound and far-reaching opportunity to improve the way that wealth is created as well as dramatically enhance social development. Unlike in America where most people were already comfortable with this technology, DDs in Bangladesh had to deal with some cultural issues in making people understand that the only way that we'll really understand both the promise and the peril of this technology is to experience it and to learn from mistakes along the way.

In Bangladesh, for example, senior managers and bureaucrats didn't like to use computers and the internet because they felt that was for junior assistants. This started to change in 2012 when the government of Bangladesh introduced a "reverse mentoring program" whereby the DDs would provide on-the-job coaching to their seniors who viewed themselves as "Digital Immigrants" (DIs). Soon enough, those with access to the internet warmed up to the possibilities of what they could do with it, and a growing number started to feel that they couldn't imagine living without it anymore.

We've indeed come a long way from the days when the initial adjustment was rather painful for many of the oldsters amongst the authors' generation who were too embarrassed to learn how to use the PC. As a result, stories—some of which may have been hoaxes—about the DI generation's awkwardness with computers proliferated among help desk operators. One help desk operator reported that when asked if she had Windows, one woman replied, "No, we have air-conditioning." Another person "hit" the keyboard so hard, he broke it. Somewhere else a secretary was asked to copy a disk and came back with a photocopy. One person was seen trying to delete files on a disk using Wite-Out. Of course, back then many high-ranking government officials in Bangladesh used to think of their desktop PCs as nothing more than expensive pieces of office furniture.

6.5 A (re)view of the shape of things that came to Bangladesh

It turns out that DDs differ from DIs not only in how intensely they interact with digital technologies, they also have a different sense of patriotism, power and membership loyalty. They belong to new "nations" of deep personal interests and dispositions: a nation of geeks, a nation of diabetics, and a nation of artists. Some of them may feel greater allegiances to these virtual nations than to their own countries, towns or villages. Things were pointing in this direction back in 2006 when the US-based Center for the Digital Future surveyed more than 2,000 people to study the attitude of individuals and the internet. The survey indicated that 43 percent of internet users felt as strongly about their online communities as they did about their offline or "real world" communities. The report concluded that the internet has become "a comprehensive tool that Americans are using to touch the world." The same can be said about our DDs in 2021.

"The philosophers have only interpreted the world in various ways. The point, however, is to change it."
– *Karl Marx (1818-1883)*

Consider this scenario: If Facebook were a country back in 2010, it would have the 3rd largest population in the world, exceeding that of the US by tens of millions. Yet people felt that it was entirely possible that Facebook would be eclipsed by another virtual community within a couple of years. The majority view was that that's how it should be.

People were also getting used to the idea that the virtual marketplace enabled by the internet is like an invisible continent that is fast dominating the world of commerce. That was when eBay and Amazon.com became the platforms for global retailing. By embracing the digital platform, BanglaDISH has managed to earn its rightful place as the one of the most visited social and commercial portals/destinations in the new and invisible continent by 2021.

Reader: *How has the way people tap into the internet changed in 2021?*

Samdani 2021: *Embedded nearly everywhere, e.g., walls, tables, chairs, desks, clothing, jewelry, and bodies, computers are now largely invisible. We do not just own one specific "Personal Computer" anymore, although computing remains a very personal activity. Instead, computing and extremely high-bandwidth communication are embedded everywhere. In some parts of the world, cables have largely disappeared, and Bangladesh is also moving in that direction.*

Quamrul 2021: *Keyboards are rare, although they still exist. People interact with computing through gestures, using hands, fingers, and facial expressions and through two-way spoken communication using natural languages. In other words, people communicate with computers the same way they communicate with their human peers, both verbally and through human expression.*

Karim 2021: *We pay significant attention to the personality of computer-based personal assistants, with many choices of personalities available in the market. We can model the personality of our intelligent digital assistants on actual persons, including ourselves, or select a combination of traits from a variety of both public personalities and private friends and associates.*

Reader: *How about the computing power of the devices? Are computers affordable enough for most people in Bangladesh and elsewhere?*

Samdani 2021: *Although not everyone can necessarily afford or need such computing power in their day-to-day lives, the computational capacity of a US$5,000 (in 2010 dollars) is approximately equal to the computational capacity of the human brain (20 million billion calculations per second). Here's a whopper that I would not have seen coming in 2010: It turns out that of the total computing capacity of the human species (that is, all human brains alive in 2021) combined with the computing technology our species has created to date, more than 10% of it resides in nonhuman devices.*

Quamrul 2021: *Electromechanical data storage and computing devices have been fully replaced with fully electronic devices. Three-dimensional nanotube lattices are now claiming a growing share of the computing circuitry market. The majority of software development efforts are now devoted to massively parallel neural nets and genetic algorithms.*

Reader: *Tell me more about what its like to be a student in 2021.*

Karim 2021: *For those who can afford them in Bangladesh, hand-held devices are extremely thin, very high resolution, and weigh only ounces each. People rarely use or access books and documents in their traditional formats. That's because most twentieth-century paper documents of interest have been scanned and made available through the wireless network.*

Samdani 2021: *Many pilot schools are propping up in Dhaka where students learn mostly by interacting with intelligent software-based simulated teachers. To the extent that teaching is done by human teachers, they are often not sitting or standing next to or in front of the student. Instead, the teachers act more as mentors and counselors rather than as sources of learning and knowledge. In most of the developed economies, this mode of learning is increasingly becoming the norm.*

Quamrul 2021: *Of course, students continue to gather together to exchange ideas and to socialize, although even this gathering is often physically and geographically remote, especially among the DDs. In addition, learning is no longer limited to the youngsters; most aspiring adult humans spend the majority of their time acquiring new skills and knowledge.*

Reader: *What about the way we conduct business in 2021?*

Samdani 2021: *There are some business transactions that include essentially a simulated person, featuring a realistic animated personality and two-way voice communication where people and the digital interface can use natural language. Often, however, there is no human interaction involved since many people have their automated personal assistant conduct transactions on their behalf with other automated personalities. In this case, the digital assistants skip the natural language and communicate directly by exchanging appropriate knowledge structures. We'll have a few vignettes to illustrate this later in this chapter.*

6.6 Education as co-created experience of knowledge and inspiration

Zooming back in 2008 you come across a video called "A Vision of Students Today," one of the hottest hits on YouTube (accessible via the link: http://www.youtube.com/watch?v=dGCJ46vyR9o) that begins in a gray, empty classroom somewhere in the US. The stark room is suggestive of the fact that nothing much has changed in the setup of the classroom since the early nineteenth century, when the blackboard was introduced as a brilliant new way to help students visualize information. When the movie was made in 2007, we see a classroom filled up with students who look bored. One after another, they hold up signs that reflect the views of the 200 students who collaborated on the project, via the internet, at their schools. In less than five minutes, these students deliver a stinging indictment of the then existing education system:

"My class size is 115."

"Eighteen percent of my teachers know my name."

"I buy $100 worth of textbooks I never open."

"I will read eight books this year, 2,300 Web pages, and 1,281 Facebook profiles."

"I will write 42 pages for class this semester and over 500 pages of e-mails."

"When I graduate, I probably will have a job that doesn't exist today."

Then a student holds up a multiple-choice test form along with a sign: "Filling this out won't get me there."

Does this look and sound vaguely familiar to you, the time traveler from Bangladesh? This goes to show that having the digital technologies available was only half the solution if we did not rethink/reform the education system fit for the twenty-first century. How did we do it? Here's how:

- Instead of focusing on the teacher, the reformed education system in Bangladesh 2021 focused on the student
- Instead of lecturing, teachers started interacting with students and helped them discover for themselves
- Instead of delivering a one-size-fits-all form of education, schools customized the education to fit each student's individual way of learning
- Instead of isolating students, the schools encouraged them to collaborate

Flash forward to 2021. Now that broadband access is nearly ubiquitous in Bangladesh, mobile phones can surf the internet, capture GPS coordinates, take photos, and swap text messages, and social networking sites let the DDs monitor their friends' every move. Technology is now completely transparent to the DDs. For them it's like what using a pencil was to their parents. Much like their parents who didn't talk about the pencil that was an "amazing technology" at some other time in history, the DDs do not talk about digital technologies when they play, build websites, text a friend, or campaign to save the rain forest. They use their mobile phones as alarm clocks, night-light, watch, and a phone. This goes to prove that computer visionary Alan Kay was right when he said that technology is "technology only for people who are born before it was invented."

There's no denying that digital technologies are not distributed equally or equitably, and digital divides are quite pronounced even within the same country, but today's DDs inhabit a flattening world where digital technologies make it as easy to send an instant message to an acquaintance thousands of miles away as to a next-door neighbor. The digital infrastructure is rapidly shrinking the world. It is becoming more and more apparent to DDs that they now live in a generation/timeframe where for the first time in history, young people around the world are increasingly becoming very much alike with the fading of the distinct localized traits that used to characterize young people from different region or countries.

> "Every man, wherever he goes, is encompassed by a cloud of convictions, which move with him like flies in a summer day."
> – Bertrand Russell (1872-1970)

Another first for the DD generation is that adults (as "Digital Immigrants") are looking to children for information and guidance on how to use digital technologies. This is even changing the role of the child in the home. In the past, parents were the authority figures when it came to anything of real value. Therefore, for the first time there are things that parents want to be able to know and do, where the kids are, in fact, the authority. Experts agree that society has never before experienced en masse this phenomenon of the knowledge hierarchy being so radically flipped on its head. But this situation has even magnified over the years with the appearance of each new digital technology, such as mobile devices and social networks. The impact has been hugely positive thus far as family members have begun to respect each other as the authorities they actually are. In many cases, this has created a more engaged dynamic within families. When managed well by the parents, this dynamic has created a more open, consensual, and effective family unit.

Back in 2009, the diffusion of parental authority spread beyond the family home when the government of Finland chose 5,000 DDs to train the country's teachers in how to use computers. For the first time ever, in one domain of digital technologies, the students became the teachers and the teachers were the students. Thus the power dynamics between students and teachers were forever altered.

Imagine what happened next as these tech-savvy DDs moved into the workforce, where many managers, especially in Bangladesh, Japan and several European countries, made little use of the internet. The successful companies were those that recognized that networked structures work more effectively than old-fashioned hierarchies as peer collaboration drove innovation and new approaches to management and government.

DDs are transforming the internet from a place where you mainly find information to a place where you share information, collaborate on projects of mutual interest, and create new ways to solve some of our most pressing problems. One way they are doing this is by creating content—in the form of their own blogs, or in combination with other people's content. In this way, DDs are democratizing the creation of content, and this new paradigm of communication has had revolutionary impact on everything it touched—from music to movies, to political life, business, and education.

6.7 The mobile phone as the all-purpose connectivity tool

By 2021, mobile phones have become sleek digital Swiss Army Knives that do a lot more than make a phone call. As mobile phones got linked to the internet, they turned into something completely different and the term mobile phone became a misnomer. As manufacturers piled on features, they turned these devices into small, powerful computers that are part voice communication, part personal digital assistant, part music player, part Web browser, part texting device, part digital camera, part video camera, part voice recorder, and part GPS compass. Since they have a persistent connection to the internet, DDs are always online.

Some parents are used to having their children use the mobile phones in more creative ways. Consider the case of Pearl, a young girl who walks several blocks to her school every day. She uses the mobile phone when she happens to be alone in the city streets to indicate—sometimes falsely—that she was engaged in a telephone conversation. In other words, Pearl uses the mobile phone as a prop or symbolic icon for connectedness. Her posture of speaking on the phone can be seen as part of a broadly understood gestural syntax. She draws upon this syntax—in a bogus form—in order to communicate to a potential harasser that she was in contact with others. Thus, her mobile phone is used both as a communication channel as well as a symbol of being connected. In turn, this provides her a vicarious protection by being used to communicate the idea to potential perpetrators that she is in touch with others and thus is not "alone."

Two of the under-reported, yet fundamental, impacts of mobile communications have been "microcoordination" and the "softening of time" in people's lives. As a result, there has been a rise in the frequency of interactions—at the expense of longer/deeper interaction/conversations—which serve to weld social groups together. Use of twitter is such a case in context. This means we know that, on a nearly perpetual basis, where our friends or partners are, we know their immediate plans, and we have a general sense of their current situation. The group knows one anothers whereabouts and has the ability to rework plans as needed. Agreements are made and frequently readjusted.

The mobile phone is competing with or perhaps supplementing the wristwatch as way to coordinate social interaction. In other words, mobile phones allow us to cut out the "middle man" (i.e., clock-based coordination). Rather than relying on a secondary system like a wristwatch, which may not necessarily be synchronized, mobile phones allow for direct interaction. This in turn provides flexibility and an efficiency that is unavailable with time-based coordination. This kind of microcoordination is a nuanced formed of social interaction. Microcoordination can be seen in the redirection of trips that have already started, it can be seen in the iterative agreement as to when and where to meet friends, and it can be seen, for example, in the ability to call ahead when we are late to an appointment.

Thus the mobile phones have the ability to "soften" schedules in that they add slack to the more precise nature of time-based agreements. For example, if you're caught in a traffic jam, you can call ahead to your potentially frustrated meeting partners and apprise them of the situation. As a result, the agenda for the meeting can be juggled to allow the meeting to proceed while you postpone your presentation a bit. Thus, the mobile phone can help to relax the scheduling of events because calling ahead provides us with the opportunity to renegotiate arrangements.

Another dimension of microcoordination is that it is iterative when it is used to progressively refine an activity. Let's say two friends agree to "do something together this weekend." While they agree to meet in general terms, they need not specify the location or the exact time for the get-together. Then, through progressively specific messages or calls, they can, in effect, zoom in on each other as the time approaches. Unlike the softening of schedules described above, this type of coordination is an ongoing activity that takes place between people when a general agreement to meet has been made and the details are progressively filled in.

A more dramatic version of the iterative coordination phenomenon is known as "swarming" where groups of people follow the movements of public personalities, coordinate protest marches, or orchestrate the actions of others on a dynamic basis, using Twitter, for example. This ability to contact others whenever and wherever adds a dynamic character to the interaction. We move away from the need to nail down a specific time or place, which can be determined in real time as the need arises. Thus mobile communication has increased the efficiency of planning meetings since the meetings can be renegotiated and redirected in real time. The device also obviates the need for contingency plans, such as "If I don't show up by 6:00 pm, go ahead without me." With access to mobile communication, we can quickly call to see if our meeting partner will make the date. Thus we move from a type of linear conception of time in which meetings, social engagements, appointments and assignments are fixed points to a situation in which these elements can, to some degree, be negotiated.

Midcourse correction is another dimension of microcoordination. It has been estimated that because of this feature of microcoordination, on the whole, the mobile phone saves more transportation than it generates. It turns out the opposite is true when considering the impact of the landline phone on the volume of transportation. Much of the savings for mobile telephony comes as a result of the ability to redirect travel that has already begun. The mobile phone allows us to receive or request information along the way, thus short-circuiting the need for meeting to exchange information. You can imagine that as programs change, you must juggle your schedule and appointments. For example, when, due to the cancellation of a meeting, one parent becomes available to pick up the children at their after-school activities, then one can call or send a text message releasing the other partner—who may already be en route—from that assignment.

Midcourse adjustment can also benefit people with hearing difficulties. Before the development of SMS (short message service or texting), these people had to rely on extremely cumbersome systems to make appointments and organize social interaction. In the past, if for some reason the hearing-impaired persons were unable to make an appointment and were marooned en route, they were unable to use the traditional telephone system to call ahead and reschedule. This was particularly true if their counterpart was also hearing-impaired. The use of SMS has revolutionized social interaction in this group because it allows the transmission and reception of written messages. In a fundamental way, the mobile device has emancipated these people and provided them greater freedom of movement.

6.8 When mobile apps rule the world

By 2021, we prefer to call the mobile phone something else, e.g., a buddy or even a digital copilot loaded with thousands of useful "apps" because everybody has come to rely on them so heavily to get through the day.

Since Apple's App Store, the most popular destination for mobile-phone programs, was launched in the summer of 2009, more than a dozen rival stores, and at least 100,000 apps were created in less than six months. When Apple started launching commercials with outlandish "There's an app for that" headlines that basically proclaimed that there's an app for everything you could ever possibly want to do, parodies such as the following started cropping up in the blogosphere:

- "If you want to write an app that makes fun of apps, there's an app for that."
- "If you want to get your drunk roommate out of bed, there's an app for that."
- "If you just murdered your friend and need to find the nearest city dump, there's an app for that."

Parodies aside, companies made money from selling apps, from ads within apps, and from selling digital goods used in apps, which were estimated to add up to at least a US $1 billion market in 2009, and headed for US $4 billion by 2012. Some startups staked their claim in the app economy to become large, lucrative businesses making popular game apps that could be played on mobile phones or social networks such as Facebook. For example, FarmVille, a farming game, where players could grow digital crops and sell them to make virtual money became one of the most popular apps in the world, with at least 60 million people playing it every month in late 2009. The game was an odd success for the digital world: Users got a virtual plot of land to farm as they saw fit. As they grew crops and earned currency, they could use the money to buy more seeds, animals, and tools like tractors. Since all players were logged in to Facebook, they could work with friends or co-workers, or they could compete against them for farmer bragging rights. There were roughly 20 times more people playing FarmVille in late 2009 than there were actual farms in the US.

The money flowing into apps was inspired by the belief that smartphones and other portable devices were transforming the tech world. The growth of mobile computing was sparking a renaissance in software development. Of course, gaming apps were the most popular programs in 2009, but mobile shopping, content, social media, communications, and productivity tools were attracting increasing amounts of capital. The prevailing thinking was that the computing that people used to do at their desks could increasingly be done on devices they can carry anywhere.

Many DDs have even started to use the mobile phones to read books. Back in 2008, mobile phone novels in Japan became a huge hit when out of that year's 10 bestselling novels, 5 started as mobile phone novels. Here's how it worked: each day the author uploads snippets of text to mobile phone novel websites, and readers download the text to their phones. One author, a 21-year-old woman named Rin, wrote "If You" over a six-month stretch while attending high school. She attracted 20 million readers with her story of tragic love between two childhood friends in the form of a 142-page hardcover that was the fifth-best-selling novel in Japan in 2007.

Economists were pointing out that the more profound changes were happening in the means of production. Think of free and open-source software and Wikipedia, and these were all models of a new form of production rather than consumption. More than that, they were influential entrants into spaces once exclusively dominated by corporate or government-based production systems. "Peer production", that is, large-scale distributed actions by many individuals, were transitioning from a curiosity to a general phenomenon by 2010. Furthermore, the next 10 years were marked by two trends. Firstly, there was systemization and widespread adoption of social practices that engaged millions of people in effective, self-directed, socially motivated production. Secondly, there was an increasing sophistication of what economists called "social contract enterprises"—organizations that learned how to become trusted platforms for productive social practices over the internet.

One could already catch glimpses of what this future might look like in 2021. Companies entering YouTube's space were seeking to differentiate themselves from it. One company, Metacafe, was building a platform that remunerated video creators for their popular videos. Another company, Kaltura, was developing an open-source collaborative video-editing platform that allowed users to edit a movie together in the same way they would edit a Wikipedia article.

One could also see this kind of peer production applied in new and surprising places. Microlending sites like Prosper and Kiva were generating peer-to-peer lending. People pulled together to post sightings of forest fires in San Diego, mapping them on Google mashups to provide information in real time. Approaching problems through peer production was thus becoming a basic tool.

All of this was pointing towards a new social contract. Over the course of modern economic history, as markets became evermore separated from social relations, people specialized and segmented their moral outlook. As a result, some actions were fine in the market, even if we would never dream of taking advantage of people in similar ways in social relations. People behaved differently when they took themselves to be acting in the market, as opposed to acting in social relationships. Peer production and other forms of collaboration reversed that by breaking down the barrier between the market self and the social self.

As companies began to see the social practices that made up peer production not as fads, but as a fundamental generational shift in consumption, they had to embrace these socially conscious values. In some sense, Professor Yunus was probably ahead of his time as he was advocating the expanding roles of social businesses since receiving the Nobel Peace Prize in 2006.

It became increasingly clear that by 2008 that the world was entering a new age in which the central economic actor is someone who both produces and consumes in the same act. This new actor came to be known as a "prosumer" or "creator," as this new kind of actor was doing something more fundamental than the mere sum of their simultaneous production and consumption. These creators were ordinary people whose everyday actions created value.

Just as the mass media were essential to the rise of the consumer economy, the emergent personal media platforms were making the creator society possible. The quintessential example of creation is a Google search. The string of text that goes into the search box seems valueless to the creator, but when aggregated with all the other search strings flowing in, it is valuable enough to make Google worth billions. A simple Google search thus typifies what drives the creator economy—creative value flowing in both directions at the same instant.

If in search for other examples of creator transactions abound—think of YouTube and Wikipedia. Interactivity is the common thread, which makes sense because interactivity is what defines the creator economy. The rise of interactivity is no more exotic than the 1950s notion of ordinary consumers being able to purchase items that had been luxuries just a few decades earlier. Now, everyone creates as they go about their daily lives. These transactions may not be art or deathless prose, but they create value. Thus, just as the time clock symbolized the producer economy and the credit card the consumer economy, the computer mouse is the symbol of the emerging creator economy.

Economists argue that not everything in the creator economy will require interaction, any more than how manufacturers rarely interacted directly with buyers during the consumer economy. However, the most successful companies will be the ones that harness creator instincts, and the biggest winners will be the companies who harness the smallest creative acts. More people watch YouTube than post videos because creating a video is work. More people read blogs than write them because long-form writing is a hassle. Meanwhile, the telegraphic sentences of tweets, texting, and Facebook updates are becoming ubiquitous acts of creator haiku. And everyone can scribble a few words to compose a Google search, which is why Google dwarfs other creator companies. If history is any guide, there will eventually be a company that dwarfs Google. We didn't know its name, but we did know how it would grow—click by click. And sure enough, BanglaDISH was incubating several contenders to the likes of Google well before 2021.

> "What was once called the objective world is a sort of Rorschach ink blot, into which each culture, each system of science and religion, each type of personality, reads a meaning only remotely derived from the shape and color of the blot itself."
> – Lewis Mumford (1895-1990)

6.9 Dropping in and out of many avatars in one lifetime

Your authors were growing up in Bangladesh in the 1960s and 1970s, when their personal identities were a fairly straightforward matter. Back then there were essentially two main forms of identity: A personal identity derived from one's more or less unique personality characteristics, special interests and favorite activities, while one's social identity was based on his or her extended family and a small circle of friends. If any one of your authors wanted to change—or altogether abandon—aspects of his social identity quickly, he would have to go beyond the small community where he grew up. If he moved to a nearby village, there would likely still be some people who would know him, or know of him through others. Some would recall how he used to express himself, and could tell stories about him. Granted, they would only tell these stories orally since there were few permanent and reliable records kept about any individual in those days. Still, word would spread.

Take the case of Belal, who is a 10th grader by day, sports multiple identities while participating in chat rooms and virtual worlds after school. He thinks having different identities online helps him discover himself and learn who he really is. For example, he uses different nicknames, called "handles," for himself online. He's a "birdie" or a "brainie" or someone else. If, for example, he says something online that is borderline sexist or disrespectful to certain groups, he gets criticized very sharply. He will then think about it and realize that that was really off and it's not really him. Now, if he did that in the schoolyard, that remark could stick with him for years. In cyberspace, he just changes his "handle" and come back as somebody else, and that somebody else is a lot closer to who he really is. Therefore, it turns out that during adolescence, it's actually a very good and helpful environment where kids can go through that process of discovering who they are.

In the internet age in which the DDs are growing up is prompting a large shift in what it means to build and manage one's identity. For example, Belal can now create a new identity on the fly and go into an online environment where people do not know who he is, at least for a while. He might create a profile of himself in a new social network. He could present himself in a way that is strikingly different from the way he presents himself in real space. He could even create an avatar in a virtual world or in a gaming environment, such as "World of Warcraft," as a way to try out an identity that is not tethered to any other identity he has had in the past. Someone would have to do some serious digging to tie these multiple identities together.

In this sense, Belal could reinvent himself many times over without leaving his desk, much less his town or village. Yet he need not explore these identities successively over time; instead, he can create them all in one day and explore them simultaneously. Furthermore, Belal's identity is not broken up into online and offline versions of himself. He establishes and communicates his identities simultaneously in the physical and virtual/digital worlds. The sixteen-year-old Belal might be bound to being a tall Bangladeshi boy in the physical world, while in the digital space he can experiment with self-representation, sometimes in modest ways and sometimes dramatically. His multiple representations create his overall identity. Studies suggest that the possibility of greater exploration in identity formation offers terrific opportunities for personal development for DDs like Belal.

Indeed, virtual worlds have become the cool destinations for Belal and the other DDs like him. The key act of identity formation in the virtual worlds is the creation of an "avatar"—a virtual representation of the computer user. In most cases, the avatar is a figure whose actions can be controlled by the user's computer mouse, keyboard or touchscreen. In many online games, the avatar is largely determined by the kind of role one chooses to play in more or less predetermined storyline of the games.

Back in 2010, Second Life was among the most promising of the virtual worlds. Once Belal was "in world", he had a great deal of freedom in the creation of his avatars, and avatar design and appearance could be a significant aspect of his in-world participation. Second Life provided tools that permitted users to tailor the appearance of their avatars, allowing them to design everything from clothing to skin color to the shape of the avatar's nose. Users could create an avatar that looked very much like themselves in terms of both physical appearance and dress. But they could also experiment with very different identities, e.g., people of one certain age could choose an avatar of an older or younger age.

Massively Multiplayer Online Games (MMOGs) play a far greater role in the formation of identity for DDs in 2021 than ever before. To see how this works, imagine that our DDs pick up a mobile device to play Forgotten Warrior, an Anime-style mobile multiplayer game where the player is a prince fighting bad guys in quest of saving the kidnapped princess. The game connects through the mobile device to a network of other gamers. This means that Belal could play with his sister sitting next to him in the family room, or with anyone else who happens to be playing at the same moment, regardless of where they are in the world. And as he plays, he is creating another part of his digital identity online, in the character of a prince.

The growth trend of the online gaming industry turns out to be one of the clearest indications that a global culture is emerging, joining DDs in countries around the world to one another. High-school students in Dhaka or Shanghai talk about many of the same online games that kids are talking about in Chicago or London. And it's not just that these games are played in multiple cultures; the connections run deeper than that. Often these kids compete with one another online across vast geographic distances. Other times, they collaborate—with money changing hands in the process. For the past several years, rich kids in the West, some of them DDs, have hired Chinese and Bangladeshi gamers to play for them to help their characters get to higher levels in the online games. It became easy to imagine that when they grow up, as captains of industry in the future, they will continue to look to outsourcing as an option to get other tricky tasks done at low cost. As kids, they're already paying someone else, halfway around the world, to do the work they don't want to do—all in the name of enhancing their identity.

The search engines have become much more sophisticated in 2021 since they are not just to help you manage information, they enable to create a "virtual you" that understands you and knows what you consider to be junk and good stuff on the internet. The "virtual you" will help you manage all these environments while you sleep, presenting you with information in a sense that you have prejudged to be helpful. It can do this because you have provided the "virtual you" with the critical aspects of knowledge, which is context.

However, there is a darker side to an over-reliance on the virtual you. Vertual identities can be abused and real electronic identities can be stolen. Just as in the physical paradigm one has to guard over one's physical assets so is the case in the vertual paradigm. Another dark aspect is that in an age of information overload, it is easy to fall back on our own prejudices and insulate ourselves with comforting opinions that reaffirm our core beliefs. Crowds quickly become mobs.

How can leaders and ordinary people challenge insular decision making and gain access to the sum of human knowledge?

It's true that the blogosphere represents an open universe of public discourse, but the flip side of the access to limitless news and information options is the apathy towards it all by many. Gravitating toward those newspapers, blogs, podcasts and other media that reinforce their own views, you can carefully filter out opposing or alternative viewpoints to create an ideologically exclusive virtual you. The sense of personal empowerment you gain—and subsequently equate with "freedom"—only fuels the "echo chamber" effect, which replaces a sense of democratic unity with accelerating polarization. To counter the effect of such polarization, you not only need to hear multiple voices, but must also cultivate a habit of wanting to hear what others have to say.

The singular issue facing the internet and media distribution in general turned out to be regulation. On the social policy side of the equation, for example, the pressures were intense when the internet as an information source was being degraded by many factors, among them the rise of extremist blogs, the widespread availability of pornography to minors, and the plain inaccuracy of vast amounts of "information" coursing over the Web. For example, Wikipedia, a widely regarded source of user-developed information, succumbed to so much noise that it became useless for anything but casual reference.

6.10 When broadband met Bangladeshi entrepreneurship

It was clear in 2010 that a digital growth strategy for Bangladesh was predicated upon three conditions, namely highly affordable broadband access, availability of cheap PCs or simple terminals (or "thin clients" which are little more than a monitor hooked up to the internet), and development of "passion-based" talent to build Web-based service businesses. The first requirement was obvious enough.

Back then the thin-client model was embraced by a company named Novatium in India where it was providing personal computing as a simple utility service. Its customers received a thin client, called a Nova netPC, as well as a set of software services, all provided through their local telephone companies and paid for through a small charge on their phone bills. Household accounts also received an hour of free internet access a day. School and various business accounts had additional software and internet options to choose from, at different prices. Not only did customers avoid the high cost of buying a multipurpose PC, they also avoided all the hassles that went along with PC ownership, from installing and upgrading software to troubleshooting problems to fighting viruses.

Looking back now from 2021, it's clear that Bangladesh managed to "leapfrog" the multipurpose PC ownership stage of the computing revolution and move straight to the mobile and thin-client model for easy and affordable access to the World Wide Computer (WWC). By leapfrogging the old PC model, we have now access to virtually unlimited online storage as well as a rich array of software services. We're also tapping into the internet through many different devices, ranging from mobile phones to televisions, and we wanted to have all of them share our data and applications. It turned out that Google and Yahoo were eager to supply us with all-purpose utility services, including thin-client devices, for free – in return for the privilege of showing us advertisements.

In addition, being an underdog in technology, Bangladesh did not have the "credentials-based" expertise internally on the scale that was needed to compete with India, for example. However, we managed to build "communities of passion"—with the virtual gathering place being BanglaDISH—to bring together the like-minded people (and even people who may vehemently disagree) from around the world and help develop or market interactively and collaboratively Web 2.0-style content and software services.

So what did all this mean for Bangladesh and Bangladeshi entrepreneurs, when it comes to being a player in the ITS and ITES space, as for example? It was clear that Bangladesh stood to gain from the internet-driven seismic changes under way, if we could make broadband access affordable and widely available. Given its small size, high population density and flat topography, it was entirely plausible that Bangladesh could achieve at least parity with India in terms of broadband access and IT infrastructure to be the credible "India+1" destination for outsourcing opportunities, for example. Furthermore, it was well-positioned to install and tap into the virtual BanglaDISH network to spur innovation and growth in ITS and ITES with its own brand as "Bangladeshoring."

As early as 2010 many NRBs were already finding out that the number of hours they spend online every week had been rising steadily for years, and as they switched from dial-up to broadband connections their reliance on the Web expanded greatly. Indeed, the

"Open Source Software" movement was pointing the way toward breaking the technical barriers for distributed or virtual collaboration. The massive lists of ongoing open-source software development projects became available at http://sourceforge.net/softwaremap, and http://code.google.com for anyone to build upon. After the concept proved itself in software development, others started testing the open-source innovation model in a number of other areas, including medical and pharmaceutical research (one case in point was the Drugs for Neglected Diseases Initiative with additional background made available at http://www.dndi.org/).

Of course, Wikipedia was one of the best-known cases of mass collaboration back in 2010. It appears that inexpensive computing and data communication tools, together with ever more advanced software programs, allowed individuals to make and share creative works and other information goods in ways that were never possible before, and they also enabled thousands, or even millions, of discrete contributions to be assembled into commercial goods with extraordinary efficiency. Back in 2006, in his book, *The Wealth of Networks: How Social Production Transforms Markets and Freedom*, Yale law professor Yochai Benkler traced the explosion in social production to three technological advances. Firstly, the physical machinery necessary to participate in information and cultural production was almost universally distributed in the population of the advanced economies. Secondly, the primary raw materials in the information economy, unlike the physical economy, were [freely available] public goods—existing information, knowledge, and culture. Finally, the internet provided a platform for distributed, modular production that "allows many diversely motivated people to act for a wide range of reasons that, in combination, cohere into new useful information, knowledge, and cultural goods."

> "The human condition can almost be summed up by the observation that, whereas all experiences are of the past, all decisions are about the future. The image of the future, therefore, is the key to all choice-oriented behavior. The character and quality of the images of the future which prevail in a society are therefore the most important clue to its overall dynamics."
>
> – *Kenneth E. Boulding (1910-1993)*

In addition, Mr. Benkler offered two useful dimensions for measuring social collaboration efforts: modularity and granularity. By modularity, he meant "a property of a project that describes the extent to which it can be broken down into smaller components, or modules, that can be independently produced before they are assembled into a whole." By granularity, he meant "the size of the modules, in terms of the time and effort that an individual must invest in producing them."

Mr. Benkler's insight was that "the number of people who can, in principle, participate in a project is therefore inversely related to the size of the smallest scale contribution necessary to produce a usable module. The granularity of the modules therefore sets the smallest possible individual investment necessary to participate in a project. If this investment is sufficiently low, then incentives for producing that component of a modular project can be of trivial magnitude. Most importantly for our purposes of understanding the rising role of nonmarket production, the time can be drawn from the excess time we normally dedicate to having fun and participating in social interactions.

To illustrate this effect of granularity, he contrasted Wikipedia with its simple entries and editing and bounded topics with the far-less successful Wikibooks, which has much larger granularity. Creators of social collaboration sites were advised to keep granularity small in order to encourage broader contributions, and if the nature of the site is complex, to increase the number of its modules. Of course, none of this guarantees the magic or timing that also lie behind the most successful sites!

Benkler estimated that the current crop of one billion people living in affluent countries have between two billion and six billion spare hours, every day! He conjectured that if a small fraction of this creative capacity could be harnessed to produce high-quality information-based goods, the output of these voluntary efforts would dwarf the output of today's knowledge-intensive industries in 2006. All it takes, he added, is the desire to create and the tools to collaborate, both of which are increasingly in abundance. Now imagine the productive capacity of billions of people self-selecting for tasks with little regard for organizational, national, cultural, or disciplinary boundaries. As a result the age of self-organization for "peer production" is born!

It has been estimated that in total a little more than one thousand serious contributors worked on the GNU/Linux kernel, and up to twenty thousand made their contributions to the overall operating system during the first decade of the twenty-first century. However, hundreds of thousands of programmers have made contributions to other Open Source Software projects, many times more than any individual firm—even as big as Microsoft—could muster.

Yet it's important to realize that the age of networked intelligence is not simply about the networking of technology, but the networking of humans through technology. It's not an age of smart machines, but of humans who, through networks, can combine their intelligence, knowledge, and creativity for breakthroughs in the creation of wealth and social development. It's an age of vast new promise and unimaginable opportunity.

Lets take into account scientific research. In the past, scientists would work with a powerful supercomputer to, say, simulate mechanisms of a biological cell membrane as a way to understand the structure of biological molecules. But as networking permeated the planet, computers everywhere could be marshaled concurrently to attack the problem. Rather than a single expensive computer supporting a single group of scientists, a global network of computers could be internetworked to support distributed teams of scientists. Again, the network as the computer is almost infinitely more powerful than a single machine. One such example is the SETI@home project, which proved the viability and practicality of the "distributed grid computing" concept since 1999, and did useful scientific work by supporting the mission of SETI (Search for Extraterrestrial Intelligence) by analyzing searches for possible evidence of radio transmissions from extraterrestrial intelligence using observational data from the Arecibo radio telescope. The data were digitized, stored and sent to the SETI@home facility, and then parsed into small chunks in frequency and time, and analyzed, using software, to search for any signals—that is, variations which cannot be ascribed to noise, and contain information. The crux of SETI@home was to have each chunk of data, from the millions of chunks, analyzed off-site by home computers, and then have the software results reported back. Thus what appeared an onerous problem in data analysis was reduced to a reasonable one by aid from a large, internet-based community. This project proved to the scientific community that distributed computing projects using internet-connected computers could succeed as a viable analysis tool, and even beat the largest supercomputers.

The good news is that the analogous concept of "mass collaboration" has been proven in several other areas as well. For example, the story of Goldcorp, a Canadian gold-mining company offers some intriguing clues to how the mass collaboration model has been working since 2000. When the company's in-house geologists failed to identify enough gold veins from 52 years worth of geological data from its Red Lake mine, the CEO decided to open up the exploration process in the same way Linus Torvalds "Open Sourced" Linux. He saw this as an opportunity to harness some of the best minds in the industry. To this end, the "Goldcorp Challenge" was launched in March 2000 with a total of US $575,000 in prize money available to participants with the best methods and estimates of gold veins. News of the contest spread quickly around the internet, as more than one thousand virtual prospectors from fifty countries got busy crunching some four hundred megabytes worth of data covering about a 55,000-acre mining property. Not only did the contest yield copious quantities of gold from 110 identified targets (of which 50 percent had not been previously identified by Goldcorp), this open source approach to exploration catapulted this underperforming US $100-million company into a US $38-billion juggernaut (in terms of market capitalization as of March 2011) while transforming a backward mining site in Northern Ontario into one of the most innovative and profitable properties in the industry.

As Professor Vijay Govindarajan (VG) from the Tuck School of Business makes clear in his recent *Harvard Business Review* piece coauthored with Jeff Immelt, CEO of GE, GE and other large industrial players based in developed countries grew for decades by making performance-rich products at home and then distributing them with some adaptations based on local conditions and needs. That process is what's termed "glocalization"—a strategy, they note, that is "so dominant today because it has delivered." They continue: "Largely because of glocalization, GE's revenues outside the United States soared from US $4.8 billion, or 19 percent of total revenues, in 1980 to US $97 billion, or more than half of the total, in 2008." However, as VG explains, despite past and current successes, companies such as GE are now doing an about-face since the strategy is only skimming the surface of potential emerging market growth.

The "disruption" that is at the center of their article can strain companies because reverse innovation requires a decentralized, local-market focus that fundamentally clashes with the centralized, product-focused structure that multinationals have evolved for glocalization. For example, GE's new handheld electrocardiogram (ECG) developed for India sells for around US $1,000 and the portable, PC-based ultrasound that was designed for China sells for as little as US $15,000. The authors note that with these kinds of products, companies like GE are "establishing lower price points, and even using the innovations to cannibalize higher-margin products in rich countries"—which is "antithetical to the glocalization model."

When it came to ultrasound technology, GE found that "in wealthy countries, performance mattered the most, followed by features; in China, price mattered most, followed by portability and ease of use." As a result, a new portable technology was developed for that market—and it's now being marketed in the US. GE's China team succeeded, in part, because it gave its local team unprecedented autonomy to develop the technology. GE has since set up more than a dozen similar operations in an effort to expand beyond the premium segments in developing countries and to preempt local companies from disrupting GE's sales, in both developed and emerging markets.

GE didn't really have a choice in embarking on the new business model. Socalled emerging giants in local markets had the technical know-how, low-cost strategies, and a deep understanding of local needs allowed them to create market-specific technologies that they could then use "to disrupt GE in rich countries" if no action was taken. However, companies pursuing reverse innovation needed a different organizational architecture if they were going to successfully shift power to where the growth was and build new products from the ground up.

6.11 Cognitive surplus put to productive use over the internet

One little-known factoid about the 2nd half of the 20th century is that after the Second World War, the developed economies of the world forced onto an enormous number of its citizens the requirement to manage something they had never had to manage before—free time. Clay Sharky, an internet expert, anointed this free time with a new moniker as "cognitive surplus."

It turns out that Americans spend about 100 million hours every weekend, just watching the ads on TV. This is a pretty big surplus. If we take Wikipedia (vintage 2008) as a kind of unit, all of Wikipedia, the whole project—every page, every edit, every talk page, every line of code, in every language that Wikipedia exist—that represents a total of about 100 million hours of human thought.

The interesting thing about a surplus like that is that society doesn't know what to do with it at first. If people knew what to do with a surplus with reference to the existing social institutions, then it wouldn't be a surplus, almost by definition. It's precisely when no one has any idea how to deploy something that people have to start experimenting with it, in order for the surplus to get integrated, and the course of that integration can transform society. This is exactly what began to happen since 2000 or thereabout as people began asking themselves, "If we carve out a little bit of the cognitive surplus and deploy it here, could we make a good thing happen?" Increasingly the answer turned positive. The results were contributions to YouTube, Wikipedia, and Galaxy Zoo, among many other such platforms for mass collaboration online.

The sobering thought is that for the first time in the history of mankind it became possible by 2021, at least in principle, to deploy the thinking power of the human race in its entirety for the benefit of all. Imagine several billion brains being logged into BanglaDISH, with lots of mirror sites located all over the world, sharing and building on new ideas from one another. It became clear that the scale and scope of innovation can be massively magnified—only if we knew how to harness the power of massively parallel human brains working together on projects people are deeply passionate about. The simple truth is that the 7.7 billion people alive in 2021 have 7.7 billion years at their disposal every single year, which is cumulatively more than the age of our Mother Earth (estimated to be only 4.5 billions years). In other words, every single year we can bring more thinking power to bear than Mother Earth could in her entire lifetime! Even if we could tap into a small fraction of the total human creativity, that would be thousands, if not millions, of years—equivalent to many lifetimes of thinking capacity of a single individual.

6.12 Internet access as a legal right for everyone in Bangladesh

By 2021 broadband access has moved from being just an economic privilege for those who can afford it to a legal right for all worldwide in the near future. As a matter of fact, the Finnish Ministry of Transport and Communications took the lead in 2009 by pushing through a law requiring telecom companies to offer speeds of at least 1 megabit per second (Mbps) to all of the country's 5.3 million citizens.

While 96% of Finland's population was already online in 2009, the ministry believed that the mandate would improve access in rural areas. Finland thus became the first country in the world to declare broadband internet access a legal right. "We think it's something you cannot live without in modern society. Like banking services or water or electricity, you need an internet connection," said the Finnish ministry.

France's highest court first declared such access a human right in 2009. But Finland went a step further by legally mandating speed. The Finnish government committed to universal access in 2008, and this was just the first step in its plan to bump the requirement to a whopping 100 megabits per second (Mbps) by 2015.

It was a view shared by the United Nations, which was making a big push to deem internet access a human right. Bangladesh took the lead in Asia with an audacious goal of ensuring access to the internet for every Bangladeshi by 2021.

Aren't you truly proud to be a Bangladeshi in 2021? So what's stopping you from realizing these dreams of a Digital Bangladesh for all? In the next chapter, we ask you to get reset with a new mindset about what "going digital" should mean for you. That means tailoring a Digital Bangladesh that suits you just right.

Chapter 7

Let's Get Reset and Go Digital!

"A journey of a thousand miles begins with a single step."
–Lao Tzu (551-479 BC)

There are two takeaways from this chapter:

How can we create our own journey as individual Digital Bangladeshis? The good news is that new economic thinking offers some guidance on how to take the road less traveled by way of creating our own economy that may defy such crude measures of economic prosperity as per capita GDP and the like.

What if you could create your own niche in the digital economy and steer clear of the economic rat race to the finish line? Yes, you can, if you can think like Warren Buffett, the world's 3rd richest man in 2011.

Throughout this book, we've made use of several overarching metaphors to make the case for faster digital development in Bangladesh. For example, we've started with acknowledging Bangladesh's marathon-like race toward becoming a middle-income country by 2021. To this end, we've introduced the concepts of roadmaps and bridges to help us leapfrog toward a renewed nation as Digital Bangladesh. We invite you to keep us posted on how things are moving on your own personal as well as our national fronts toward fulfilling the visions of Digital Bangladesh by posting any and all initiatives and accomplishments—no matter how large or small—at www.goingdigitalbook.com

However, those who are expecting quick payoffs in terms of immediate GDP growth from investments in digital infrastructure in Bangladesh are probably setting themselves up for disappointment. That's because too often we confuse ends with means. Much like the financial sector, the ICT sector is a means to a more productive economy, not an end in itself. At another level, our economy is supposed to increase our well-being. Thus it, too, is a means and not an end in itself.

7.1 How to keep going and not stop short of the finish line

Our concern as it relates to the ongoing digital journey in Bangladesh is that many projects will get started and then be quickly abandoned because the sponsors become disillusioned from the poor progress or inadequate performance of haphazardly designed prototypes. Too often, inexperienced investors/sponsors will stop short only yards away from the finish line, especially if the finish line is defined too narrowly, say in terms of short-term GDP growth alone.

Those who succeed will take a different approach. They will start with a project with maybe slightly better than a 50% chance of success—broadly defined—and then keep at it until it delivers on 100% of its potential. The name of the game here is to make the necessary commitment to endure the many steps of incrementally refining our approach through successive "crawls and walks" until we can run like pros toward the finish line.

In the spirit of full disclosure, we the authors who happen to be engineers and applied scientists by schooling and professional orientation would like to admit to our bias for action over introspection. Here's a joke to make our point: An engineer, a geologist and an economist stranded on a desert island find a can of food. Ravenously hungry, the engineer proposes to smash it open with a rock. The geologist calmly suggests that natural forces, e.g., rusting of the metal can, will eventually do the job. Enthusiastically offering to break the deadlock, the economist says, "Let's assume we have a can opener..."

> "An invasion of armies can be resisted, but not an idea whose time has come."
> – Victor Hugo (1802-1885)

Alright, the joke is at the expense of the economists amongst our readers, but the point is that flawed assumptions lead to flawed decisions and actions, which we can no longer afford. The fact that millions of people in Bangladesh are bearing the brunt of these flawed assumptions as they struggle to eke out a subsistence living is evidence that there is something wrong with the assumptions behind traditional economic development.

What if GDP is a flawed metric to begin with? As it happens, several alternative economic performance indicators have been proposed, e.g., the UN's Human Development Index (HDI) that combines GDP with social indicators with an emphasis on life expectancy, adult literacy, and school enrollment; the Chinese government's Green GDP (GGDP) that attempts to correct GDP by monetizing (or internalizing, as opposed to externalizing, in economics lingo) environmental factors; and Genuine Progress Indicator (GPI), proposed by Redefining Progress, a non-profit think tank, that tries to correct GDP by monetizing both environmental and social factors.

To their credit, however, economists are increasingly coming to the conclusion that flawed or biased statistics may lead us to make incorrect inferences or conclusions. In particular, metrics that seem out of sync with individual citizens' perceptions are problematic. For example, if the country's GDP per capita is increasing, but most people feel they are worse off, they may worry that governments are manipulating the statistics, in the hope that by telling them that they are better off, they will feel better off.

In a recent 2009 report by the Commission on the Measurement of Economic Performance and Social Progress, Nobel Laureate Joseph Stiglitz almost states the obvious in saying that in our increasingly performance-oriented society, metrics matter. What we measure affects what we do. If we have the wrong metrics, we will strive for the wrong things. In the quest to increase GDP, for example, we may end up with a society in which citizens are worse off. As economists attempt to draw inferences about the desirability of policies by making comparisons over time or between countries, there is a risk of biased, distorted, and flawed inferences if the metrics employed are incorrect.

> "Millions who long for immortality do not know what to do with themselves on a rainy Sunday afternoon."
> – Susan Ertz (1894-1985)

Mr. Stiglitz concedes that the purposes of our statistical systems are multiple, and a metric that is designed for one purpose—meaning market activity—may be ill-suited for another. On this count, GDP provides neither a measure of income of households nor a measure of well-being.

Many of the problems of GDP statistics are well known to economists, especially given the evolving income structure and changing profiles of the economic activity in our society. For example, if there is increasing inequality, there may be an increasing disparity between average income and median income (the income of the representative citizen), and one may be increasing while the other is declining.

In addition, globalization itself has meant that the difference between the well-being of the citizens within a country may differ markedly from the output produced within a country. When problems of globalization and environmental and resource sustainability are combined, GDP metrics may be especially misleading. For example, a developing country that sells a polluting coal mining concession with low royalties and inadequate environmental regulation may see GDP increase but well-being decrease. There are concerns too that a focus on the material aspects of GDP may be especially inappropriate as the world faces the crisis of climate change. Should we "punish" or downgrade a country—in terms of, let's say, its GDP performance—if it decides to take some of the fruits of the increase in productivity from the advancement of knowledge in the form of leisure, rather than just consuming more and more goods? This is a question each of us can answer on behalf of ourselves individually as we personalize our digital journeys.

7.2 Always play fair and square

Another important sportsmanlike quality is ensuring everyone gets a fair chance to participate in the digital journey. How can we achieve this? Many years ago Nobel Laureate Kenneth Arrow proposed a brilliant solution by twisting the traditional thinking about competitive market efficiency on its head. This solution was inspired by a famous thought experiment—dubbed "original position behind the veil of ignorance"—designed by John Rawls, a leading American moral and political philosopher, to resolve the paradox or tension between the unerring efficiency of the free market and the moral imperative that some kind of fairness should prevail. In this Rawlsian theory of social justice, we are asked to imagine that societal roles and positions were completely re-fashioned and redistributed, and that from behind our pre-birth veil of ignorance we do not know what role we will be assigned upon birth. According to this theory, only then can we truly consider the

> "Life would be infinitely happier if we could only be born at the age of eighty and gradually approach eighteen."
> – Mark Twain (1835-1910)

morality of an issue. For example, the pre-Civil War whites in the southern United States did indeed condone slavery, but they most likely would not have done so had there been a re-fashioning of society so that they would not know if they would be the ones enslaved.

An important feature of this thought experiment is that you don't get to keep any aspects of your current role, position or privilege, including even those aspects that are an integral part of your self. As John Rawls put this himself, "No one knows his place in society, his class position or social status; nor does he know his fortune in the distribution of natural assets and abilities, his intelligence and strength, and the like." For example, in the imaginary society, you might or might not be intelligent, rich, or born into a preferred class. Since you may occupy any position in the society once the veil is lifted, this theory encourages thinking about society from the perspective of all members.

> "It is a paradoxical but profoundly true and important principle of life that the most likely way to reach a goal is to be aiming not at that goal itself, but at some more ambitious goal beyond it."
> – Arnold Toynbee (1852-1883)

Dear reader, we never promised to provide counsel on getting rich overnight in this book. But we recognize that this is a "hot topic" for many of our readers. So let's share with you another take of the above thought experiment from the world's 3rd richest man in Warren Buffett. Here's his version dubbed "the luck of the draw":

Imagine it's 24 hours before your birth, and a genie appears to you. He tells you that you can set the rules for the world you're about to enter—economic, social, political—the whole enchilada. Sounds great, right? What's the catch?

Before you enter the world, you will pick one ball from a barrel of 6.8 billion (the number of people on the planet). That ball will determine your gender, race, nationality, natural abilities, and health—whether you are born rich or poor, sick or able-bodied, brilliant or below average, American or Bangladeshi.

This is what Buffett calls the "ovarian lottery." As he explained to a group of University of Florida students, "You're going to get one ball out of there, and that is the most important thing that's ever going to happen to you in your life."

We should be designing a society that, as Mr. Buffett says, "doesn't leave behind someone who accidentally got the wrong ball and is not well-wired for this particular system." He points out that he is designed for the American system—and he was lucky to be born into it. He can allocate capital, and he lives in a place and at a time when those skills are well rewarded. (His pal Bill Gates is quick to point out that if Buffett had been born in an earlier time, he'd be some animal's lunch because the Oracle of Omaha can't run fast or climb trees.)

When Mr. Buffett talks about this lottery, he often concludes by asking:

> "If you could put your ball back, and they took out, at random, a hundred other balls, and you had to pick one of those, would you put your ball back in? Now, of those hundred balls ... roughly five of them will be American. ... Half of them are going to be below-average intelligence, half will be above. Do you want to put your ball back? Most of you, I think, will not. ..."

As we craft our own journey as Digital Bangladeshis, this is a good perspective to keep in mind if we're tempted to bemoan our lot in this world. Many of us live better than most people, and even better than Americans from 20 years ago, who didn't have the internet, email, cell phones, iPods, and GPS devices, not to mention scores of medical and pharmaceutical advances.

Mr. Arrow proved that not only are all perfect markets efficient, all efficient outcomes can be achieved using a competitive market, by adjusting a starting position. The direct implication of Arrow's analysis is that instead of focusing on the enormous complexity of a real economy, think of a very simple 100-meter sprint. By definition, the fastest sprinter will win the race. But you could move some starting blocks forward and some starting blocks back, so that although each participant in the race was running as fast as he or she could, obeying the usual rules and objectives of sprinting, the fastest had to cover extra ground that he would end up breaking the tape at the finish line neck-and-neck with the slowest.

With due respect to Mr. Arrow and our other economist friends, we do not think this "head start theorem" is practicable. At this juncture, we side with Lily Tomlin, an American actress and comedian, who observed back in 1977, "The trouble with the rat race is that even if you win, you're still a rat." Hence the better idea is to create your own race and to run at a pace of your own toward the finish line that you've set for yourself. The more important point is to start today and be there first! And this is the reason we have all along been deliberate in steering clear of a "rat race" mentality in this book.

7.3 Dare to care for what constitutes your digital legacy

Whether it's text messaging via the nearly ubiquitous mobile phone, microblogging on Twitter or making friends on Facebook, we are creating our own races by breaking down our consumption and production of information goods into ever-smaller tidbits, ordering and reordering them in our minds and external digital devices to meet our very own specific needs. For example, we

> "I wish to live as to derive my inspiration from the commonest of events, so that what my senses may perceive, my daily walk, the conversation with my neighbors, may inspire me and I may dream of no heaven but that which lies about me."
>
> – Henry David Thoreau (1817-1862)

buy single songs on iTunes and arrange them on playlists, instead of albums prearranged by commercial producers and artists. In other words, we can now more than ever shape our lives to match our deepest satisfactions, and in turn, make profoundly valuable contributions to those around us, be they next-door neighbors or friends from half way around the world. This is indeed the best of times to create our personalized economic race and live smarter, happier, fuller lives in the process.

Perhaps one extreme example of creating your own race is the MyLifeBits project sponsored by Microsoft. Designed to allow people to record everything they see and hear—and even things they cannot sense—and to store all these data in a personal digital archive, the project will try to collect a lifetime of storage on and about its first "experimental subject" in Gordon Bell, a luminary computer scientist. Since 1998, the project has attempted to record all of Bell's communications with other people and machines, as well as the images he sees, the sounds he hears and the Web sites he visits—storing everything in a personal digital archive that is both searchable and secure.

Bell's personal digital archive thus far has captured a lifetime's worth of articles, books, cards, CDs, letters, memos, papers, photos, pictures, presentations, home movies, videotaped lectures, and voice recordings and he has stored them digitally. He is now paperless, and is beginning to capture phone calls, IM transcripts, television viewings, and radio listenings. Equipped with an automatic camera and an arm-strap that logs his bio-metrics, this experiment and the software system created to support it can now put anyone at the center of a movement studying the creation and enjoyment of their very personal e-trails.

Well, Mr. Bell got started with his MyLifeBits project back in 1998. What about your next project in advancing the cause of your digital journey? When are you going to blaze your very own e-trails? It's your call now.

Maybe you'll choose to leave some snippets of your path-breaking e-trails by dropping us a note or two culled from your very own digital journey at www.goingdigitalbook.com

Bon voyage, dear reader !

Appendix

Additional Background Information

The history of the current Digital Bangladesh concept can be traced to a simple clause from the Bangladesh Awami League (AL) 2008 election manifesto

AL's "Vision 2021" statement (clause V under item #10 on Human Resource Development) articulates the important roles information and communication technology (ICT) will play toward accelerating the economic development of Bangladesh, which later became known as the visions of "Digital Bangladesh": *The potentials of the ICT sector will be realized. Software industry and IT services will be developed by providing all possible assistance to talented young people and interested entrepreneurs. This measure will increase export and promote employment opportunities. Our vision is to make Bangladesh digital in 2021. IT education will be made compulsory at secondary level by 2013 and at primary level by 2021. The task force on ICT that was established during the Awami League rule but rendered ineffective by the BNP-Jamat Alliance will be reactivated. High-tech park, software technology park, ICT incubator and computer villages will be set up at suitable locations in the country.*

Source: http://www.albd.org/autoalbd/index.php?option=com_content&task= view&id= 367&Itemid=1

Bibliography

For online access to additional archived background materials and the latest news and updates pertaining to this book, please visit us at http://www.goingdigitalbook.com

——— Access to Information (A2I) Program, Prime Minister's Office, *Strategic Priorities of Digital Bangladesh* (October 2010 Draft), accessible at http://www.digitalbangladesh.gov.bd/blog.php?ID=181

——— *A Charter for Change: Election Manifesto of Bangladesh Awami League-2008*, accessible at http://www.albd.org/autoalbd/index.php?option=com_content&task=view&id=367&Itemid=1

——— GoogleBooks online, sample "limited preview" sections of the many books listed in this bibliography are accessible at http://books.google.com

——— *The Economist* magazine, full content available online through subscription and registration; limited content available for free at http://www.economist.com/index.html

——— The World Bank, *Information and Communications for Development: Global Trends and Policies*, 2006

——— The World Bank, *Bangladesh: Strategy for Sustained Growth* (Bangladesh Development Series, Poverty Reduction and Economic Management Unit, The World Bank Office, Dhaka, 2007)

——— The World Bank, *Information and Communications for Development: Extending Reach and Increasing Impact*, 2009

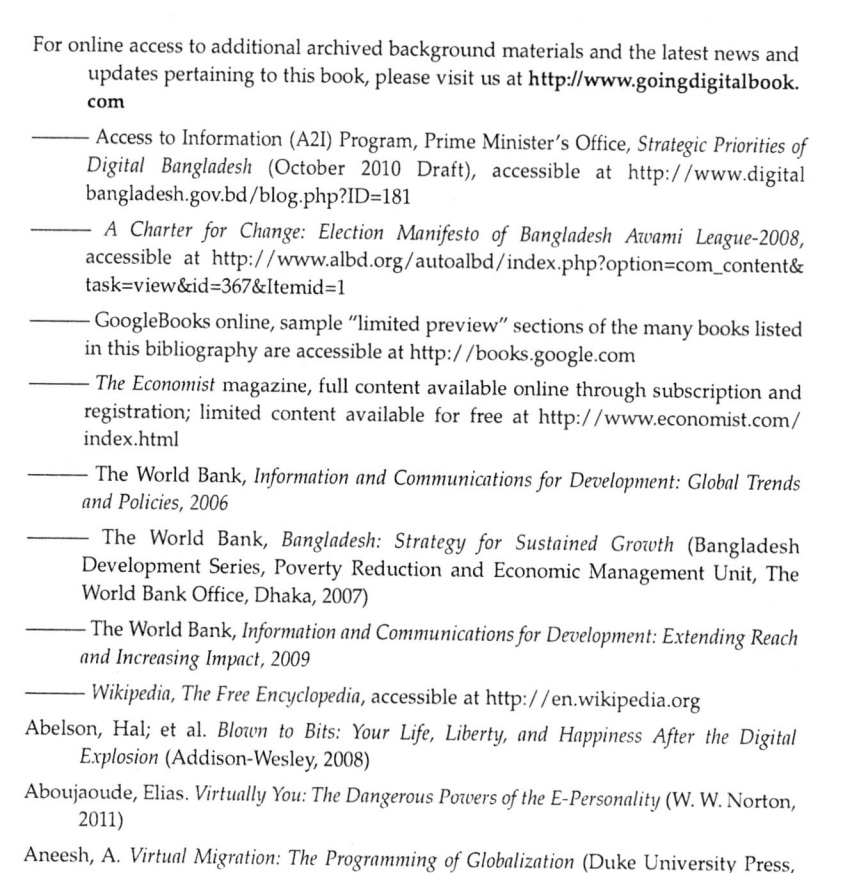

——— *Wikipedia, The Free Encyclopedia*, accessible at http://en.wikipedia.org

Abelson, Hal; et al. *Blown to Bits: Your Life, Liberty, and Happiness After the Digital Explosion* (Addison-Wesley, 2008)

Aboujaoude, Elias. *Virtually You: The Dangerous Powers of the E-Personality* (W. W. Norton, 2011)

Aneesh, A. *Virtual Migration: The Programming of Globalization* (Duke University Press, 2006)

Auletta, Ken. *Googled: The End of the World as We Know It* (Penguin Press, 2009)

Barabasi, Albert-Laszlo. *Linked: How Everything Is Connected to Everything Else and What It Means for Business, Science, and Everyday Life* (Penguin, 2003)

Barnes, Peter. *Capitalism 3.0: A Guide to Reclaiming the Commons* (Berrett-Koehler Publishers, 2006)

Bartle, Richard. *Designing Virtual Worlds* (New Riders Press, 2003)

Basalla, George. *The Evolution of Technology* (Cambridge University Press, 1988)

Beattie, Alan. *False Economy: A Surprising Economic History of the World* (Riverhead Books, 2009)

Beniger, James R. *The Control Revolution: Technological and Economic Origins of the Information Society* (Harvard University Press, 1986)

Benkler, Yochai. *The Wealth of Networks: How Social Production Transforms Markets and Freedom* (Yale University Press, 2007), also available online at http://www.benkler.org

Berlinski, David. *The Advent of the Algorithm: The Idea That Rules the World* (Harcourt, 2000)

Blaxill, Mark; and Ralph Eckardt. *The Invisible Edge: Taking Your Strategy to the Next Level Using Intellectual Property* (Portfolio, 2009)

Boellstorff, Tom. *Coming of Age in Second Life: An Anthropologist Explores the Virtual Human* (Princeton University Press, 2008)

Boer, F. Peter. *The Real Options Solution: Finding Total Value in a High-Risk World* (Wiley Finance, 2002)

Boer, F. Peter. *Technology Valuation Solutions* (Wiley Finance, 2004)

Brand, Stewart (editor). *Whole Earth Catalog: Access to Tools* (Portola Institute, 1969)

Brand, Stewart. *Whole Earth Discipline: An Ecopragmatist Manifesto* (Viking Press, 2009)

Brooks, David. *The Social Animal: The Hidden Sources of Love, Character, and Achievement* (Random House, 2011)

Brown, John Seely; and Paul Duguid. *The Social Life of Information* (Harvard Business School Press, 2000)

Burrus, Daniel. *Flash Foresight: How to See the Invisible and Do the Impossible* (Harper Business, 2011)

Carr, Nicholas. *The Big Switch: Rewiring the World, from Edison to Google* (W. W. Norton, 2009)

Chaplin, Heather; and Aaron Ruby. *Smartbomb: The Quest for Art, Entertainment, and Big Bucks in the Videogame Revolution* (Algonquin Books, 2005)

Chanda, Nayan. *Bound Together: How Traders, Preachers, Adventurers, and Warriors Shaped Civilization* (Penguin, 2007)

Christensen, Clayton M., et al. *Seeing What's Next: Using Theories of Innovation to Predict Industry Change* (Harvard Business School Press, 2004)

Cowen, Tyler. *Creative Destruction: How Globalization is Changing the World's Cultures* (Princeton University Press, 2002)

Cairncross, Frances. *The Death of Distance: How the Communications Revolution Is Changing Our Lives* (Harvard Business School Press, 2001)

Crundwell, F. K. *Finance for Engineers: Evaluation and Funding of Capital Projects* (Springer, 2008)

Davis, Philip J.; and David Park, editors. *No Way: The Nature of the Impossible* (W. H. Freeman, 1988)

Davis, Stan; and Christopher Meyer. *Blur: The Speed of Change in the Connected Economy* (Addison-Wesley, 1998)

Dertouzos, Michael. *What Will Be: How the New World of Information Will Change Our Lives* (HarperCollins, 1997)

De Soto, Hernando. *The Mystery of Capital: Why Capitalism Triumphs in the West and Fails Everywhere Else* (Basic Books, 2000)

Dossani, Rafiq. *India Arriving: How This Economic Powerhouse Is Redefining Global Business* (Amacom, 2008)

Downey, Gary Lee. *The Machine in Me: An Anthropologist Sits Among Software Engineers* (Routledge Press, 1998)

Drucker, Peter F. *Innovation and Entrepreneurship: Practice and Principles* (Harper and Row, 1985)

Dyson, Esther. *Release 2.0: A Design for Living in the Digital Age* (Broadway Books, 1997)

Eskelsen, Grant, et al. *The Digital Economy Fact Book, 10th Edition, 2008-2009* (The Progress & Freedom Foundation, 2009)

Florida, Richard. *The Rise of the Creative Class: And How It's Transforming Work, Leisure, Community and Everyday Life* (Basic Books, 2002)

Ford, Martin. *The Lights in the Tunnel: Automation, Accelerating Technology, and the Economy of the Future* (Create Space, 2009)

Friedman, Thomas L. *The Lexus and the Olive Tree: Understanding Globalization* (Farrar, Straus and Giroux, 1999)

Friedman, Thomas L. *The World Is Flat: A Brief History of the Twenty-First Century* (Farrar, Straus and Giroux, 2005)

Friedman, Thomas L. *Hot, Flat, and Crowded: Why We Need a Green Revolution – and How It Can Renew America* (Farrar, Straus and Giroux, 2006)

Gates, Bill. *The Road Ahead* (Pearson ESL, 1999)

Gilder, George. *Microcosm: The Quantum Revolution in Economics and Technology* (Simon and Schuster, 1989)

Gleick, James. *Chaos: Making a New Science* (Viking Penguin, 1987)

Gleick, James. *The Information: A History, a Theory, a Flood* (Pantheon Press, 2011)

Hammond, Allen L., et al. *The Next 4 Billion: Market Size and Business Strategy at the Base of the Pyramid* (World Resources Institute, and International Finance Corporation, 2007)

Heller, Michael. *Gridlock Economy: How Too Much Ownership Wrecks Markets, Stops Innovation, and Costs Lives* (Basic Books, 2008)

Hobart, Michael E.; and Zachary S. Schiffman. *Information Ages: Literacy, Numeracy, and the Computer Revolution* (Johns Hopkins University Press, 1998)

Hofstadter, Douglas. *Metamagical Themas: Questing for the Essence of Mind and Pattern* (Basic Books, 1985)

Hubbard, Douglas W. *How to Measure Anything: Finding the Value of Intangibles in Business* (Wiley, 2007)

James, Geoffrey. *Business Wisdom of the Electronic Elite: 34 Winning Management Strategies from CEOs at Microsoft, Compaq, Sun, Hewlett-Packard, and Other Top Companies* (Times Business, 1996)

Jensen, Rolf. *The Dream Society: How the Coming Shift from Information to Imagination Will Transform Your Business* (McGraw-Hill, 1999)

Johnson, Steven. *Where Good Ideas Come From: The Natural History of Innovation* (Riverhead Books, 2010)

Karim, Habibullah N, *Poverty Reduction Through Information Technology* (Poverty Reduction Strategy Paper, Government of Bangladesh, 2002)

Karim, Habibullah N, *Bangladesh – at the cross-roads of information technology* (The Commonwealth Ministers Reference Book, 2006)

Karim, Habibullah N, *Catching a ride on the IT gravy train* (*The Daily Star*, 2008)

Karim, Habibullah N, *Of Software and Soft-tears* (*The Daily Star*, 2008)

Karim, Habibullah N, *The IT song and dance routine in Bangladesh* (*The Daily Star*, 2008)

Karim, Habibullah N, *Towards A Digital Bangladesh* (*The Daily Star*, 2008)

Karim, Habibullah N, *IT In Graft Battle* (*The Daily Star*, 2009)

Karim, Habibullah N, *Bangladesh IT Industry Going Global* (*The Daily Star*, 2010)

Karim, Habibullah N, *Digital Promise Unmade* (*The Daily Star*, 2011)

Kelly, Eamonn, et al. *What's Next: Exploring the New Terrain for Business* (Perseus Publishing, 2002)

Khanna, Tarun. *Billions of Entrepreneurs: How China and India are Reshaping Their Futures and Yours* (Harvard Business School Press, 2007)

Kinsley, Michael (editor). *Creative Capitalism: A Conversation with Bill Gates, Warren Buffett, and Other Economic Leaders* (Simon and Schuster, 2008)

Koch, Richard. *The Natural Laws of Business: How to Harness the Power of Evolution, Physics, and Economics to Achieve Business Success* (Currency, 2001)

Kurzweil, Raymond. *The Age of Intelligent Machines* (MIT Press, 1990)

Kurzweil, Raymond. *The Age of Spiritual Machines: When Computers Exceed Human Intelligence* (Viking Penguin, 1999)

Kurzweil, Raymond. The *Singularity Is Near: When Humans Transcend Biology* (Penguin Books, 2005)

Lammers, Susan. *Programmers at Work: Interviews* (Microsoft Press, 1986)

Leebaert, Derek (editor). *Technology 2001: The Future of Computing and Communications* (MIT Press, 1991)

Ling, Rich. *The Mobile Connection: The Cell Phone's Impact on Society* (Elsevier, 2004)

Mahajan, Vijay; and Kamini Banga. *The 86% Solution: How to Succeed in the Biggest Market Opportunity of the 21st Century* (Wharton School Publishing, 2006)

Malaby, Thomas. *Making Virtual Worlds: Linden Lab and Second Life* (Cornell University Press, 2009)

Malone, Michael S. *The Future Arrived Yesterday: The Rise of the Protean Corporation and What It Means for You* (Crown Business, 2009)

Marber, Peter. *From Third World to World Class: The Future of Emerging Markets in the Global Economy* (Basic Books, 1999)

Marber, Peter. *Seeing the Elephant: Understanding Globalization from Trunk to Tail* (Wiley, 2009)

Martin, James. *The Meaning of the 21st Century: A Vital Blueprint for Ensuring Our Future* (Riverhead Books, 2006)

McKenzie, Richard B. *Digital Economics: How Information Technology Has Transformed Business Thinking* (Praeger, 2003)

McGrath, Rita Gunther; and Ian MacMillan. *The Entrepreneurial Mindset: Strategies for Continuously Creating Opportunity in an Age of Uncertainty* (Harvard Business School Press, 2000)

McMillan, John. *Reinventing the Bazaar: A Natural History of Markets* (W.W. Norton, 2002)

Menzel, Peter; and Faith D'Aluisio. *Robo sapiens: Evolution of a New Species* (MIT Press, 2001)

Micklethwait, John; and Adrian Wooldridge. *A Future Perfect: The Challenge and Hidden Promise of Globalization* (Crown Business, 2000)

Minsky, Marvin. *The Society of Mind* (Simon and Schuster, 1985)

Mirchandani, Vinnie. *The New Polymath: Profiles in Compound-Technology Innovations* (John Wiley & Sons, 2010)

Mohammad, Mahathir. *A New Deal for Asia* (Pelanduk Publications, 1999)

Moore, James F. *The Death of Competition: Leadership & Strategy in the Age of the Business Ecosystems* (HarperBusiness, 1996)

Morgan, Gareth. *Imaginization: The Art of Creative Management* (Sage Publications, 1993)

Nasr, Vali. *Forces of Fortune: The Rise of the New Muslim Middle Class and What It Will Mean for Our World* (Free Press, 2009)

Nilekani, Nandan. *Imagining India: The Idea of a Renewed Nation* (Penguin Press, 2009)

Pacek, Nenad; and Daniel Thorniley. *Emerging Markets: Lessons for Business Success and the Outlook for Different Markets* (The Economist, 2004)

Palfrey, John; and Urs Gasser. *Born Digital: Understanding the First Generation of Digital Natives* (Basic Books, 2008)

Penrose, Roger. *The Emperor's New Mind: Concerning Computers, Minds, and the Laws of Physics* (Oxford University Press, 1989)

Petzinger, Thomas. *The New Pioneers: The Men and Women Who are Transforming the Workplace and Marketplace* (Simon and Schuster, 1999)

Pickover, Clifford. *Computers and the Imagination: Visual Adventures Beyond the Edge* (St. Martin's Press, 1991)

Popcorn, Faith, and Adam Hanft. *Dictionary of the Future: The Words, Terms, and Trends that Define the Way We'll Live, Work and Talk* (Hyperion, 2001)

Porter, Michael. *The Competitive Advantage of Nations* (The Free Press, 1990)

Prahalad, C.K. *The Fortune at the Bottom of the Pyramid: Eradicating Poverty through Profits, and Enabling Dignity and Choice through Markets* (Wharton School Publishing, 2006)

Ray, Paul, et al. *The Cultural Creatives: How 50 Million People are Changing the World* (Harmony Books, 2000)

Reeves, Byron, and J. Leighton Read. *Total Engagement: Using Games and Virtual Worlds to Change the Way People Work and Businesses Compete* (Harvard Business School Press, 2009)

Rifkin, Jeremy. *The Age of Access: The New Culture of Hypercapitalism Where All of Life Is a Paid-for Experience* (Penguin Putnam, 2000)

Rohwer, Jim. *Asia Rising: Why America Will Prosper as Asia's Economies Boom* (Simon and Schuster, 1995)

Robin, Harry. *The Scientific Image: From Cave to Computer* (W.H. Freeman, 1993)

Sachs, Jeffrey D. *Common Wealth: Economics for a Crowded Planet* (Penguin Press, 2008)

Sahlman, William A., et al (editors), *The Entrepreneurial Venture* (Harvard Business School Press, 1999)

Samdani, Gulam (editorial). "Managing Knowledge," *Chemical Engineering*, April 1992, p. 5 (McGraw-Hill)

Samdani, Gulam (with Ken Fouhy). "Smart Software: Expert Systems Are Now Sharp-witted Assistants to CPI Engineers," *Chemical Engineering*, April 1992, pp. 30-33 (McGraw-Hill)

Samdani, Gulam. "Turning the Trickle of Private Equity 'Smart Money' into a Torrent," *Dinar Standard*, September 10, 2005 (republished with permission from *The Executive Times*), accessible at http://www.dinarstandard.com/current/PrivateEquity010905.htm

Samdani, Gulam. "Six Faces of Entrepreneurial Finance," *Dinar Standard*, October 20, 2005 (republished with permission from *The Executive Times*), accessible at http://www.dinarstandard.com/finance/privateequityfaces1005.htm

Samdani, Gulam. *Beyond Bonsai: Catalyzing a Transformation of the Economic Pyramid into a Diamond in Bangladesh*—an essay submitted for consideration for the Quadir Prize, an annual global contest to strengthen Bangladesh (Hosted by the Center for International Development at Harvard University, 2007), accessible at www.goingdigitalbook.com

Schoemaker, Paul J. H., and Joyce A. Schoemaker. *Chips, Clones, and Living Beyond 100: How Far Will the Biosciences Take Us?* (FT Press, 2009)

Schrage, Michael. *Serious Play: How the World's Best Companies Simulate to Innovate* (Harvard Business School Press, 2000)

Shurkin, Joel. *Engines of the Mind: The Evolution of the Computer from Mainframes to Microprocessors* (W.W. Norton, 1996)

Simon, Herbert. *The Sciences of the Artificial* (MIT Press, 1969)

Smith, Douglas K. *On Value and Values: Managing Ourselves in a Fragmented World—Thinking Differently About We in an Age of Me* (FT Prentice Hall, 2004)

Smith, Janet Kiholm, et al. *Entrepreneurial Finance* (John Wiley & Sons, 2004)

Smith, Phil, and Eric Thurman. *A Billion Bootstraps: Microcredit, Barefoot Banking, and the Business Solution for Ending Poverty* (McGraw-Hill, 2007)

Standage, Tom (editor). *The Future of Technology* (The Economist, 2005)

Stewart, Thomas A. *Intellectual Capital: The New Wealth of Organizations* (Currency, 1997)

Stewart, Thomas A. *The Wealth of Knowledge: Intellectual Capital and the Twenty-First Century Organization* (Currency, 2001)

Stiglitz, Joseph E., et al. *Report by the Commission on the Measurement of Economic Performance and Social Progress* (available online at http://www.stiglitz-sen-fitoussi.fr)

Strassmann, Paul A. *The Business Value of Computers* (The Information Economics Press, 1990)

Taleb, Nassim Nicholas. *The Black Swan: The Impact of the Highly Improbable* (Random House, 2007)

Tanaka, Graham. *Digital Deflation: The Productivity Revolution and How It Will Ignite the Economy* (McGraw-Hill, 2003)

Tapscott, Don. *Growing Up Digital: The Rise of the Net Generation* (McGraw-Hill, 1998)

Tapscott, Don, and Anthony D. Williams. *Wikinomics: How Mass Collaboration Changes Everything* (Portfolio, 2007)

Tapscott, Don. *Grown Up Digital: How the Net Generation is Changing Your World* (McGraw-Hill, 2009)

Tapscott, Don, and Anthony D. Williams. *Macrowikinomics: Rebooting Business and the World* (Portfolio Penguin, 2010)

Thaler, Richard H., and Cass R. Sunstein. *Nudge: Improving Decisions About Health, Wealth, and Happiness* (Yale University Press, 2008)

Thurow, Lester C. *The Future of Capitalism: How Today's Economic Forces Shape Tomorrow's World* (Penguin Books, 1996)

Toffler, Alvin, and Heidi Toffler. *Revolutionary Wealth: How It Will be Created and How It Will Change Our Lives* (Alfred A. Knopf, 2006)

Viguerie, Patrick, et al. *The Granularity of Growth: How to Identify the Sources of Growth and Drive Enduring Company Performance* (Wiley, 2008)

Warsh, David. *Knowledge and the Wealth of Nations: A Story of Economic Discovery* (W.W. Norton, 2006)

Weinberger, David. *Everything Is Miscellaneous: The Power of the New Digital Disorder* (Times Books, 2007)

Yunus, Muhammad (with Karl Weber). *Creating a World Without Poverty: Social Business and the Future of Capitalism* (Subarna, 2007)

Yunus, Muhammad (with Karl Weber). *Building Social Business: The New Kind of Capitalism that Serves Humanity's Most Pressing Needs* (Public Affairs, 2010)

Zack, Lynch. *The Neuro Revolution: How Brain Science is Changing Our World* (St. Martin's Press, 2009)

Acknowledgements

The collaboration that has produced this book extends beyond the authors to many professionals, friends and colleagues who gave generously of their time and provided guidance and insights without which this effort would not have been nearly as much fun and intellectually satisfying. We owe them an incalculable debt of gratitude.

Sultan Ahmed of Austin, Texas, took on the task of leading the efforts of designing the book's comprehensive website at www.goingdigitalbook.com. We thank him deeply for helping us take our message to the world via the web!

And to all among the "digital elite" and thought leaders in Bangladesh and beyond who shared their views and ideas with us during the research phase of this book project, we say a big THANK YOU! They include:

Mr. Mahfuz Anam, Editor, *The Daily Star*, Dhaka

Mr. Tarek Barkatullah of Bangladesh Computer Council

Dr. Jamilur Reza Choudhury, former Vice-Chancellor (CEO) of BRAC University, Bangladesh

Mr. Anir Chowdhury, Policy Adviser at A2I Project, Prime Minister's Office, Bangladesh

Mr. David Edelstein, Director of the Grameen Foundation Technology Center, USA

Dr. Omar Ishrak, President & CEO at GE Healthcare Systems, USA

Mr. Mustafa Jabbar, President, Bangladesh Computer Samity

Dr. A. Moyeen Khan, past Science and ICT Minister, Government of Bangladesh

Ms. Edith Myers, VP at Pragma Systems, USA

Mr. Yeafesh Osman, State Minister of Science & ICT, Government of Bangladesh

Mr. Mahbub Zaman, President of BASIS

Glossary of Terms

Algorithm
: A sequence of rules and instructions that describes a procedure to solve a problem and is often used for calculation, data processing, and automated reasoning. A computer program expresses one or more algorithms in a manner understandable by a computer.

Analog
: When referred to an electronic signal, it means a variable quantity that is continuously varying in time and amplitude, as opposed to varying in discrete steps (as is the case for a digital signal or quantity). Most phenomena in the natural world are analog. When we measure and give them a numeric value, we digitize them. The human brain uses both digital and analog computation.

Apps
: Also known as application software, software applications, or applications for short, they represent computer software designed to help the user perform a particular task. Typical examples are word processors, spreadsheets, media players and database applications. Since Apple's introduction of the App Store in 2008, apps became a major service category that allows users to browse and download tens of thousands of applications from the iTunes Store. Depending on the application, they are available either for free, or at a cost.

AI
: The field of research that attempts to study and design intelligent agents where an intelligent agent is a computing system that perceives its environment and takes actions that maximize its chances of success. Fields within Artificial Intelligence (AI) include knowledge-based systems, expert systems, pattern recognition, automatic learning, natural-language understanding, robotics, and others.

Big bang theory
: The prevailing cosmological theory about the early development of the Universe that stipulates a cosmic explosion, from a single point of infinite density, marked the beginning of the Universe 13.7 billions of years ago.

Bit	A contraction of the phrase "binary digit." In a binary code, one of two possible values, usually zero and one. In information theory, it's the fundamental unit of information.
Broadband	Technically speaking, broadband refers to a class of communication channels capable of supporting a wide range of frequencies, typically from audio up to video frequencies. A broadband channel can carry multiple signals by dividing the total capacity into multiple, independent bandwidth channels, where each channel operates only on a specific range of frequencies. Although various minimum bandwidths have been used in definitions of broadband, ranging from 64 kbit/s up to 2.0 Mbit/s, the US Federal Communications Commission (FCC) as of 2009 defines "Basic Broadband" as data transmission speeds exceeding 768 kilobits per second (Kbps), or 768,000 bits per second, in at least one direction: downstream (from the internet to the user's computer) or upstream (from the user's computer to the internet).
Byte	A contraction for "by eight." A group of eight bits clustered together to store one unit of information on a computer. A byte may correspond, for example, to a letter of the English alphabet.
CD-ROM	Compact disc read-only memory is a laser-read disc that contains up to a half billion bytes of information. "Read only" refers to the fact that information can be only read, but not deleted or re-recorded, on the disc.
Chip	A collection of related circuits that work together on a task or set of tasks, residing on a wafer of semiconductor material (typically silicon).
Cloud computing	Inspired by the cloud symbol that's often used to represent the internet in flow charts and diagrams, cloud computing is a general term for anything that involves delivering hosted services over the internet. These services are broadly divided into three categories: Infrastructure-as-a-Service (IaaS), Platform-as-a-Service (PaaS) and Software-as-a-Service (SaaS). A cloud can be private or public. A public cloud sells services to anyone on the internet (such as, Amazon Web Services). A private cloud is a proprietary network or a data

center that supplies hosted services to a limited number of people. Private or public, the goal of cloud computing is to provide easy, scalable access to computing resources and IT services without large upfront investments.

Infrastructure-as-a-Service provides virtual server instances with unique IP addresses and blocks of storage on demand. In the enterprise, cloud computing allows a company to pay for only as much capacity as is needed, and bring more resources online as soon as required. Because this pay-for-what-you-use model resembles the way electricity, fuel and water are consumed, it's sometimes referred to as 'utility computing'.

Platform-as-a-service in the cloud is defined as a set of software and product development tools hosted on the provider's infrastructure. Developers create applications on the provider's platform over the internet. PaaS providers may use APIs, website portals or gateway software installed on the customer's computer. Force.com, (an outgrowth of Salesforce.com) and GoogleApps are examples of PaaS.

In the software-as-a-service cloud model, the vendor supplies the hardware infrastructure, the software product and interacts with the user through a front-end portal. SaaS is a very broad market. Services can be anything from Web-based email to inventory control and database processing. Because the service provider hosts both the application and the data, the end user is free to use the service from anywhere.

Computation The process of calculating a result by use of an algorithm (e.g., a computer program) and related data. It also refers to the ability to remember and solve problems.

Computer A machine or device that implements an algorithm. A computer transforms data according to the specifications of an algorithm. A programmable computer allows the algorithm to be changed.

Computer language A set of rules and specifications for describing an algorithm or process on a computer.

Cybernetic poet A computer program that is able to create original poetry that is apparently as inspiring as that created by a human poet.

Database	The structured collection of data to enable easy storage and retrieval with an information retrieval system. A database management system (DBMS) allows easy monitoring, updating, and interacting with the database.
Debugging	The methodical process of discovering and correcting errors to reduce the number of "bugs" or defects in computer hardware and software. The first "bug" was an actual moth, discovered by Grace Murray Hopper, the first program of the Mark I computer.
Digital	Derived from the word digit or *digitus* (Latin for "finger") since fingers are used for discrete counting. The use of combinations of bits to represent data in computation. Contrasted with analog.
DVD	Digital video disc is a high-density compact disc system that uses a more focused laser than the conventional CD-ROM, with storage capacities of up to 9.4 gigabytes on a double-sided disc. A DVD typically has sufficient capacity to hold a full-length movie.
Encryption	Encoding information so that only the intended recipient can understand the message by decoding it. PGP (Pretty Good Privacy) is an example of encryption.
Evolutionary or genetic algorithm	Computer-based problem-solving systems that use computational models akin to the process of evolution shaped by some selection mechanisms as key elements in their design. Within a program, a population of simulated entities are created that undergo a process of evolution in a simulated competitive environment.
Exponential growth	Much like the compounding of interest on a principal amount, this is characterized by growth in which the size of the output increases by a fixed multiple of itself over time.
Exponential trend	Any trend that exhibits exponential growth, such as an exponential trend in population growth.
Hologram	An interference pattern, often using photographic media, that is encoded by high-power laser beams and read by means of low-power laser beams. This interference pattern can reconstruct a three-dimensional image. An important property of a hologram is that the information is distributed throughout the hologram. Cut a hologram in half, and both

halves will have the full picture, only half the resolution. Scratching a hologram has no noticeable effect on the image. Human memory is believed to be distributed in the brain in a similar way.

ICTs   Information and communication technologies designed to help users find, explore, analyze, exchange and present information. ICTs allow users to participate in a rapidly changing world in which work and other activities are increasingly transformed by access to varied and developing digital technologies. They also give users quick access to ideas and experiences from a wide range of people, communities and cultures around the world. Thus almost by definition, ICTs are a key driver of economic growth, designed to satisfy the needs and wants of a community over time. ICTs have been identified by many international development organizations as a crucial element in developing the world's poorest countries, by integrating them into the global economy and by making global markets more accessible.

Image processing   The manipulation of data representing images, or pictorial representation on a screen, composed of pixels. The use of a computer program to enhance or modify an image.

Information   An ordered sequence of data that is meaningful in a process, such as the bits in a computer program or the DNA code of an organism. Information can be contrasted with "noise," which is a random sequence and inherently unpredictable. However, information is also unpredictable in the sense that we cannot predict future information from past information. If we can fully predict future data from past data, then that future data stops being information.

Information theory   A mathematical theory concerning the difference between information and noise, and the ability of a communications channel to carry information. The landmark paper, entitled "A Mathematical Theory of Communication" by Claude Shannon in the *Bell System Technical Journal* not only introduced the concept of communication theory, but also analyzed the concept of information in 1948. The opening sentence of that paper explained the crux of the issue involved in communication: "The fundamental problem of communication is that of reproducing at one point either exactly or approximately a message selected at another point."

According to Mr. Shannon, "information" is part of a message, data set, picture, or group of sounds that is not predictable. Rolling a dice that had a 6 on each of its faces would not reveal any information, since the outcome is totally predictable. Such a view of information immediately shows a way of reducing the volume of data that need to be stored or transmitted. If this dice is rolled 100 times, you don't need to record 100 sixes. Instead, you just say 100 times 6. This, after all, was the information in the sequence, and this approach "compresses" the data. Similarly, sorting or transmitting a number like ∂ does not require you to send the infinite set of numbers down the line—they are predictable if you send the appropriate algorithm that can calculate it at the other end. Thus the numbers in ∂ are predictable once you have the algorithm.

Intelligence Perhaps best defined as "that faculty of mind by which order is perceived in a situation previously considered disordered." Also can be defined in terms of a process comprised of learning, reasoning, and the ability to manipulate symbols. The problem of defining "artificial or machine intelligence" becomes a matter of defining intelligence.

Internet A global system of interconnected computer networks that use the standard Internet Protocol Suite (TCP/IP for Transmission Control Protocol and Internet Protocol) to serve billions of users worldwide. It is a network of networks that consists of millions of private and public, academic, business, and government networks of local to global scope that are linked by a broad array of electronic and optical networking technologies. The internet carries a vast array of information resources and services, most notably the inter-linked hypertext documents of the World Wide Web (WWW) and the infrastructure to support electronic mail.

Most traditional communications media, such as telephone and television services, have been reshaped or redefined by the technologies of the internet. It has given rise to such services as Voice over Internet Protocol (VoIP) and Internet

Protocol Television (IPTV). The internet has enabled or accelerated the creation of new forms of human interactions through instant messaging, internet forums, and social networking sites.

Luddite One of a group of early-nineteenth-century English workmen who destroyed labor-saving machinery in protest. They were the first organized movement to oppose mechanized technology of the Industrial Revolution. Today, the Luddites are a symbol of opposition to technology, digital or otherwise.

Micro-processor An integrated circuit built on a single chip containing the entire central processing unit (CPU) of a computer.

MIPS Million instructions per second is a method of measuring the speed of a computer in terms of the number of millions of instructions performed by the computer in one second. An instruction is a single step in a computer program as represented in the computer's machine language.

Moore's Law First postulated by the former Intel CEO Gordon Moore in 1965, it is the prediction that the size of each transistor on an integrated circuit chip will be reduced by 50% every 24 months. The result is the exponentially growing power of integrated circuit-based computation over time.

Nano-technology A body of technology in which products and other structures are created through tightly controlled manipulation of matter on an atomic and molecular scale, which represents the quantum realm. As a result, novel quantum mechanical effects manifest themselves at this scale. "Nano" refers to a billionth of a meter, which is the width of about five carbon atoms.

Nanotubes Elongated carbon molecules that resemble long tubes and are formed of the same pentagonal patterns of carbon atoms as buckyballs. Nanotubes can perform the electronic functions of silicon-based components. Since nanotubes are extremely small, they provide very high densities of computation. Nanotubes are a likely technology to continue to provide the exponential growth of computing when Moore's law on integrated circuits runs out of steam by the year 2020. Nanotubes are also extremely strong and heat resistant, thereby permitting the creation of three-dimensional electronic circuits.

Network neutrality Also known as Net neutrality or internet neutrality, it is a principle that advocates no restrictions on content, sites, or platforms, the kinds of equipment that may be attached, and on the modes of communication allowed. Since the early 2000s advocates of net neutrality have raised concerns about the ability of broadband providers to use their last mile infrastructure to block certain internet applications and content (e.g. websites, services, and protocols), particularly those of competitors. Neutrality proponents claim that telecom companies seek to impose a tiered service model in order to control the digital pipeline and thereby remove competition, create artificial scarcity, and oblige subscribers to buy their otherwise uncompetitive services. Many believe net neutrality to be primarily important as a preservation of current freedoms. Vinton Cerf, co-inventor of the Internet Protocol, Tim Berners-Lee, creator of the World Wide Web, and many others have spoken out in favor of network neutrality.

Opponents of net neutrality characterize it as "a solution in search of a problem," arguing that broadband service providers have no plans to block content or degrade network performance. Critics of net neutrality also argue that data discrimination of some kind, particularly to guarantee quality of service, is not problematic, but is actually highly desirable.

Neural computer A computer with hardware optimized for using the neural network paradigm. A neural computer is designed to simulate a massive number of models of neurons in a human brain.

Operating system A software program that manages and provides a variety of services to application programs, including user interface facilities and management of input-output and memory devices.

Pattern recognition Recognition of patterns with the goal of identifying, classifying, or categorizing complex inputs. Examples of inputs include images such as printed characters and faces, and sounds such as spoken language.

Glossary of Terms

Personal computer A generic term for a single-user computer using a microprocessor, and including the computing hardware and software needed for an individual to work autonomously.

Pixel An abbreviation for picture element. The smallest element on a computer screen that holds information to represent a picture. Pixels contain data giving brightness and possibly color at particular points in the picture.

Program A set of computer instructions that enables a computer to perform a specific task. Programs are usually written in a high-level language, such as "C" or "FORTRAN" that can be understood by human programmers and then translated into machine language using a special program called a compiler. Machine language is a special set of codes that directly controls a computer.

RAM Memory that can be both read and written with random access of memory locations. Random access means that locations can be accessed in any order and do not need to be accessed sequentially. Random access memory (RAM) can be used as the working memory of a computer into which applications and programs can be loaded and run.

Robot A programmable device, linked to a computer, consisting of mechanical manipulators and sensors. A robot may perform a physical task normally done by human beings, possibly with greater speed, strength and/or precision.

Semi-conductor A material commonly based on silicon or germanium with a conductivity midway between that of a good conductor and an insulator. Semiconductors are used to manufacture transistors. Semiconductors rely on a phenomenon of quantum physics called tunneling.

Simulator A program that models and represents an activity or environment on a computer system. Examples include a flight simulator used to train pilots and a simulated patient to train physicians. Simulators are also used for entertainment.

Software Information and knowledge used to perform useful functions by computers and other digital devices.

Transistor A switching and/or amplifying device using semiconductors, first created in 1948 by John Bardeen, Walter Brattain, and William Shockley of Bell Labs in the US.

Tunneling	In quantum mechanics, the ability of electrons (negatively charged particles orbiting the nucleus of an atom) to exist in two places at once, in particular on both sides of a barrier. Tunneling allows some of the electrons to effectively move through the barrier and accounts for the "semi" conductor properties of a transistor.
Turing Test	A procedure proposed by Alan Turing in 1950 for determining whether or not a system (generally a computer) has achieved human-level intelligence, based on whether it can deceive a human interrogator into believing that it is human. A human "judge" interviews the (computer) system, and one or more human "foils" over terminal lines (by typing messages). Both the computer and the human foil(s) try to convince the human judge of their humanness. If the human judge is unable to distinguish the computer from the human foil(s), then the computer is considered to have demonstrated human intelligence. Turing did not specify many key details, such as the duration of the interrogation and the sophistication of the human judge and foils. Some futurists predict that computers will pass the Turing Test by the late 2020s, although the validity of the test remains a point of controversy and philosophical debate.
Virtual reality	A simulated environment in which you can immerse yourself, currently with a convincing replacement for the visual and auditory senses, and expected to be able to provide the tactile and olfactory senses by the 2020s. The key to realistic visual experience in virtual reality is that when you move your head, the scene instantly repositions itself so that you are now looking at a different region of three-dimensional scene. The intention is to simulate what happens when you turn your real head in the real world: The images captured by your retinas rapidly change. Your brain nonetheless understands that the world has remained stationary and that the image is sliding across your retinas only because your head is rotating. Currently the crude virtual reality systems require the use of special helmets to provide the visual and auditory environments. Futurists predict that by the 2020s, virtual reality will be provided by ubiquitous contact-lens systems and implanted retinal-imaging devices.

WWW World Wide Web (WWW) is a highly distributed (not centralized) communications network allowing individuals and organizations around the world to communicate with one another. Communication includes the sharing of text, images, sounds, music, video, software and other forms of digital information. The primary user interface paradigm of the Web is based on hypertext, which consists of documents (which can contain any type of data) connected by "links," which the user selects by a pointing device, such as a mouse. The Web is a system of data-and-message servers linked by high-capacity communication links that can be accessed by any computer or mobile device user with a "web browser" and internet access. Sir Tim Berners-Lee, a British engineer and computer scientist is credited with the creation of the WWW in 1989, making it so easy to use the internet that anyone with a personal computer and a telephone line could join in. This concept of "adding the Web to the Net" has led to one of the most remarkable communication revolutions, and in so doing has altered the way that people interact.

Index

Academic Earth, 60
Access to Information (A2I), 21-22, 87, 117-118, 134, 189, 197
Ahmed, Abu, 6
Ahmed, Fahim, 104
Ahmed, Mohiuddin, iv
Ahmed, Sultan, 197
Ahmed, Tofael, 83
Ahmed, Zia, 103-104
Alam, Nurul, 114
Anders, Bill, xvii
Angel funding, 100
apps, 74, 138, 150, 199; "apps for democracy", 74
Arrow, Kenneth, 182, 184
Asian Development Bank (ADB), 28, 102, 106
Atomic Energy Commission (AEC), 4
Automated Check Handling (ACH), 137
Avatar, 46
Average Revenue Per User (ARPU), 39
Azim Premji Foundation, 103

Bangalore, 37, 83, 101, 129-130
Bangladesh Association of Software and Information Services (BASIS), 10-13, 16-19, 21, 84-85, 101, 141, 143, 197
Bangladesh Awami League (AL), 4, 119, 187, 189
Bangladesh Bank (BB), 22, 68
Bangladesh Computer Council (BCC), 15, 17, 21, 22, 82-85, 90, 126-127, 143, 197
Bangladesh Computer Council Act, 82
Bangladesh Computer Samity (BCS), 4-5, 7, 11, 13, 19, 85, 143, 197
Bangladesh Inc., 114
Bangladesh Nationalist Party (BNP), 15, 119, 136
Bangladesh Railway (BR), 6
Bangladesh Rural Advancement Committee (BRAC), 16, 22, 103, 121, 132, 197
Bangladesh Telecom Regulatory Commission (BTRC) Act, 84-86
Bangladesh Telecom Regulatory Commission (BTRC), 11, 84-86, 89, 122, 124-125, 143
Bangladesh Telegraph and Telephone Board (BTTB), 12, 86, 122; *presently known as* Bangladesh Telecommunications Company Limited (BTCL)
Bangladesh University of Engineering and Technology (BUET), 83, 121, 132
Bangladesh army, 7; caretaker government of, 7, 15
BanglaDISH, 151, 156, 166, 171, 177
BanglaLion, 125, 143
bank financing, 102
banking mobile, 66-68, 136-137; virtual, 66
Bardeen, John, 207
Barisal BM College & University, 121, 132
Bartle, Richard, 190
Basalla, George, 190
BDeshTV.com, 31, 99, 143
Bell Labs, 207

Bell System Technical Journal, 203
Bell, Gordon, 185-186
Benkler, Professor Yochai, 172-173, 190
Berlinski, David, 190
Berners-Lee, Sir Tim, 33, 206, 209
Bhatti, Zubair, 77
Bill & Melinda Gates Foundation, 103
Bils, Mark, 80
Blaxill, Mark, 190
Board of Investment (BOI), 143
Bouissou, Brigitte, 59
BRAC University, 16, 121, 132, 197
BRIDGE framework, 93
broadband connectivity, vii, 35, 43, 114, 121, 124, 140
Broadband over Powerline (BPL), 46
Brooks, David, 190
Brown, John Seely, 190
Brummer Fund, 103
Buffett, Warren, 179, 183-184, 192
Bulwer-Lytton, Edward, 81
Business Process Outsourcing (BPO), 92

capital, viii, xv, 15, 29-30, 40, 68, 79, 83, 94-95, 97-102, 104-110, 112-113, 121, 126, 138, 164, 184, 190-191, 195; management funds, 101; venture, 95-96, 98, 100, 107-108, 110, 113, 121
capitalists
venture, 100, 107, 110; vicious, 113; virtual, 113; virtuous, 112-113; viscous, 113; vulture, 111
Carr, Nicholas, 190
CellBazaar, 65
Central Processing Unit (CPU), 205
Chen, Steve, 33
China, 2, 19, 26-27, 37-39, 51, 53, 57, 105, 114, 126-127, 130, 141-142, 175-176, 192
Chittagong University, 121, 132

Choudhury, Professor Jamilur Reza, 16, 21, 83-84, 197; JRC report by, 83
Chowdhury, Anir, 197
Chowdhury, Nurul Ghani, 5
cloud computing, xv, 138-140, 145, 148-151, 153, 200-201
cognitive surplus, ix, 176-177
connectivity, viii, 23, 42-43, 52, 72, 87, 98, 133, 146, 160
convergence, 31, 37, 43, 88-89
Cost of Goods Sold (COGS), 55

Daiyan, Shaikh Abdud, 105
data privacy and electronic security laws, 88
Davis, Philip J., 191
Dell (a multinational computer company), 5, 37
democracy, 27, 35, 57, 74, 78, 94, 114
Department for International Development (DFID), 68
Dhaka Chamber of Commerce & Industry (DCCI), 26
Dhaka Exchange Next (DENext), 121
Dhaka University, 121
Dhaka-Chittagong Economic Corridor (DCEC), 28
Digital Bangladesh, iii, vii-viii, xiv, xviii, 1, 3-4, 7, 16, 22-23, 26, 35, 56, 75, 80-81, 84, 87-88, 90-92, 94-95, 114, 117-121, 124-125, 132-133, 135, 139-141, 143-144, 178-179, 184, 187, 189, 192
Digital Deshis (DDs), 145-146, 148, 154-155, 157-160, 164, 167-169
digital
age, 1, 36, 148; divide, xi, 30-31, 35-36, 42, 89, 148, 159; doctor, 69; going, xviii, 93, 117, 135, 178; immigrants, 159; lifestyle initiatives, 23; technology, xi, xvi, 43, 72, 159
Discounted Cash Flow (DCF), 78-79

Index

e-commerce, 22, 49, 88, 136, 137
Edelstein, David, 197
education as co-created experience, viii, 157
e-government, 14, 21, 76, 87, 141, 143
e-health, 69, 135
Einstein, Albert, 3, 61
e-learning, 135
Entrepreneurs Equity Fund (EEF), 100-101
Ershad, H.M., 82
Esar, Evan, 95
e-services, 22, 133-134
Estonia, 75-76
Export Promotion Bureau (EPB), 17-18, 83

Facebook (a social networking service), xviii, 1, 31, 48, 74, 88, 97, 119, 121, 124, 139, 151, 155, 158, 163-164, 166, 185
FarmVille (a farming game), 163-164
Feynman, Richard, 59
Fiber@Home (a domestic private company), 122-124, 143
Flickr (a photo-sharing service), 152-153
Florida, Richard, 191
Friedman, Thomas, 37, 62, 191

Gates, Bill, 1, 60, 148, 184, 191-192
GE Healthcare (GEHC), 71, 197
Genuine Progress Indictor (GPI), 181
Ghana, 28-29, 76
Gibson, William, 32
Gilder, George, 191
Globalization 3.0 (software), 37
globalization, 1, 37, 40, 52, 182
Globalpur, 44-45
Goingdigitalbook.com, xiv, 87
Goldcorp Challenge, The, 175
Google Earth, The, 57, 150

Google Maps, The, 56-57, 75
Google.org, 56; from Edison to, 190
Govindarajan, Professor Vijay, 175
Grameen Bank (GB), xi, 63-64, 71, 102, 105-106
Grameen Foundation, 64-65, 73, 103, 197
Grameen Fund, 105-106
GrameenPhone, 63, 124-125, 133, 137
Graphic Design Services (GDS), 17
Gross Domestic Product (GDP), 11, 25-29, 38-40, 42, 51, 115, 137, 179-182

Harvard University, 190, 194
Hasina, Sheikh, 119
Hassan, Prof Kabir, 27
Heinla, Ahti (Skype guru), 75
High-Definition Television (HDTV), 34
HP, 5, 97
Human Development Index (HDI), 181
Hurley, Chad, 33

IBM, 4, 71, 139-140, 147
ICT Capacity Development Company (ICDC), 17
Imam, Hasan, 105
Immelt, Jeff, 175
Imperial Chemical Industries (ICI), 6
India+1, 171
Infocomm Authority, 88
Information & Communication Technology (ICT); Act, 86, 87, 88, 92; Policy Review Committee, 16; Policy, 15-16, 21, 26, 85, 87, 90, 92, 118; Task Force, 16, 21-22, 84
Intel (BD) Ltd., 4
International School Dhaka (ISD), 62
Internet Protocol (IP), 12, 30, 45-46, 113, 201, 204, 206
Ishrak, Syed Omar, 71, 197
Islam, Ifty, 105

Islam, Kazi Nazrul, 61
Islamic University of Technology, 132
IT parks, 96, 101, 126-127, 129

Jabbar, Mustafa, 5, 197
Jahed, Abu Nayeem M, v
Jahed, Sultana Zabinda A., v
Japan International Cooperation Agency (JICA), 8, 14, 19
John Wiley & Sons, 195
JP Morgan, 17

Kandiah, Thevakumar, 106
Karim, Habibullah N., iii, v, xiv-xviii, 5, 10, 16, 18, 21, 29, 156-157, 192
Karim, Jawed, 33
Kenya, 56, 67, 69, 75, 90-91
Keystone Digital Ltd (KDL), 114-115
Khan Academy, 60
Khulna University, 121, 132
Kibria, Reza, 8
Kibria, Shah A.M.S., 7
Kinsella, Ray, 44
Kiva (a microlending e-commerce firm), 165
Klenow, Pete, 80
Knopf, Alfred A., 195
knowing-doing gap, 117
Koch, Richard, 192
Korea Trade and Investment Promotion Office (KOTRA), 29
KPMG (an international accounting firm), 23
Kurzweil, Raymond, 192

Lammers, Susan, 192
leapfrog, vii, xviii, 1
Low Income Country (LIC), 3, 27, 81

Machine Dialogue, 5
Mahajan, Vijay, 192
Malaby, Thomas, 193
Mark I computer, 202
Massachusetts Institute of Technology (MIT), 59-60, 71, 192-194
Massively Multiplayer Online Games (MMOGs), 47, 168
McKenzie, Richard B., 193
McKinsey & Company, 10
McLuhan, Marshall, xvii
McMillan, John, 193
Mehta, Dewang, 7
Meyer, Christopher, 191
mHealth, 69-71
microcredit, 102, 106, 195
Microsoft, 5, 9, 37, 55, 60, 115, 140, 148-151, 173, 185, 192
Middle Income Country (MIC), 1, 3, 26-27, 42, 81
Millennium Development Goals (MDGs), 2-3
Mina, Quamrul, iii, v, xiv-xvii, 31, 156, 157
mKrishi, 65
Moore, Gordon, 53, 205
Morgan, Gareth, 193
Mother Earth, 177
M-PESA (a mobile-phone based money transfer service), 67
multilateral financial institutions, 102
MyLifeBits Project, 185-186
MySpace (a social networking service), 31

NASSCOM (Indian software industry association), 7
National Computer Committee, 6, 14
National Telecom Policy, 84
Negroponte, Nicholas, 72

network readiness index, 12
New York University (NYU), 60
Nokia Life Tools, 65
Nolvak, Rainer, 75
Non-Resident Bangladeshis (NRBs), 98-99, 142
North, Alfred, 117
North-South University, 121, 132

OfCom, 89
offshoring, 9, 51
Okolloh, Ory, 75
OpenCourseWare (OCW), 59
Oral Rehydration Therapy (ORT), 37
Original Equipment Manufacturer (OEM), 5
Orwellian dictator, xvii

Park, David, 191
patents and trademarks laws, 88
Personal Digital Assistant (PDA), 52
Petzinger, Thomas, 193
Prime Minister's Office (PMO), 16, 21-22, 87, 91, 117-119, 189, 197
Princeton University, 190
private equity, 95, 100-102, 108-110, 113
prosumer, 165
Public Key Infrastructure (PKI), 86
Public-Private Partnership (PPP), 27, 101, 132

Quadir, Iqbal, 63-64, 72-73
Quadir, Khalid, 100, 103

Rahman, Colonel (Retd) Azizur, 14, 82
Rahman, Hossain Zillur, 26
Rajshahi University, 121, 132
Rawls, John, 182-183
Ray, Paul, 194
Really Simple Syndication (RSS), 153

Rizhao city, 2
Rochester Institute of Technology, 97
Rockefeller Foundation, 72
Rofiquzzaman, Dr., 82

Sahlman, William A., 194
Samdani, Gulam (aka "Sam"), iii, v, xiii-xviii, 10, 156-157, 194
Samsung, 5, 9, 91
Science & ICT Ministry, 15
SEAF Bangladesh Ventures, 99, 104
Second Life, 47, 168, 190, 193
Shahjalal University of Science and Technology (SUST), 121, 130, 132
Shaw, George Bernard, 108
Shockley, William, 207
Singh, Dr. Manmohan (Prime Minister of India), 7
Singh, Nirvikar, 11
Skype, 31, 75
Small, Micro and Medium Size Enterprises (SMMEs), 96
social
 business, 101-102, 165; funds, 101-102; networking, 34, 47-48, 151, 158, 205
South Korea, 26, 28-29, 32, 36, 89, 126
Stanford University, 133
Stewart, Thomas, 195
Stiglitz, Joseph, 181, 195

Taleb, Nassim Nicholas, 195
Tarzan strategy, xiv
Tata Consultancy Services, 65
Technohaven Company Ltd., 6-7
technology parks, 85, 120, 126, 130-131
Thaler, Richard H., 195
Twain, Mark, xiii
Twitter (a social networking service), 31, 34, 74, 97, 119, 124, 139, 162, 185
Tzu, Lao, 179

Uganda, 64, 66-69, 73
UK-Intellect, 20
United Bank Limited (UBL), 4
United Nations Development Program (UNDP), 22, 87
University of California at Berkeley, 60, 133
University of Chicago, 80
University of New South Wales (UNSW), 60
University of Rochester, 80
University of Southern California (USC), 60
US National Center for Remanufacturing and Resource Recovery (NCR3), 97
USAID, 29
US-Bangladesh Investment Group, 104
Ushahidi, 74, 75

van Winkle, Rip, 30, 82, 146
Venture Investment Partners Bangladesh Ltd, 103, 110
Vicki Davis (10th grade Computer Science class at Westwood Schools in Camilla), 62
Vision 2021, 27, 187
Voice over Internet Protocol (VoIP), 30, 46, 204
Volvo example, 5
Vonage (an internet phone operator), 31

Warburg Pincus LLC, 106
Warsh, David, 195
Watson, Thomas, 147
Weinberger, David, 195
Whitehead, Alfred North, 117
Wikipedia, 135, 164-166, 170, 172-173, 176-177, 189
Williams, Anthony D., 195
Williams, Evan, 34
WiMax, 98, 124-125, 143
WordPress (a blog-publishing service), 152
World Bank (WB), 13, 16, 19, 24-27, 38, 68, 93, 102, 106-107, 189
World Economic Forum (WEF), 12
World Intellectual Property Organization (WIPO), 88
World Wide Computer (WWC), 147-148, 154, 171

Yale University, 190, 195
YouTube (a video sharing service), 1, 33-34, 48, 58-60, 139, 150-152, 157, 165-166, 177
Yunus, Professor Muhammad, xi, 64, 77, 101, 106, 165, 195